S0-BNZ-248

THAT THEY MAY HAVE LIFE

THAT THEY MAY HAVE LIFE

/\

The Episcopal Church in South Dakota

1859-1976

Virginia Driving Hawk Sneve

THE SEABURY PRESS·NEW YORK

The Episcopal Church in South Dakota
P.O. Box 517
Sioux Falls, South Dakota 57101

The Seabury Press
815 Second Avenue
New York, N.Y. 10017

Copyright © 1977 by The Episcopal Church in South Dakota

All rights reserved. No part of this book may be reproduced,
stored in a retrieval system, or transmitted, in any form or
by any means, electronic, mechanical, photocopying, recording,
or otherwise, without the written permission of The Episcopal
Church in South Dakota.

Printed in the United States of America

Library of Congress Cataloging in Publication Data

Sneve, Virginia Driving Hawk.
   That they may have life.

   "A Crossroad book."
   Bibliography: p.   Includes index.
   1. Protestant Episcopal Church in the U.S.A.—South Dakota.
   2. South Dakota—Church history.
I. Title.
BX5917.5.S8S65 1977   283'.783   76-55342
ISBN 0-8164-2141-2

This book was written for South Dakota and in memory of
THE REVEREND JAMES HENRY DRIVING HAWK
1913–1948

Contents

The Rt. Rev. Walter H. Jones, seventh Bishop of South Dakota.

Foreword

I

We cannot change the past. Men and women who were grasping and evil can be viewed objectively. What was petty and transitory will have practically faded away. What will be studied and considered above all is what has lasted. What lasts is the sound and noble actions of people who base their response on pure and generous motives. You will find many of them herein. Herein you will find great and noble individuals from two distinct cultures who were involved in the Church's day by day work. Together these people laid the foundations of faith that make today's tasks possible. Nowhere in the Church's geography can you find such a mixture striving together for the whole Church. Nowhere has such leadership evolved to be shared with the whole Church.

Virginia Driving Hawk Sneve has captured this truth in this history of the Church in South Dakota. She does so as one who understands both cultures represented in this history. And this history is offered to this nation in our Bicentennial year with a prayer that we may learn from it how to live in harmony without losing the values of our ancestors.

Walter H. Jones
Seventh Bishop of South Dakota

⋀⋀⋀⋀
Foreword

II

As I was raised in the home of my grandparents, William and Rebecca Holmes, missionaries in the District of South Dakota, it was my great privilege not only to know and observe them, but also their fellow Christians—clergy and lay; to see their faith, courage, enthusiasm, and joy in living. I am confident that their lives were rooted in a commitment to the Risen Lord Who was their Leader. These courageous people were strengthened by the living streams of love emanating from Him Who is Love.

Those early Christians saw the Church as a Living Community of which the Living Christ is Head, with no partiality and a deep concern for everyone. The Church, in its sacramental life, helped them attain a self-respect. Our Missionary District had some of the finest men and women in Christendom.

I am grateful to Almighty God that a story can be written about the Church in a century of intense activity, and further, that the author is one of ours, whose father was one of our outstanding native priests. It is my prayer that this history will help us all to see that truly Our Blessed Lord is the Way, the Truth, and the Life.

Harold S. Jones
Suffragan Bishop of South Dakota

Foreword

III

I rejoice that *That They May Have Life* has come into being. It is a rich history, full of romantic features, exhibiting spiritual life, vigor, and progress. It reveals periods of adversity along with periods of relative calm and less dramatic advance. All of the time, the same divine direction and support has been manifest. We who have had our opportunity granted us to share a part in the growing Church in South Dakota, give especial thanks. We remain ever grateful for the companions of those twenty-five years, 1945–1970, and for the friendships which do so long endure.

Indeed, we all are rightly cheered by the history-making advances presently to be witnessed as the Church in South Dakota moves from strength to even greater strength.

Conrad Herbert Gesner
Sixth Bishop of South Dakota

/\./\./\./\.|
Introduction and Acknowledgements

South Dakota has had the strongest and most extensive missionary work of the Protestant Episcopal Church in the United States, and there has been a long over-due need to tell the story of this work, since its beginnings over one hundred years ago. I am grateful to the Church in South Dakota for giving me the opportunity to tell this story.

This book is not a compilation of parish and mission histories, but I thank the many willing persons who wrote and submitted the histories of their individual parishes or missions. These small parts of the larger story were an invaluable source material, and a springboard for further research.

I cannot begin to list the people who contributed and helped with the research of one hundred and seventeen years, but special thanks must go to a few: Mr. Harold Shunk, who contributed to the research of the early days; Mrs. R. E. (Betty) Furois, who gathered data on women; Mrs. George (Coke) Meyers, who pestered parishes into writing their histories; the Reverend James D. Marrs, who did the same with the reservations and missions; the Reverend Robert D. Wright, Diocesan Historiographer, who permitted me to disrupt and create havoc in the Archives; the staffs of the Historic Resource Center, Pierre, the Minnesota State Historical Society, and the South Dakota State Library, who found ancient and obscure references for me through their Interlibrary Loan connections.

Inexpressible gratitude goes to retired clergymen, the Reverend Frank Thorburn, former Historiographer, who delved into his diaries (bless him for keeping one); the Reverend Paul H. Barbour, who answered my foolish questions with erudite recollections; and the Reverend Vine V. Deloria, whose family made much of the history of the Church in South Dakota.

Thanks to Bishop Harold, who conceived the idea of the history and asked me to write it; to Bishop Walter, who gave me unlimited use of the Bishop's library and unlocked the door to the attic; to Bishop and Mrs. Gesner, who so promptly responded to my plea for help; to Mrs. Limpo, Jeanne Olson, Dewey Knowlton, and Archdeacon Davis in the Diocesan offices, who didn't mind the dust I brought down from the attic at Dexter House and who helped in so many ways.

Thanks be to God for all of these people, but especially for the Venerable Edward Ashley, deceased, who wrote an unpublished history of the Church in Dakota Territory; and for my husband, Vance, who read my manuscript and gave me criticism and suggestions, and loving encouragement when one hundred and seventeen years threatened to overwhelm me.

Virginia Driving Hawk Sneve

/\\/\\/\\/\\

THAT THEY MAY HAVE LIFE

1

/\.\/\.\/\.\

God Is Wakantanka

When the missionaries brought Christianity to the Dakota or Sioux Indians, there was a great change in the native value system. Some Indians were able to retain old values and integrated them into Christian beliefs, so that the old was combined with the new and conversion to a new religion was an easy extension of the old. For others the conflicts were insurmountable and there was hostility and resistance to the missionaries and to Christianity.

Religion permeated every aspect of the Dakotas' life. It was impossible to differentiate between the social, economic, and religious phases of the Dakota culture. Religion was inextricably interwoven with every pattern of individual behavior.[1] Thus, the Dakota held a special reverence and respect for all religions. The early missionaries were welcomed and their message reverently heard. It was only later when the Indians saw that not all white men followed the doctrines of Christianity, that the motives of the missionaries were questioned.

The early missionaries insisted that their converts repudiate the most basic elements of their culture. To the Dakota, a man was destined to be a warrior and hunter. To refuse to fight or hunt and agree to plow the land was a sign of weakness. The male who voluntarily submitted to these shameful things—which he must do to become a Christian—made great personal sacrifices in the face of degrading ridicule from his people. Women became the first converts, for their acceptance of Christianity did not mean an abandonment of their former role as wife and mother.

However, the Dakota came to respect the missionaries, for these were the first white men who did not come to exploit them. Still, many were dubious of the Christians claim to a higher morality. "We are not sinners,"

3

a chief told Bishop Whipple. "It is his people (the whites) who bring firewater and corrupt our daughters."[2]

The Dakotas acceptance of Christianity was at first an acceptance of the God of their conquerors and a search for the white man's power, without completely abandoning the old beliefs.[3] The missionaries attempted to make it easier to reconcile the different beliefs by calling the Christian God *Wakantanka,* the Dakota name for the Great Spirit.

Christianity was the one part of the white man's life in which an Indian was accepted as an equal—all people were held to be the same before God. In a time when the happiness and freedom of the old life was being destroyed, just when the Dakotas needed a friend, the Church came to them. Ella Deloria, a faithful churchwoman, described the need:

And what good was it now anyway, in pieces? The sun dance—without its sacrificial core; festive war dances—without fresh war deeds to celebrate; the Hunka rite of blessing little children—without the tender Ring of Relatives to give it meaning—who would want such empty leavings?
And then the church came and filled that emptiness to overflowing.[4]

It was unfortunate that the early missionaries believed that the Dakota had to change his entire way of life to become a Christian. Their whole purpose was to civilize, and they indiscriminately tried to drive out all Indian ways. Modern Christians realize how much faster the civilization process would have been if the early missionaries had used the native religion as a frame of reference, instead of trying to eradicate it.

With the election of Ulysses S. Grant, a new era began for the Indians and the Episcopal Church. One of Grant's first acts as President was the establishment of the Peace Policy, an unusual and controversial departure in the government's relationship with the Indians. In his first inaugural address in 1869, Grant said:

The proper treatment of the original occupants of this land—the Indians—is one deserving of careful study. I will favor any course toward them which tends to their civilization and ultimate citizenship.[5]

In 1869, Grant placed the superintendency of Nebraska, Kansas, and Indian Territory, Oklahoma, under the care of the Society of Friends. Grant appointed Jacob D. Cox, an Episcopalian, as Secretary of the Interior. Cox was sincerely interested in developing an efficient, honest civil service system. Up until Cox's appointment, the Indian Bureau had been a nest of corruption, whose agents too often used their offices to their own advantage. Congress established a Board of Indian Commissioners composed of religious leaders and philanthropists. The Board was headed by William Welsh, a Philadelphia businessman, philanthropist, and an Episcopalian, who had an interest in the Dakota Indians. Welsh was the only member of the nine-man board who had personal knowledge and experience of Indians. Felix R. Brunot, Pittsburgh, was another Episcopalian member of the board.

The Board would check the Indian Bureau to make sure that the goods purchased for the Indians was of high quality, and that no fraudulent arrangements were made with contractors. They would also tour the Indian agencies to gain first-hand knowledge of the work.

Grant's Peace Policy was enacted by Congress on April 10, 1869, and contained the following major provisions:

1. The Indians were to be placed on reservations as quickly as possible so that the dictates of humanity and Christian civilization could be met. On the reservations, they were to be taught as fast as possible the arts of agriculture and civilization through the aid of the Christian organizations of the country actively engaged in the work, acting in harmony with the federal government. The Indian's intellectual and moral character was to be developed with kindness and humanity through Christian principles.

2. It would be the policy of the President to punish with severity any tribe which refused to live on the reservation and determined to continue their nomadic way of life.

3. All supplies of every kind needed by the Indians on the reservations should be purchased at fair and reasonable prices in such a way that supplies would arrive when and where needed and without having the government funds squandered in their purchase. No longer should profiteers be allowed to make money on Indian supplies.

4. It was the purpose of the government, with the advice of religious organizations, to procure competent, upright and moral religious agents to care for the Indians on the reservations and to distribute the goods and provisions purchased for them by the government. The church groups were to aid in the intellectual, moral and religious culture and thus assist in the humanity and benevolence which the peace policy meant.

5. It was the policy of this peace enactment to establish schools, churches and Sabbath schools through the instrument of the church organizations so that the Indian might be taught a better way of life and be trained to be citizens of this great nation.[6]

The policy was proclaimed as a great step in the direction of solving the Indian problem. On July 15, 1870, Congress added an act to the Peace Policy which made it mandatory that religious groups appoint Indian agents. Congress also acted to make it unlawful for an Army Officer to hold civil office. On March 3, 1871, Congress determined that the Indians would no longer be treated as sovereign tribes or nations, but as individuals under the United States Government. This act extended the control of the agents, who would now be worthy of such because they were religious men.

In 1870, William Welsh visited the various reservations and made a detailed report of his travels, talks with chiefs, and made recommendations to the Secretary of the Interior. Welsh also reported to the Episcopal Church, where he made a plea for missionaries and money. The Church responded to his eloquence and established the Indian Commission of the Domestic Commission of the Board of Missions.[7] On December 12, 1871, the new commission assumed the care and control of the Indian field.

Offices were established in the Mission Building, New York City, and three of the Church's missionary organizations, the Domestic Committee, the American Church Missionary Society, and the Indian Hope Association of Philadelphia, all turned over monies from their treasuries to the Indian Commission.[8] Colonel E. C. Kimbel was the first secretary, and he was succeeded by the Reverend R. C. Rogers.[9]

Seven agencies were assigned to the Episcopalian Indian Commission: five among the Dakota, one with the Poncas, and one among the Shoshones and Bannocks in Wyoming Territory.[10] The Commission nominated agents for these tribes, and all but one appointment was accepted by Congress. In their first annual report, the commission listed the names and localities of the agencies, agents, tribes and their number[11]:

Agency	Locality	Agent	Tribe	No. of Indians
Ponka	Dakota	C. P. Birkett	Ponka	750
Yankton	Dakota	Rev. J. G. Gasman	Yankton	2,500
Crow Creek	Dakota	Dr. H. F. Livingston	Yanktonais	1,200
Crow Creek	Dakota	Dr. H. F. Livingston	Lower Brules	2,200
Cheyenne	Dakota	H. W. Bingham	Two Kettles	
Cheyenne	Dakota	H. W. Bingham	Minneconjous	2,000
Cheyenne	Dakota	H. W. Bingham	Sans Arcs	
Red Cloud's	Dakota	Dr. J. W. Daniels	Ogalallas	2,500
Spotted Tail's	Dakota	D. R. Risley	Upper Brules	2,500
Shoshone and Bannocks	Wyoming	J. Irwin	Shoshones and Bannocks	1,500

The Ponca and Santee Agencies were under the care of a Quaker agent; Standing Rock was Roman Catholic; Sisseton and Flandreau under the Presbyterians.

The Commission requested that their clerical members preach sermons in behalf of the cause, and sympathetic congregations were urged to form associations to promote its growth and minister to the needs of the missionaries.[12] Fifty churches responded with donations, but workers from the clergy were lacking.

The Commission went to Berkeley Divinity School, Connecticut, and made an appeal to the young seminarians who were "enthusiastic, unmarried, and unworried about the trials of survival among the heathen and hostile Indians in the west." Three young men, the Reverends Henry Swift, William J. Cleveland, and Heckaliah Burt, answered the call, and after their graduation left immediately for the field. Already in Dakota was the Reverend J. Owen Dorsey, who had responded to William Welsh's plea for a missionary for the Poncas, and the Reverend Samuel Hinman, who had followed the Santee from Minnesota. The area they served was under the jurisdiction of Bishop Clarkson of Nebraska, and covered one hundred and fifty-three thousand miles. Clarkson said of his vast charge, "It would be as reasonable to expect efficient Episcopalian oversight and administration of the Diocese of Massachusetts or New York from a Bishop resident in London."[13]

In 1873, the Jurisdiction of Niobrara was established by the Church, and William Hobart Hare was named its Bishop. The area he oversaw was bounded on the East by the Missouri River; on the South by the State of Nebraska; on the West by the 104th Meridian, the Territory of Wyoming, and Nebraska; on the North by the 46th degree of north latitude; including also the several Indian reservations on the left bank of the Missouri, North and East of said river.[14] In addition, Hare had transferred to him the care of the Oneidas in Wisconsin, and the Santee in Nebraska.[15]

Hare described his feelings about his Dakota charges:
These Sioux Indians are heathens, heathens not far off but lying cold on the Churches' bosom. Our people have seen them lying dead—they have not pitied them but have beaten and stamped on their dead humanity. The government now shames us taking a noble, yea a Christian stand. The Church must respond. She has responded by calling me to head in her name, a movement in their behalf.[16]

In his third annual report of 1875, to the Board of Indian Commissioners, Hare wrote of the Church's work:

The responsibility which the Church has assumed in undertaking to nominate to the Government men suitable for agents among the Indians is seen with each year's experience to be graver and graver. A chance visitor to our Indian Agencies would see, perhaps, only large room for improvement; but few candid persons who were familiar with the condition of affairs before the present system was adopted, and who are acquainted with their condition now, would hesitate to affirm that most marked improvement has been effected by the present system— alike in the discouragement of drunkenness and gambling, in the improved character of the white employees, in the progress of schools and churches, in the protection of the Indians from extortion and corruption, and in the humanity and honesty of agents.[17]

Hare went on to complain that at times the imperfections of the present system vexed his spirit and at times, he was ready to welcome a change in policy. "But," he wrote, "my deliberate conviction is that any one of the changes proposed which is more than simply a modification of the present system, would be most decidedly a change for the worse."[18]

The peace policy began because Grant was unwilling to accept political appointees and Congress was unwilling to take constructive action on behalf of the Indian service. The policy, or non-policy, placed the responsibility upon the different denominations for nominating and supervising the agents.[19]

The policy seemed to fail because of the incompetence of the agents and growing paternalism of the churches and their nominees.[20]

However, in 1876, Rutherford B. Hayes was President, and Grant's peace policy was considered a definite failure. The new administration brought the shortcomings into the open. The Indian Service had all the while been unhappy that they no longer had complete control of the Indians, and now they openly expressed their adverse opinions of the churches' management of the agencies.[21]

Hayes was also determined to tighten up the Indian Service, and take over Indian education in order to speed assimilation and a general intensification of the government's program of civilization. Hayes appointed E. A. Hayt as Commissioner of Indian Affairs, who began to ferret out misbehavior in the church-appointed agents.[22] Hayt moved to destroy the churches' influence by making emergency appointments and established rigid requirements, and rejected church nominees, and by 1880, the churches' role in administering the Indian agencies was finished.[23]

Hayt sent General J. H. Hammond to Dakota, where he seized the records of three Episcopalian agencies and charged the agents with the misuse of office. Bishop Hare vigorously protested Hammond's action, and declared that the Church would believe the men innocent, until it was proven otherwise.

Dr. H. F. Livingston, Agent at Crow Creek, was put on trial in Yankton, but was acquitted. There was evidence of mismanagement at his agency; but whether Livingston was responsible, or was merely careless about keeping records, his persecution served to break down the influence of the Episcopal Church. Blame was placed on the Church, and on Bishop Hare, even though the agents were found innocent.[24]

The Department of the Interior now came into conflict with the Department of the Army who had, ever since it had lost control of the Indians in 1849, attempted to regain power. Bishop Hare and the Episcopal Church favored the Indian Service because they felt the Army control would be detrimental to the Indians. The Indian Service was the lesser of the two evils. William Welsh, however, felt that the Army should have control, as the officers were well paid, and would be less tempted to corruption than the ill-paid civil servants. The Indians themselves feared the Army, remembering the corrupting atmosphere around forts where their women were prostituted and liquor was plentiful.

The Indian Service retained control of the Indians, and criticized the missionaries for thinking that the Indians should first be Christianized and then educated. Now, education would proceed without Christianization. The Church and the State would again be separated, and the cooperative relationship of the Grant period would never be again.

Very early in their contacts with the Dakotas, Episcopalian missionaries realized that religion and the satisfaction of everyday needs could not be separated by the Indians. When the missionaries spoke of building schools and churches, the Indians replied, "We think it strange that you should speak of schools when we asked for other things first. We cannot eat schools and churches."[25] The Episcopalians did not make a distinction between philanthropy and evangelization. Episcopalians were often accused of being lax with their Indian charges by permitting them to continue some of their old practices, such as placing food on the graves of the dead. The other denominations of the more puritanical Calvinistic creeds attempted to maintain a tighter control over their Indians; but the early Episcopalian missionaries felt that too much discipline would make Christianity unpalatable to the Indians. Samuel Hinman, in his work with the Santee, was conscious of the criticisms of missionaries to the Sandwich Islands, who made religion too austere.[26]

Bishop Hare gained an early understanding of his Indian charges. "The

Indian's old life," Hare wrote, "was like his moccasin—soft and easy-fitting. The new life is like a tight hard leather boot. It rubs him and makes him sore."[27]

The color and richness of the Episcopal ritual appealed to the Dakotas, because they could associate such with their native ceremonies. Feast Days and holidays were important in the Church, and provided festivities to a people who needed diversion to relieve the drab drudgery of their days.

In addition, the Church had ceremonies for the transition from one stage of life to another, which the Dakota could relate to their native ceremonies. Baptism for the babies and confirmation for those who were passing into adulthood were acceptable substitutes for the Hunka and Puberty rites. The service of the Burial of the Dead had within it the proper honor and mystery which the Dakota gave in their old funeral ceremonies. The Church also permitted the give-away and final feast given by relatives of the deceased to be held in church guild halls.

The Dakota managed in their own fashion to fit the values of the old into Christianity, and could understand, by their knowledge of the Sun Dance, the asceticism and the torture of the crucifixion for the good of others. Giving to others, especially to the poor, was common to them. The high honor the Church accorded virginity was similar to Dakota custom. Putting money in the collection plate on Sundays was a semblance of giving honor to another person and gaining prestige in the Dakota give-away pattern.[28] The Niobrara Convocation, although it had no Indian ceremonials within it, served the same social function as the old Sun Dance, when friends and relatives came together in the summer from all directions. The convocation custom of the Indians from the different reservations camping together was not unlike the traditional spots held in the camp circle by the various tribes.

Still, in times of crisis and disorder, many Dakota slipped back to the old traditions and religions. Christianity among the Indians became very much like Christianity among the whites. Those who remained faithful Christians and accepted the new order realized that the old Dakota way of life was doomed; it could not stand against the stronger white civilization. They knew if they were to survive, they must adopt Christian standards and behavior.

Thus, by 1890, there were many devout Christian Indians who adhered to the practice of non-violence and good works, but also another group who were superficial and transitory Christians who readily donned the Ghost Shirts and accepted the Messianic movement, which promised

the return of the buffalo and the departure of the whites from the land.
Bishop Hare wrote:

A delusion has taken possession of the minds of the wilder elements among the
Indians. The leaders in the movement have invigorated old heathen ideas with
snatches of Christian truth and have managed to excite an amount of enthusiasm
which is amazing. They teach that the Son of God will presently appear as the
avenger of the cause of the wild Indian. . .[29]

The Ghost Dance religion incorporated Christian teachings into its
philosophy:

Previously, the crucified Christ, for example, would have been rejected by the
conquered Indians; but now He would return as an avenger of the wrongs which
had been done them, serving much the same purpose as their guardian spirits. In
these ways, the Ghost Dance was effective during this great crisis in unifying
some basic Christian beliefs with those of the pre-existing Teton system of
religion.[30]

The Messianic Craze had its tragic consequences at Wounded Knee,
and it was "virtually the final flicker of the ancient spirit of the Sioux."[31]
The *Church News* of April 1891 reported on the Christian Indians' activities during the troubled times:

The conduct of the Christian Indians in South Dakota during the recent uprising
of the hostiles was beyond all praise. They were loyal to the government, loyal to
the Church; and exemplary in their Christian conduct, extending ministrations to
the wounded and sick, and sharing with them the gifts which friends in the East
had sent them. Our chapel at Pine Ridge, under the missionary Charles S. Cook,
was turned into a hospital for the wounded and dying. Our faithful workers became brothers and sisters of mercy. Two chapels and a rectory were destroyed,
but yet the work of the mission was carried forward with steadiness through all the
disturbance. No better proof could be given of the real value of our Church work
among the Indians, and no stronger argument for the extension of the work than
the bearing of the Christians under the severe strain of that trying ordeal.[32]

The periodical went on to admit, "One mistake we make is to class all
redskins together as equally bad—the same mistake by the way, which
they make regarding us."[33]

Years later the reduction of rations, crop failures, starvation, and over-
all frustration—conditions similar to those which had fostered the rise of
the Messianic movement—would generate another movement which was
also a combination of native religion and Christianity.[34] This was the
Peyote Cult, which had its basis in the invocation of power from a sup-

reme being who is identified with the Christian God and symbolized by the peyote button or seed pod of the mescal cactus plant.[35] The trance, which results from the ingesting of peyote, was likened to that of the old vision quests in which the seeker of a guardian spirit attempted to get outside of himself, or into an abnormal state.[36]

The Episcopal Church, along with other denominations, viewed the cult as being heretic and pagan. The Venerable Edward Ashley, Archdeacon of Niobrara, wrote to the Commissioner of Indian Affairs in 1925, stating his concern with the increased use of peyote in the Indian country through the devise of the Native American Indian Church and its use in sacramental service. Ashley formed the Continuation Committee, made up of Father Bernard Strassmaier, Roman Catholic; Jessie Williamson, Dakota Indian Presbytery; the Reverend A. F. Johnson, Presbyterian; Mr. Fred B. Riggs, Santee Normal; Mr. Wright, Santee; and the Reverend R. Hertz, Congregational. Ashley was chairman of the committee, which was formed with the purpose of discouraging Indian dances, divorces, and especially peyote eating.[37]

The Reverend Frank Thorburn, who was at Pine Ridge when the Peyote Cult was at its height, recalled:

On the Pine Ridge we had a representative meeting at Porcupine of Roman Catholics, Presbyterians, Episcopalians, and Peyote members. All had their say. The outcome was a question of Church policy. Should Peyote users be excommunicated? What should be done when and if our Church families who went to the Peyote Cult requested baptism of children, the Holy Communion, marriage, burial? How should penitents be received and restored to the Church?

There was no official Church policy set forth by the Bishop or the Niobrara Convocation to deal with Peyote. Father Joyner (Nevill Joyner, Superintending Presbyter of the Pine Ridge Mission), counselled us, the clergy, catechists, and helpers to "not slam the door on those who stopped coming to church. Visit them with loving Christian concern so they would return to the Church."[38]

The only continuing cult of the old Dakota religion is the *Yuwipi* meeting, in which four manifestations of *Wakantanka* are worshipped and supernatural power is invoked for curing the sick, finding lost articles or persons.[39] However, the *Yuwipi* meeting has undergone changes which reflect the Indians' adaptation to reservation life. Father Thorburn recalled his experience, and that of other Episcopalian clergy, with the *Yuwipi* on the Pine Ridge:

I tried to find the right approach as a Christian to dealing with the problem. My experiences in being told of participation in *Yuwipi* and talks with Clayton High

Wolf (a native priest) led me to the conclusion that the *Yuwipi* touched on the question of angels and devils, good and evil spirits, physical and mental ills, temptation, and that social phenomenon of astrology, mediums, and claims of spirit possession.

During this time (after the 1934 reorganization act) of revival of the open practice of *Yuwipi* and Peyote, I was asked by Church (Indian) families to exorcise their homes from the "spirits" that were disturbing them.[40]

Being a baptized Christian and a confirmed attending member of a church, and also attending Peyote and *Yuwipi* ceremonies, apparently did and does not bring conflict to the Indians who have multiple religious affiliations.

Individuals pass from one group to another as the personalities of the leaders appeal to them or neighbors report unusual success in curing.

The shifting from one religion to another of apparently conflicting concepts becomes more understandable when it is realized that there are certain elements fundamental in the native pre-Christian religion which are carried over into the contemporary religions. The first is the seeking of divine power for strength and assistance in meeting the problems of earthly life. The second is the seeking of social interaction and social participation which gives to the individual a sense of security and membership in a larger group not attained regularly in other institutions.[41]

In addition to the conflict, and at times, fusing of Christian beliefs and native cults, there was also competition and demand for exclusiveness among the Christian denominations, which brought confusion to a once single, strongly integrated people. This competition was injurious to social acculturation, and has, in contemporary times, brought strong criticism from Indian activists.

In the summer of 1873, three young Indians, David Tatiyopa, 21; Felix Bronut, 20; and Philip Deloria, 19; saw the cultural division growing between Indians attempting to continue the nomadic life and those adopting the new agricultural life, as well as the divisions in religion from the various denominations.[42]

In 1873, most of the Dakota tribes were still living in the old way, and these roaming people were called "hostiles," because they sought to retain the old way of life. The other group was termed, "the friendly Indians," who settled near agencies and forts, farmed, raised stock, sold cord wood, hay and ice, and worked as carpenters, blacksmiths, policemen, and in other frontier jobs. The three young men from this latter group were also Christian converts and Episcopalians.[43]

The three formed the *Wojo Okolakiciye,* "The Planting Society." Ten

A Brotherhood of Christian Unity Annual Meeting, Crow Creek Agency, 1890.

years later it was changed to "Brotherhood of Christian Unity," or BCU, as it became widely known. Their organizational structure was based on two goals:

1. We Indians, before the coming of the whiteman, knew what was good, but not what was very good. We knew what was bad, but not what was very bad. The whiteman has brought us the very good and the very bad. However, the very good they have brought us is so very, very good, we firmly believe that this good will overcome the very bad ultimately. Our Blessed Lord and Savior, Jesus Christ, is the very, very good. Nevertheless, we clearly see that before the coming of our Lord, strangely, we were more united than we are now. Jesus Christ is here, but His representatives are competing against one another as Roman Catholics, Episcopalians, Presbyterians, and Congregationalists. By doing this, they are dividing us. Therefore, through this brotherhood club, let us try to stay together.
Let us try to show the whiteman that we can continue as brothers at the same time we are denominational Christians.
2. Let us look on the chain of Indian life, try to spot the weakest link, concentrate upon that with what resources we may have in material, energy, and wisdom, for the temporal welfare of our Indian people, until stronger people than ourselves come to our assistance—like the Government and the Churches—and then all of us together will be able to achieve some good results.[44]

The first project of the three young men was to begin in farming themselves. They built log houses and barns near Greenwood on the Yankton reservation, and their efforts were mocked by the "hostiles" who, on their visits to the agency, turned their horses into the gardens of the "brotherhood" to trample the potatoes and corn.

Despite this harrassment, the three recruited men for the Brotherhood from both the friendlies and the hostiles, telling them that "they had better settle down and try to learn the whiteman's way of learning to live on a smaller piece of ground."[45]

The three sought Bishop Hare's approval of their club, but he did not give them much encouragement other than saying, "Go and Try It."[46] The Bishop's statement became the rallying slogan of the group.

In its first century, the BCU spread from the Yankton reservation to every reservation in South Dakota. At one time, it had a membership of over a thousand men and the majority were from denominations other than Episcopalian. By 1940, the membership was down to 400, was predominately Episcopalian, and the constitution and bylaws were revised, and the membership requirement was changed from "Anyone who believes in Almighty God, the Father, the Son, and the Holy Ghost may become a member," to belief in the Trinity, plus baptism and confirmation in the Episcopal Church. But in 1957, the BCU again restored the original membership requirements.

The BCU's first effort was in the Farm Program, next in teaching the Indian people the use of money. Following projects were the importance of education, encouragement of young men to enter Christian ministry of some denomination, and in later years, assisting Indian people to adjust to town life and working to bring industries to the reservations.

The Venerable Vine V. Deloria, son of Philip who was one of the BCU founders, has been active in the work of the Brotherhood and says of its present status, "BCU is at a low ebb. The main reason is inflation and the need of new goals. The old goals do not exist except in a few isolated reservation areas."[47]

2

ʌʌ.ʌʌ.ʌʌ

Lower Missouri and Eastern Dakota

SANTEE

The work of the Episcopal Church in Dakota Territory, and what would become South Dakota, began with the appointment of Henry Whipple as Bishop of Minnesota on October 11, 1859.[1] The next year Bishop Whipple and Doctor James Lloyd Breck visited the Lower Agency of the Santee Dakota, or Sioux, at Redwood, Minnesota, and heard the Indians plea for a missionary and a school. A young man, Samuel Dutton Hinman, destined to play an important and controversial role in Dakota, had come to Bishop Whipple's divinity school from Connecticut as an orphan. In 1859, he was ordained deacon, and sent with his bride, Mary, to Redwood, where they established a Santee Mission.[2]

Hinman was with the Santee for two years, but his progress in Christianizing them was slow. He did not have the support of a regular mission board, and he and Bishop Whipple constantly struggled to obtain funds to maintain the Redwood station. Hinman was also at first hindered in his work by not knowing the Indians language or customs. But he soon won their respect by his unselfish labors with the sick and poor, and a few began coming to his school, which received partial support from the government.[3]

The work at Redwood ended on August 18, 1862, when the Santee broke out of the narrow confines of their Minnesota Valley reservation in a desperate, doomed uprising against long years of government treachery and deceit. Many of the Christian Santee saved white missionaries and settlers, but all were considered equally guilty of the white settlers' deaths and were imprisoned at Fort Snelling. Hinman accompanied the Santee to the fort to give what comfort he could in the face of the angry white residents of Minnesota who were demanding extermination of the "merciless" savages or, barring that, their complete removal from Minnesota.

The Rt. Rev. Henry Whipple.

The Rev. Samuel Dutton Hinman. By permission of the Minnesota Historical Society.

Bishop Whipple confirming Santee Indians at Fort Snelling, Minnesota, April, 1863.

Hinman and the Presbyterian missionaries who ministered to the Santee were the victims of the vindictiveness of the white population. Hinman was beaten unconscious by a band of roughs who broke into the
stockade. He, and others who defended the Indians, were called avari-
cious priests and denounced as mawkish sentimentalists and contempti-
ble fools.[4]

The Santee, in the misery of their destitution, turned to the missionaries
for aid. Many now realized the need for strong faith in their lives in this
time of distress, and accepted the Christian God. Hinman lived at the
fort, opened a school, baptized 149, and had as many as 300 Indians under
his care. When Bishop Whipple visited the prison, he confirmed 100
Santee.[5]

On February 16, 1863, the United States Government abrogated all
treaties with the Mississippi Sioux, and gave their annuity payments to
the white families of those who were killed. Minnesota never wanted a
Sioux Indian within its borders again.[6]

The Santee were assigned a new reservation in Dakota Territory, near
Crow Creek on the Missouri River, and a stockade was built which enclosed the agency buildings and barracks. The journey to their new home
began at Fort Snelling, where the Indians were herded onto steamers and
shipped down the Mississippi, like loads of cattle, to St. Joseph, Missouri. There they were crowded into a smaller craft, the *Florence,* which
forced them to sleep in shifts because there was not enough room for all to
lie down.[7] The conditions were insufferable and the food bad, as they
moved up the Missouri to their new home.

They reached Crow Creek on May 30th, and in a matter of days, the
hills around the agency were covered with the graves of women and
children who had died as the result of the over-crowding on the small
boat, and who had no medical attention on their arrival at Crow Creek.
The situation at Crow Creek was one of the worst ever inflicted on pris-
oners of the United States.

It was a horrible region, filled with the petrified remains of the huge lizards and
creeping things of the first days of time. The soil is miserable; rain rarely ever
visits it. The game is scarce, and the alkaline waters of the streams and springs are
almost certain death.[8]

The Indians arrived too late to plant crops, which would not have
produced enough harvest in that arid land to support them. The govern-

ment had to feed them and this was difficult because of the distance from the source of supply.

Hinman joined the Santee at Crow Creek and traveled with them when they were again moved to the mouth of the Niobrara River in Nebraska. This time, they journeyed overland and arrived on June 11, 1866, to a hostile reception from white settlers in the area whose lands had been appropriated by the government for the new Santee reservation.[9]

The Santee, now denied any annuities and forbidden to leave the reservation to hunt, built a log chapel at Bazille Creek under Hinman's direction. He lived among them without any financial aid from the Church Mission Board, and had to rely solely on voluntary gifts from white persons in the East who felt kindly towards the Indians.[10]

In 1864, Mr. Hinman translated a large part of the *Book of Common Prayer* into the Santee dialect, and it was published in 1865.[11] The Santee came to love the book, as more of them learned to read their own language.

During the time from 1866 to 1868, the chapel at Bazille Creek was used, and the congregation was visited by Bishop Robert H. Clarkson of Nebraska shortly after it was built. In the spring of 1868, the chapel was flooded out, and all records were destroyed.

A generous gift, from a woman of New Bedford, Massachusetts, made possible the building of the Chapel of our Most Merciful Savior in 1868. The new chapel was considered to be one of the most beautiful small church buildings in the West.[12]

At about this time, Mr. Hinman took a small group of Santee East, where they impressed the white people in Philadelphia to form an association for the Santee's relief. The association was made up of a large number of members of the Society of Friends who were interested in Indian work. Hinman was also able to influence the Sherman Peace Commission to have Article Six inserted in the 1868 Treaty with the Sioux, which allowed the Santee to remain permanently in their new homes, to acquire title to farms, and to be made citizens in three years.[13]

On October 5th and 6th, 1870, the first convocation of the Dakota missions was held at Santee. In attendance were two white and three Indian clergy, four lay delegates, four catechists, representatives of Santee bands, one Ponca, and five headmen of the Yanktons.[14]

With the new chapel, the work of Hinman and his wife, assisted by Miss Emily West, was making great progress when a tornado struck on June 1, 1870, and destroyed the mission house and chapel.[15] Mr. William Welsh visited the Santee shortly after the disaster and reported:

Mission of Our Most Merciful Savior, Santee Agency, Nebraska, 1873.

After crossing the river into Nebraska, it was impossible to resist the depressing influences attendant upon witnessing the devastation caused by a whirlwind.... Small fragments of the new hospital, mission-house and the chapel, and their furniture, books, etc., were scattered everywhere. The log buildings attached to the mission-house shared the same fate. We were soon cheered, however, by meeting the Missionary (Hinman) and his family, though buried in the ruins, yet by God's special Providence now in the fullness of bodily health, and with faith that God will bring good out of seeming evil.[16]

In 1871, through Mr. Welsh's aid, a new chapel and mission house was built, as was a schoolhouse with laundry, kitchen, and twelve sleeping rooms. The mission now also had a vegetable garden and twenty-five acres of wheat. In the same year, Sister Anna Prichard arrived to work in the school.[17]

A second station of the Santee mission was built on the land of Chief Wabasha, six miles from the first. Wabasha, a hereditary chief, was a zealous early Christian convert who had a great deal of influence with his people. The chapel was built as a gift from Mr. and Mrs. Samuel Nettleton of Watertown, Connecticut.[18]

Bishop Clarkson, in December, 1871, wrote of his impression of the mission: "In every visit with that wonderful Santee Mission I am more and more impressed with the marvelous evidence of the work of God's Holy Spirit among the people."[19] Clarkson had ordained the first full-blood Dakota, Paul Mazakute, Iron Shooter, as deacon in 1868, and for five years, Mazakute ministered to his people. In an account of his work, Mazakute wrote:

> In 1862 I made my Christian vows. For seven years I was a Catechist, and for five years I have been a Minister. One year I was a Deacon, and for four years I have been a Priest. When I was made a Priest, I went to the Yankton people (1869).
> Though I have never been far away, yet among the Dakotas—at Yankton Agency, and White Swan, and Choteau Creek, at Ponka, at Santee, and on the Bazille—six villages I have proclaimed the glad tidings of the Gospel.[20]

Mazakute contracted tuberculosis and had to resign his active and arduous work. He took a claim in 1871 on the Bazille Creek, eighteen miles from the Santee mission, and farmed a small plot to feed his family. Even in his retirement, Mazakute began ministering to the Santee farming near him who were without Christian influence. He built a "bough house" for his church, and his rectory was a tipi. Women in New York, members of the Society of the Double Temple, heard of Mazakute's self-sacrifice, and raised money to build him the Chapel of the Blessed Redeemer and a log cabin for his home on Bazille Creek (later known as Howe Creek). On May 12, 1873, Mazakute succumbed to his illness after only a few months in the new chapel.[21]

Two other young Dakotas, Daniel Hemans and Luke C. Walker, were ordained deacons by Bishop Clarkson in 1871. Walker became Hinman's assistant, and Hemans was assistant and interpreter to the Reverend J. W. Cook at Yankton. Heman's work had just begun when he died in the smallpox epidemic which raged through the Santee Agency and mission in 1873. He had returned to help at the school, which was turned into a hospital in which the clergy and teachers ministered to the sick around the clock. By the end of the year, 105 had died.[22]

Christian Taopi, once a fierce warrior as a youth, whose name, *Taopi*, Wounded One, was earned when he was wounded in a Santee-Chippewa battle, was another ordained deacon who assisted in the work of the Santee

The Church and Rectory of Rev. Paul Mazakute, Bazille River, Nebraska, June, 1872.

Mission. He, as was Mazakute, was afflicted with tuberculosis, and although he suffered for years, he continued ministering to his people while his strength lasted. He succumbed to the disease, "a valiant Christian soldier,"[23] in 1872.

Philip Johnson Wahpehan (Wahepan), another Santee, was ordained to the deaconate in 1869, but died on November 24, 1871. Wahpehan, called Philip the Deacon, had left his home and family at Bazille Creek to hunt when he was caught in a terrible blizzard. When he did not return, a search was made, and his frozen body was discovered a week later. He was associated with the Yankton Mission, and the chapel at White Swan was renamed the Church of Phillip the Deacon after his death.[24]

Samuel Hinman's influence over the Indian clergy was great, and they thought highly of him. However, he did not get along with the other white protestant missionaries at Santee and there was a great deal of conflict between them. ". . . A difficulty seems to have arisen between them and it is notorious in the tribe that the missionaries themselves, have of late years, not been upon terms of ordinary civility and courtesy with each other."[25] Hinman apparently possessed a personality and temperament which made it difficult for him to work with other ministers of his own race.

On Ash Wednesday, March 1, 1876, Hinman suffered the loss of his devoted wife, Mary. She had been with him in the beginnings of his ministry to the Santee in Minnesota and worked with him in Nebraska.

He gave her credit for doing more toward Christianizing and civilizing the people than he himself accomplished. Mary Hinman had been afflicted for three years with a painful "disease which attacked her throat. Medical skill proved unavailing. . . . Yet her long sickness, borne with utmost patience and meekness and resignation to the will of our heavenly Father, was in itself a most impressive sermon and example before the people."[26] She was greatly loved by the Santee, and after David Weston's band moved to Flandreau, they named their chapel "St. Mary's," in honor of Mary Hinman.

Hinman continued at Santee for two more years, and perhaps, the loss of the calming influence of his beloved wife was one of the causes of increasing conflict with Bishop Hare. Hare, on the other hand, had heard rumors of Hinman's immorality ever since the bishop's first years in Niobrara. The persistent rumors were damaging to the Church's work, and Hare finally decided that it would be in the best interests of all of the missions to remove Hinman. On March 25, 1878, Hare, "only from a sense of duty and with the most painful reluctance," exercised his authority and severed Mr. Hinman's connection with the Santee Mission.[27]

Hinman felt that his life work among the Santee had been destroyed, and his character defamed by the Bishop's action. Before the coming of Bishop Hare, Hinman had had total responsibility for the Santee Mission, with only minimal attention from Bishop Clarkson. Hinman remembered the criticisms against white missionaries to the Sandwich Islands of making religion too austere, and as a result, was criticized by the Presbyterian missionaries at Santee who tried to maintain tight control over their Indian converts. He permitted the Indians to continue their traditional practice of placing food on the graves of the dead and to attend native dances until his own Indian catechists dissuaded him, because they knew firsthand of the fighting and drinking which accompanied the dances.[28]

Hare's arrival and introduction of a firmer and more direct control of the Indians was intolerable to Hinman, who was jealous of his position in the mission field. After his dismissal, Hinman said, "How can I but remember that I am the founder of all the missions to the Dakotas, that they were built by years of patient and lonely toil and that but for me—I speak as a man—they would not have been?"[29]

Hinman did not renounce his ministry and demanded a trial before a court of presbyters, which was appointed for June 4, 1878, but did not convene until July.[30] The charges against Hinman were of "gross immorality, misconduct and the dishonest and unfaithful use of money entrusted to him for the work of the mission."[31] The court rendered a guilty verdict, but took no disciplinary measures other than to expel him from the reservation.

Mr. Hinman then took his case to the Board of Managers of the Domestic and Foreign Missionary Society, and in a letter to them, detailed his grievances and charges against Bishop Hare's action. The letter was printed into a pamphlet and widely circulated.[32]

Bishop Hare, feeling the need to defend his actions, retaliated with his "Rehearsal of Facts" which detailed the grave offenses "against the morality credibly imputed"[33] to Hinman. Hare made use of the hand printing press recently installed at St. Paul's School at his home in Yankton Agency, and printed the pamphlet and it, as was Hinman's, was widely circulated. As a result of the pamphlet's circulation, Hinman brought suit in the courts of New York State for libel, charging a malicious intent in the publication of the "Rehearsal of Facts" and claimed damages of twenty-five thousand dollars.[34] The court ruled against the Bishop, but reduced the damages to ten thousand dollars. Hare appealed, but the unpleasant situation was still not resolved. The Appeals Court reversed the decision of the lower court and recommended that the case be "left to the wise and judicious arbitrament of mutual friends."[35]

Hare and Hinman then appeared before the Presiding Bishop in 1887, and both signed papers prepared by him to end the nine years of scandal. Hare's paper stated:

That while the acts imputed to the Rev. Samuel Dutton Hinman in my Rehearsal were not established at the first trial, I, nevertheless, fully believed the testimony on which they were reported to me to be credible, and thought then, and think now, that, with my convictions of duty, I could *not* do otherwise than believe and act on it.[36]

Hinman, in his signed statement, declared:

That I brought the action in the suit above-named, to furnish an opportunity for giving all the evidence that could be given affecting my character, and not for any money damages, none of which do I ever expect to receive. And, further, that while I assert my innocence in respect to all the imputations contained in the Rehearsal made by Bishop Hare, and think that he will ultimately come to that conclusion, I have no doubt that Bishop Hare has fully believed me to be guilty and has acted on that belief.[37]

Years later, the Reverend Edward Ashley wrote of the Hare-Hinman episode, "It is not for me to say anything in regard to the merits of the case, except this, that Bishop Whipple of Minnesota stood by Mr. Hinman."[38]

Samuel Hinman, in his years as a missionary also used his knowledge of the Dakota Indians and their language in behalf of the United States government. As noted earlier, he had been influential in the inclusion of an article in the 1868 Treaty to benefit his Santee, and served as the official interpreter for the treaty commission. He was a member of the 1876 treaty commission, "one of the praying men who mourned over the fallen tribe and neatly abstracted from it the Black Hills, the Powder River and Bighorn lands."[39] In 1877, Hinman and Hare were in agreement that the Ponca Indians, who had been placed under the jurisdiction of Niobrara, be removed to Indian Territory, Oklahoma.[40]

Hinman left Dakota after his removal from the administration of the Santee Mission, and was employed by the U.S. Census Bureau, Washington, as an Indian specialist.[41] The severest criticism of him was yet to come with his involvement as the official interpreter during the unscrupulous work of the 1882 Sioux Land Commission under Newton Edwards. Again, Bishop Hare was in opposition to Hinman, and wrote letters to influential persons in the East, strongly protesting the methods used by the commission to obtain the signatures of the Sioux.[42] Hinman was personally accused by Indians from Pine Ridge of making threats to frighten men into signing.[43]

This man, whom the Santee affectionately called, "Hemani,"[44] who had devoted most of his adult life to bringing the Dakota to Christ, was now a disgraced and dishonored man. The Hare-Hinman controversy split the Santee Agency into three factions. The other protestant missionaries were against Hinman, most of the Indian Episcopal clergy supported the Bishop, but most of the Indian congregation remained loyal to Hinman. The Reverend W. W. Fowler, who succeeded Hinman, believed that Bishop Hare was arbitrary and unfair in his punishment of the Indians who supported Hinman. All who did so were expelled from the church.[45]

Bishop Whipple stood by Hinman and received him back into the Minnesota diocese. Hinman applied to Bishop Hare for a Letter Dimissory, which the Bishop wrote on September 17, 1887.[46] The press concluded from the Letter Dimissory that Hare had changed his mind about Hinman, and implied that the Bishop had been misinformed when he first made the charges. This led Hare to write a letter to the clergy and laity of his district in which he wrote:

I held that a Bishop is bound to grant such a request (for Letter Dimissory) unless he has evidence of the misconduct of the Presbyter concerned, within the three years immediately preceding the request.[47]

Hinman returned to Minnesota where he died a broken man in 1890, and was buried at Birch Coulee, not far from where his missionary work began.

Hinman was replaced by the Reverend W. W. Fowler, who stayed at Santee until 1887. The Reverend C. R. Stroh was the next missionary to the Santee, and in a short time, he learned Dakota and became well acquainted with his charges. He contracted typhoid fever in 1892, and was taken to Springfield for medical treatment. In the middle of the night on August 21, he got out of bed, and it was theorized that he tried to swim across the river to Santee. His body was found forty-five miles downstream.[48]

Stroh was succeeded by an Indian catechist, Smith Robinson, and the administrative supervision of the Santee was placed under the Reverend Joseph Cook across the river at the Yankton Mission.[49]

In 1909, the Santee Mission was under the administration of the Reverend William Holmes. Holmes continued the supervision of Santee from Springfield, where he moved in 1924, to become the vice-warden of Ashley House. In 1925, he transferred to the Standing Rock reservation. The Reverend Paul H. Barbour came to Springfield and was in charge of the Santee Mission until 1930, when he moved to Rosebud, and Santee was again administered from the Yankton Mission by the Reverend H. H. Whipple.

FLANDREAU

In the spring of 1869, twenty-five families left the Santee reservation without official authorization from the government agent. They traveled overland and settled on unoccupied land in the Big Bend valley on the Big Sioux River.[50]

Several reasons have been advanced as to why the band, under the leadership of David Weston, left Santee. Many of them had been imprisoned in Minnesota after the 1862 Uprising, and had undergone not only a religious conversion, but also a psychological transformation, that substituted the white man's individualism for the Indian attitude of common ownership.[51] In Nebraska, the government re-established the old chiefs' power, whom the Weston group rebelled against. They were also aware of the provisions, under the terms of the 1868 Treaty, which permitted Indians to take up homesteads outside of the Great Sioux Reservation.[52]

Other reasons the band had for leaving Santee were that the Nebraska land was poor, and the small particles allotted to them were inadequate. The land around the Big Bend was not only fertile, but also more like the Minnesota home they had loved. Then there was the fear common to all of the Santee, that the Nebraska reservation was not a permanent one, and the Indians could again be uprooted and moved at the government's whim.[53]

The small band began their trek with little food, because the Santee agent refused to issue rations to those who would not accept the leadership of the old chiefs. They had only a few ponies and most of the people walked; one woman froze to death when they were caught in a spring snow storm.[54] They could not plant any crops that first year, but were able to secure credit from businessmen in Sioux Falls to purchase food and clothing. During the winter they trapped muskrats, which they sold and earned money to buy seed, and with oxen hired from white settlers in the area, they broke ground and planted their first crop.[55] The group was joined by twenty-five more families from Santee during the first year, and fifteen more in the second spring.

Commissioner Parker, of the Indian Bureau, had ruled that in order for the band to homestead, they must permanently and wholly dissolve all tribal connections and benefits due them as members of their tribe.[56] However, the Indian Office did assume some responsibility when, under Grant's Peace Policy, the Presbyterian Church was given jurisdiction over them. A few people of the Flandreau colony, who had been Episcopalians in Santee, continued to hold services in their new home with David Weston as catechist. They built a log cabin as their chapel, but conflict soon arose as to who should be catechist and the group, small as it was, broke into two factions.[57]

In 1874, the Weston group sent a delegation to Bishop Hare asking him to visit them. Hare started but was driven back by a snow storm, and he was reluctant to infringe on the official Presbyterian responsibility for the colony. However, the Reverend J. W. Cook of Yankton did not agree with his bishop, and wrote in his diary that it was an "outrage to the Flandreau people by the Bishop turning them over to the tender mercies of the Presbyterians."[58]

Finally in 1877, Bishop Hare visited Flandreau, and when one of the women donated a horse and the Indians gave 200 dollars, he was convinced of their sincerity to have an Episcopal mission at Flandreau. The parish of St. Thomas, New York, contributed $1,200, and Dr. Henry of Flandreau gave two acres of land, and the Indians six adjoining acres. St.

Mary's Chapel, named as a memorial to Mary Hinman, serving both whites and Indians, was built on the west end of town.[59]

The first service was held in December, 1878, and the church was consecrated on April 20th, 1879. In a letter from Flandreau, dated April 21, 1879, Bishop Hare tells of interruption of that service:

Sunday, April 20, a roaring gale prevailed, but the congregation, who gave undivided attention until I had advanced about ten minutes in my sermon, when frightened glances of two or three of the men who were sitting near the windows which look toward the town (about an eighth of a mile distant) turned my attention in that direction. I saw in an instant that a fire was raging there, an alarming event always in this windy region when the country has been long without rain. . . . I immediately told the men that I thought we could best honor God by going at once to the assistance of the people of the imperiled town, doffed my robes, as did Rev. Mr. Young his surplice, and ran with him and the rest of the people toward the flames. . . .

Our Indians won, by their hearty and efficient efforts to check the flames and save property, the admiration of the most cynical. . . . Not withstanding the exhaustion which excited efforts of the Indians had produced, a fair-sized congregation assembled in the church in the afternoon, when Rev. Mr. Young presented a class of eight for confirmation.[60]

The Reverend H. St. George Young was in charge of St. Mary's Church until January, 1880, and with his departure, the attendance dropped from one hundred and twenty to forty. The catechist, David Weston, again assumed charge under the jurisdiction of the Reverend W. W. Fowler of Santee who, because of the distance, was unable to give regular attention to the new congregation.

In 1884, the Reverend Edward Ashley visited Flandreau and reported to Bishop Hare that the Flandreau Mission was weak. The Indian congregation had again split into factions over the choice of catechists and many joined the Presbyterians.[61]

Bishop Hare made an effort to revive the good beginnings and assigned Mrs. M. E. Duigan to assist the Indians. Her main emphasis was working with the women in teaching the proper use of medicines, regular bathing, and good care of their children and homes.[62] The Indian catechists continued to hold services, and in 1888, when the Reverend William Joshua Cleveland was assigned to Grace Church, Madison, Flandreau was placed in his charge. The Bishop reported:

Tuesday morning, the Indian congregation (of Flandreau) came together, a body of decent looking people, about 50 in number, a large attendance considering that they live on scattered farms six to ten miles distant from the church and from each other. Mr. Cleveland presented a class of 9 for confirmation.[63]

In 1891, St. Mary's chapel was moved to its present location just to the south of the Indian School campus.[64] Later, in 1894, the white members of the Church separated and built their Church of the Redeemer and the St. Mary's Mission continued its ups and downs of attendance.

Cleveland ministered to the Flandreau congregations for ten years. In 1910, Bishop Johnson reported that St. Mary's had a membership of twenty-eight, and was in the charge of the Reverend Dr. Robert Doherty, with William Jones as a catechist and Zenas Graham as helper.[65] From that time on, St. Mary's and the Redeemer congregations were in the charge of one priest who usually did not reside in Flandreau, but visited from Dell Rapids, Madison or Brookings. The two congregations declined until it became economically infeasible to maintain both. They merged into St. Mary's and Our Blessed Redeemer in 1964, and the chapel of St. Mary's was closed. In 1972, St. Mary's was assigned to the Association of Christian Churches for use as the student chapel of the Religious Education Program for the Flandreau Indian School. The Chapter of Calvary Cathedral retained ownership of the land and building.

SISSETON

The Sisseton and Wahpeton Santee Indians had been settled on their reservation near Lake Traverse in Dakota Territory after the 1862 Minnesota Uprising. In the late fall of 1868, Bishop Whipple visited the reservation and was so appalled by the destitution he found that he issued food and clothing without regard to the terms of the 1867 Treaty, which stated that no rations would be given to those Indians who would not work.[66]

Bishop Whipple, a powerful friend to the Sisseton tribes, was granted the responsibility of distributing federal funds to the Indians. The Sisseton-Wahpetons had been under the influence of the Presbyterian missionaries, Riggs and Williamson, in Minnesota and on the new reservation. Riggs began building a church and ignored orders from the Interior Department to stop until it was officially decided which denomination was to have charge of the reservation.[67]

Jared W. Daniels, an Episcopalian, succeeded the first agent in 1869,

and although he was well liked by the Indians and was an effective ad-
ministrator, he was removed and replaced by a Presbyterian when that
denomination assumed control of the reservation.[68]

In 1877, a Sisseton delegation made a 300 mile, ten day journey to
attend the Niobrara Convocation at Yankton Agency, and presented the
following petition to the convocation and Bishop Hare:

> From Sisseton, Wahpeton and Lake Traverse some of the men says, every man
> on earth wants to live well, and if he knows one thing good, he wants to have it.
> We hear and know from the white men they have laws and great many strong
> words, so they live well.
>
> But there is one great and strong law they have and that is the Word of God.
> And so we hear this great and strong law and wish to live well and have the
> Protestant Episcopal Church here in this place to teach us and our children that
> great law, and so we ask a young man to tell his works, his name is Daniel J.
> Robertsons, and then we want to tell the truth so we put down our names.[69]

Bishop Hare, reluctant to trespass into the Presbyterian controlled reservation, and there being no funds to establish a new mission, did not act
upon the petition. The Sisseton Episcopalians continued to request a
missionary, and so in 1881, Hare visited the Agency and received permission from the agent and the Presbyterians to establish a church.[70]

The agent gave land and from women in the East came money to build a
chapel. On June 1, 1881, the Reverend Edward Ashley arrived and began
his work with a membership of thirteen.[71]

Ashley, whom the Sisseton called, *Psehtecin*, Ashwood,[72] had come to
Dakota Territory from England in his teens and worked as a carpenter,
and later, as a teacher at the Yankton mission. He studied on his own and
was ordained deacon in 1876. Bishop Hare sent Ashley to Seabury Divinity School, Faribault, Minnesota, where he studied for two years. After
his graduation and ordination to the priesthood, Ashley held the first
service in St. Mary's Church at the Agency in 1882. In 1884, he reported
to Bishop Hare:

> I have gained one thing which is a satisfaction to me, the confidence of the
> people. There is considerable ignorance and apathy to overcome and it is uphill
> work, but then it is God's work and in his own good time He will give the increase
> of our Planting and Watering.[73]

Ashley made progress, and in 1885, St. James, Waubay was built, in
1886 St. John the Baptist was established west of Brown's Valley, and in
the same year, St. Luke's at Veblen was built.

In 1889, Ashley was transferred to Fort Bennett, on the Cheyenne River reservation, as Rural Dean of the Niobrara Deanery. In 1922, he became Archdeacon of Niobrara. He later moved to Aberdeen, from where he traveled all over the Niobrara Deanery. He is credited with understanding the Indians far better than any other white man. He was a student of their language and customs and spoke and wrote better Dakota than the Indians did themselves. When he died in 1931, after fifty-seven years of continuous service for and with the Indians, his title, Archdeacon of Niobrara, died with him.[74]

The Reverend John Robinson became the Superintending Presbyter of the Sisseton Mission in 1900. In 1913, the Reverend Paul H. Barbour came to Sisseton where he served until 1915. The following is Father Barbour's account of his years at Sisseton:

We (Barbour and wife Mary) landed in Sisseton about September 1st. The Rev. John Robinson *Mato Sapa*, Black Bear, my superior during my deaconate, was quite old, the real director of the Sisseton Mission was Mrs. Robinson. The physical plant (at St. Mary's) was in good sturdy shape. South of it was a good two-story rectory and barn-cum-icehouse. Mary and I settled down in the guild hall, a shack which had been divided into three 12x24 rooms with attached garage and a *tankan tipi* (privy). Brr!

The first year I had some Religious Education teaching at the government boarding school northwest of St. Mary's with Father Robinson. As of now, there were four chapels and in the following year I started a Robertson-Wetherstone family mission on a farm near Rosholt.

The Dakota name I had at Sisseton was *Mato Cistinna*, Little Bear (contrast with *Mato Sapa*). Mrs. Robinson's reaction to the name was, "I knew he was a cub and should be slapped."

After Mary's death in September, 1914, Dave Clark and I lived in the rectory at St. Mary's that winter. The third winter, Frank Rhea, then a deacon, later Bishop of Idaho, lived in the rectory and I, with a young government clerk, Homer Johnson, lived in the guild hall.

That third year I had two deacons, young Frank Rhea and old Victor Renville. After Bishop Biller's death, I carried on until Rhea was priested, then back to Hartford to live with my mother and son until 1923.

In my Sisseton years, the roads were not too difficult, except right after a heavy rain or blizzard. Just the usual quantity of pre-graveled South Dakota roads. I had a team of mares, two saddles, a buggy, and a home-made sleigh to carry me on my rounds.

In my innocence, I took it for granted that in another generation or two the Dakotas would be absorbed and assimilated into the surrounding civilization. I remember asking someone for the Dakota word for "civilization" and he gave me *wasicuniciyapi*, "taking on the white man's way."[75]

YANKTON MISSION

The Yankton Indians of the Dakota Indians were a friendly tribe, and had a history of cooperative relationships with the whites. Lewis and Clark, in 1804, recorded them as living near the mouth of the James River. As more white settlers moved into the area, the United States government negotiated a treaty, signed on April 19, 1858, in which the Yanktons ceded 11,200,000 acres and moved to a 400,000-acre reservation between Choteau Creek and the Missouri River.[76]

Major A. H. Redfield, the first agent assigned to the Yanktons, held the first Protestant Episcopal service in Dakota Territory at the Yankton Agency on July 17, 1859.[77] The work of the Church with the Yanktons, was, however, the natural outgrowth of that to the Santees.

There was some intercourse between the two tribes while the Santee were still in Minnesota and the Yanktons were roaming over the vast territory of Dakota, western Iowa, and Nebraska. When the Santee were moved to Crow Creek, which was only about one hundred miles distant from the Yankton reservation, and on the regular route that the Yanktons used in going back and forth to visit their Teton relatives or to hunt buffalo, the two tribes became more intimately acquainted.[78]

The Reverend Samuel Hinman made it a point to make the acquaintance of the Yankton headmen, and spoke with them about their interests, and advised them to seek the establishment of an Episcopal mission on their reservation.[79]

In 1863–64, some of the young Santee men sought work at the Indian agencies and military posts along the Missouri. Among them was Paul Mazakute, a catechist at Santee, who came to work in the saw-mill at the Yankton Agency. He began holding services and classes of instruction for the Yankton Indians, and his efforts laid the foundations for the work of the Episcopal Church on that reservation.[80]

The Indians from the Yankton Agency frequently visited the Santee, and sometimes attended the services at Bazille Creek and witnessed the teaching of the children in the Mr. Hinman's school. A half-breed, Frank Vassar, *Seaswena*, entered the school to learn to read and write his own language and to know of the ways of the Church. Vassar, with encouragement from Hinman, tried to unite the Yanktons in wanting an Episcopal Mission among them.

The Yanktons, according to J. W. Cook, were divided into three groups:

First, those headed by the old Head Chief, *Padaniapapa*, Struck-by-the Ree, who desired a Romish Mission. This desire had been aroused by Father DeSmet, a Jesuit Missionary, who many years in succession visited the tribes living along the Missouri river. . . . Father DeSmet promised them a Mission, and year by year renewed the promise, and urged them to prevent any other religious body from undertaking any Mission or school work among them.

The second party was composed of those who were attracted by the work of the (Episcopal) Church among the Santees, the simple beauty of her services, the singing, the instruction of the children, and the use of vestments by the minister when celebrating divine service. They said: "We don't want that church where ministers wear only their ordinary dress, but we want that church whose ministers wear white robes." Above all, the improvement which they saw in the Santee attracted them.

The third party, and perhaps the largest of all, was that of the distinctly heathen element, utterly opposed to the white man's ways and religion, and wishing to be left entirely to their dancing and grotesque rites and ceremonies.[81]

Frank Deloria, chief of the half-breed band, visited Mr. Hinman and said, "I am sent by four Chiefs, four Head Soldiers, and eight sons of Chiefs, to pray you and the brethren of your Holy Fellowship to build up a mission among our people."[82]

Mr. Hinman replied to the request by saying when the three parties were united in their desire for an Episcopal Mission, and formally requested its establishment, he would do what he could to help them.

Finally, the Struck-by-the Ree group and the hostile party said they would not oppose an Episcopal Mission, and a council was called on April 30, 1868, at which a formal request was made of Samuel Hinman.[83]

Bishop Clarkson, who had jurisdiction over the Yankton reservation, urged the Board of Missions to respond to the Yanktons' plea, but the man and the means were not yet available. However, the Yankton Indians' request was known to the American Board of Missions, and they immediately sent the Reverend John P. Williamson to establish a Congregational Mission at the Yankton Agency.[84]

In the summer of 1869, William Welsh, whom the Indians called *Wapaha Hota*, Gray Hat, visited Santee, and Hinman took him to the Yanktons to personally hear their request for an Episcopal Mission. Welsh responded encouragingly, and the Indians began gathering logs for the building of a church. After Paul Mazakute was ordained deacon, he was sent in November 1869, to begin work at the Mission at Yankton. With him Hinman sent a group of Santee Indians who were skilled in building log structures to prepare the timbers for a church and mission house.

The Reverend Joseph W. Cook, who had been a missionary in

Cheyenne, Wyoming, answered the call for a white missionary and took charge on May 10, 1870.[85]

By the end of August, the church was completed, and Cook, called *Kuk*, by the Yanktons, employed an old man, *Navkain*, as a crier, who started some miles below the Agency crying aloud to the people that the church was now complete and urging them to come for service.[86]

The Reverend Joseph W. Cook, who wrote (in the third person) a historical sketch of Church at the Yankton Mission, and also kept a detailed diary from 1875 to 1902, said of the beginnings of the work at Yankton:

. . . We had a powerful friend and helper in Frank Deloria. His presence could be counted on almost without fail, and his efforts to bring to church all whom he could influence; and often before services or after its close, and sometimes at the request of Mr. Cook, he would rise in his place with his immense form and powerful voice, and with all his eloquence plead with the people to be attentive to learn the new doctrine and to conform to the proprieties of the public worship of God.

They (the Indians) came in crowds, doubtless mostly impelled by curiosity, yet it kept up for many months.

Our teaching and preaching was of the most elementary character, the foundation truths of Christianity. . . . As we were able we visited about among the people, especially where we learned there was sickness and distress, speaking to them the comforts of the Gospel, and urging upon them the advantages of education and Christianity.

That fearfully hot, dry summer there was a great deal of sickness among the people, especially among young children. Mr. Cook having had a good deal of experience in hospitals and in the compounding of medicines and putting up prescriptions, out of pity prescribed for some children with remarkable success, which so raised his reputation for skill in that line that from that time for years after he was constantly sought to prescribe for the sick.[87]

The year, 1870, was one of many "firsts" for the Yankton Mission.[88] In addition to the arrival of Cook and the starting of the school, Paul Mazakute first ministered the Sacrament of Infant Baptism when Josephine, daughter of Frank Vassar, was baptized on May 8th. On July 10th, the first Christian marriage was solemnized in the Dakota language by Mr. Hinman, when Frank Vassar and Mary Tasagylduta were married. On August 21st, Hinman held the first service of Holy Communion in the Church of the Holy Fellowship. The first Episcopal burial service was held by Mazakute when John Itewauyakapi, a baptized boy, was interred. Walter S. Hall joined the mission as a teacher on September 27th, and Sister Anna Prichard, from Memorial House, Philadelphia, also began her work that fall. On December 4th, Andrew Botkin, the first adult, was baptized by Mr. Cook.

"In December," wrote Cook, "to the great joy of Deloria, his son Philip was taken into the Mission family. He was the first of five Dakota boys to whom in the course of a few years we sought to give special advantages, by living among us and then by being educated among white people."[89]

The other of the five boys were Charles S. Cook, half-breed son of a Virginia military officer, who chose to be called by the Reverend Mr. Cook's surname; William T. Selwyn, who disappointed Cook by not utilizing the opportunities given him; Felix T. Brunot, a young chief who, after his education, became a man of great influence among his people; and the fifth was Alfred C. Smith, also an early pupil at St. Paul's school, who became a government Day school teacher at Yankton and on other reservations.[90]

In 1871, St. Matthew's Chapel was built on March 20th near *Magaska*, White Swan, at the upper end of the reservation. The Reverend Philip Johnson Wahpehan was in charge until he was moved to Choteau Creek to replace Paul Mazakute in September. John E. Chapman and Amos Ross, Santee catechists, remained in charge. The Chapel was renamed Philip the Deacon, in memory of Wahpehan, who froze to death on November 24th.[91]

On January 3rd, Sister Lizzie Stiteler, from Memorial House, Philadelphia, joined the Yankton Mission. On May 12th, Bishop Clarkson confirmed twenty-four Indians in the first confirmation in what would become the state of South Dakota.[92]

Six miles below the agency, the Church of the Holy Comforter was built at Point of the Timber in 1872, and the Reverend George Young, assisted by catechist Salos R. Walker, was in charge. In the spring of 1881, the log chapel was swept away in a flood and was not rebuilt.[93]

William Hobart Hare, Bishop of the newly created Missionary Jurisdiction of Niobrara, arrived at the Yankton Mission on May 8, 1873.[94] He chose for his cathedral the Church of the Holy Fellowship, the log chapel at the Agency, and made his home in a small room added to its side. In 1886, a framed structure replaced the original and was consecrated on October 3rd.

In 1893, the Santee and Ponca Missions were assigned to the charge of Mr. Cook, and he administered the vast area from Yankton Mission until his death in 1902.

Yankton Mission, Greenwood, Dakota Territory. L-R; Rectory, Cathedral of the Holy Fellowship, St. Paul's School. This was the site of Bishop Hare's first home and cathedral in Dakota.

PONCAS

"These Indians in council evinced much pratical common sense. They see that civilization is their only hope. They were delighted to learn that the Church would furnish teachers without diminishing their small annuity"[95] wrote William Welsh of the Ponca Indians in his 1870 report to the Secretary of the Interior and the Protestant Episcopal Church. Welsh became a staunch friend of this once proud and powerful tribe who had been reduced in number by smallpox, starvation, and frequent raids by their Sioux neighbors.[96]

In a treaty of March 12, 1858, the Poncas ceded their land to the government in exchange for a strip of land six miles wide and twenty miles long on the Niobrara River and Ponca Creek. There they farmed and built homes, but in March, 1865, they were forced to abandon the site and moved to a reservation twenty miles north of the Santee on the west side of the Missouri River.[97] There they were visited by the Reverend Samuel Hinman in 1869, who sent Paul Mazakute to hold services for them on every other Sunday.

The tribe had promised in their treaties never to take up arms, and had never broken their word, despite constant Sioux harassment. When Welsh visited them in 1870, they expressed to him their confusion that the government rewarded the Sioux, who preyed upon them, whereas the peaceful Indians were destitute and their plight ignored. Welsh reported:

They (Poncas) behaved so well under the very trying circumstances in which they are placed, that I told the agent to pledge them this month a money annuity of five dollars a head, say, $3,750. I felt sure the Government would not withhold it, but I would not have promised it had I not been willing to make the payment in case of disappointment. A visitor must have a heart much harder than mine, to refuse a helping hand to Indians who are intelligently striving after Christian civilization. . . .[98]

When Welsh returned East, he sought a missionary for the Poncas. J. Owen Dorsey, a young deacon from Maryland, responded to the call and went to the reservation in the spring of 1871. The Poncas received him "as one sent by the Great Spirit for their good."[99] For four or five months he used an interpreter, and the Indians listened to his teachings, and encouraged their children to attend his school. However, in that short time, Dorsey acquired enough knowledge of their language, which was similar to the Omahas, to write it, and translated the Lord's Prayer and Apostles' Creed.[100]

Dorsey soon realized that he needed female help to teach the women and young girls of the tribe to increase the efficiency of the Mission, by "carrying civilization to the Indian homes," as had been done by Mrs. Hinman and Miss West at Santee. In November, 1871, he was joined by his mother, Mrs. M. C. Stanforth.[101] Welsh reported:

Mrs. Stanforth, Mr. Dorsey's mother, a zealous Southern matron who had acquired skill by caring for the spiritual and bodily requirements of slaves. . . . Mrs. Stanforth's qualifications for such work are great . . . she learned how to vaccinate, to probe and sew up wounds, to bandage and to perform all the other duties of a skilled surgical nurse.[102]

By the next summer of 1872, a mission house and chapel had been built, and Dorsey and his mother were joined by Sister Mary Graves, Miss M. Ives, and Miss Eugenie Nichols. By the end of one year, some students (adult and children) were reading the McGuffey reader, and all but two or three knew the alphabet.

On June 19, 1872, at the first public baptism of the tribe, there were twenty-nine persons baptized: seventeen adults and twelve children, and two others received into the Church.[103]

One of the Ponca chiefs, Antoine, "a graceful orator, and perhaps the wisest counsellor and best friend of our work in the tribe," spoke of the work of the missionaries:

When I see you, my friends, I am made wise and can look far ahead. When Mr. Hinman came to us, he brought the Great Spirit to our hearts. I find to-day that you are stronger than all other friends sent to us by our great Father (the president). Do not lose heart—still strive for us. The sight of you raises our eyes—your presence makes us stronger. . . . You brought our mother (Mrs. Stanforth) to us. We are glad to see her here today. We want our children made wise. We are the poorest tribe on this river. You have been up the country to make friends with the Dakotas; but you see what a people they are; how they have stolen our horses. I do not know whether you believe what they say or not. They are provided for by our great father. Now, will you say when you reach Washington that we are justly dealt with?[104]

Antoine was referring to the continued forays of the Sioux against whom the Poncas had no arms to defend themselves. In 1872, the government was considering removing the Poncas to live with their Omaha relatives. However, the full-blood chiefs had their way, and they remained on their reservation, even though hemmed in by the Sioux.

There was, in the spring of 1872, heavy rains which washed away the grain fields, and the resultant flood swept away many houses. In addition to this calamity, Mr. Dorsey and "their mother," Mrs. Stanforth, contracted malaria and had to leave the reservation and return East to recuperate. Bishop Hare reported:

It has seemed advisable to suspend our work among the Ponkas, pending their proposed removal, especially as the Government has been obliged to call upon us to surrender the house which the Mission family were permitted to occupy, and there is no other in which the Mission family could live. It is probable that the Ponkas will be removed to a Reservation not under the control of our Church. . . .[105]

The work was suspended until October, 1874, when Dr. Richard Gray, a candidate for the ministry and a practicing physician, took charge.[106]

In the fall of 1876, the Poncas were a peaceful and happy community, striving, as they had always done, to live peacefully under the terms of their treaties with their government.

One Sunday the Indians (Ponca) went to their church as usual, to hear the words of the minister, but some of the words which he said that tribe will never forget. He told them that he had heard that they were to be driven from their homes and sent far to the south, never to come back again. He said he was exceedingly sorry for them as they had been honest, industrious, frugal, hard working, and had just gotten themselves nice houses and farms. He did not know that he could help them. He could only pity them.[107]

In 1877, the government, following the advice of Bishop Hare, removed the Poncas against their will to the Quapaw River, Indian Territory, in Okalahoma. There the Poncas were placed under the jurisdiction of another denomination. Bishop Hare's advice was apparently based on his belief that the Poncas would be better off away from the constant harassment of the Sioux, and the indifference of the government to their plight.[108]

"I trust," Hare wrote, "that those who have given money for the benefit of the Poncas will allow what remains on hand to be expended for the good of other Indians within the Jurisdiction of Niobrara."[109]

However, the Poncas made powerful friends in Nebraska and in the East, who were appalled by their illegal removal from their homes. Their plight received wide press coverage which raised a public outcry, so that in a historic legal opinion handed down by the court on May 12, 1879, in the case of the Poncas, Indians were established as persons having the same rights as other Americans.[110]

White Thunder, chief of the Upper Brule, gave back to the government the land which had been given him after the Poncas left, and in turn, it was "given" back to the Poncas who wished to return.[111] Bishop Clarkson of Nebraska, along with A. F. Sherrill, Congregational minister of Omaha, and W. J. Harsha, pastor of the Presbyterian Church, Omaha, headed the Ponca Relief Committee, which worked for the Poncas return.[112] The Church's work among them remained under the Diocese of Nebraska, but never regained the strength of its early days. In 1939, at the request of the Executive Council of the Diocese of Nebraska, and with the Presiding Bishop's approval, Bishop Roberts was given oversight of the Ponca and Winnebago reservations. The Reverend Walter V. Reed took charge of the work, which was to be a temporary arrangement.

3

∧∧∧∧∧

Upper Missouri and Western Dakotas

CROW CREEK

The Crow Creek reservation had originally been established for the Santee exiles from Minnesota. After the Santees' removal to Nebraska in 1866, bands of Two Kettles and the Lower Yanktonais more or less took over the buildings at Fort Thompson and were allowed to remain. By 1869, the Lower Yanktonais and Two Kettles were reported as "peaceable and trying to farm at Fort Thompson."[1]

William Welsh, after his 1870 visit to the area, reported:

These Indians long for a minister, for schools, and for instruction in agricultural handicraft, with such appliances as will enable their people to draw support from the soil, instead of being fed like tame cattle. . . . The women here have been more demoralized than elsewhere by the immoral conduct of those whom the government has placed over them.[2]

In 1872, Welsh, with a delegation from the Executive Committee of the Church, again visited the Crow Creek reservation:

The Agent at Crow Creek is Dr. H. F. Livingston, nominated to the post by our Board of Missions, to whom the oversight of these Indians was assigned two years ago . . . a great change has been effected in the short time that has elapsed since the new policy went into operation. The present Agent, by his activity and personal courage, has entirely broken up the infamous whiskey traffic, which threatened the utter ruin of the tribe. The Reverend Samuel D. Hinman accompanied the delegation and held a service in the Dakota language for the Indians which was the first many of them had attended.[3]

In October, 1872, the Reverend Heckaliah Burt went to the Crow Creek reservation and lived first at Medicine Crow's camp, three miles

The Rev. Heckaliah Burt, Crow Creek Mission,
with his horse team, Charley and Billy.

above the present Fort Thompson.[4] He was soon joined by Sister Anna
Prichard who opened a school for girls and the building of a church was
started. The school and Sunday services were first held in the government
buildings at Fort Thompson, and services were also held in the government buildings at White Ghost's camp, six miles above the agency.[5] At
Upper Camp, the Indians were so receptive to the Church's work, that
the Executive Committee built Christ's Church, a mission house, and a log
house for Sister Anna. Sisters Olive Roberts and Sophia Pendleton were
in charge of the new boarding school.[6]

In 1875, Bishop Hare wrote glowingly of the Crow Creek work:

Quiet progress has during the past year marked the stations comprised in this
Mission. The instrumentalities in operation are: a Day-school at the Upper Camp
(average attendance twenty); a Day-school at the Lower Camp (average attendance six); a Boarding-School at the Agency (average number of boarders eight);
a Sewing school at the Upper Camp under the care of Sister Anna (average
attendance twenty); besides religious services at all points named. At both places
of worship, the attendance has been remarkably good, considering that these
Indians never knew anything about the Church till recently.[7]

Hare also reported that in 1875, Edward Ashley was a teacher at the Lower Camp. Burt was transferred to Lower Brule in 1876; Ashley remained at Crow Creek as a lay reader and teacher.

Burt was assigned to Pine Ridge in 1879, where he met and married Harriet Blanchard in 1882. Harriet was from Hopkinton, New Hampshire, and her brother, George, had operated the trading post at Pine Ridge.[8]

In 1881, Burt returned to Crow Creek, and Christ's Church was moved to old Fort Thompson because the larger building was needed to accommodate the shift in the Indian population.[9]

In 1881, white settlers had pushed into the borders of the Crow Creek reservation, and Dakota newspapers were demanding that the land be opened to settlement and the reservation abolished. "The only friend the frightened Crow Creek Indians seemed to have left was their Episcopal missionary, Reverend Heckaliah Burt, one of God's good common men who had devoted his life to the service of these poor Sioux. It was on his suggestion that the Crow Creek chiefs (April 15, 1882) signed a petition beseeching the Great Father (Chester A. Arthur) for protection from the Dakota whites. . . ."[10]

The Indians gave the Burts many beautiful things for safekeeping, and the missionary home became a small museum where the Indian children had free access to learn of their old Dakota heritage which the older people feared would be forgotten.[11]

On October 2, 1914, Bishop Biller, after a visit to Crow Creek, recorded in his journal:

With Messers. Burt and (E. B.) Mounsey, I celebrated Holy Communion, confirmed and preached. Again the church was packed, children sitting on the floor of the chancel. After the service I had conferences with several persons. The door of the Mr. Burt's house is always unlocked and from early morn until late at night Indian callers may be found in the "living-room." Always they are welcome and no member of the family seems ever to be too tired or too busy to confer with them.[12]

Bishop Biller offered Burt a six-month furlough, "in view of his nearly forty-five years of continuous service. I do not know if he will accept or whether his Indians will let him leave them for so long a time."[13]

Heckaliah Burt died at Chamberlain on June 8, 1915. The house that now stands on the ground of Christ Church at Fort Thompson was built in 1918, as the Burt Memorial Cottage. It stood near the mission house in old Fort Thompson. The Burts' collection of Indian artifacts was passed on to David Clark, "because he understood that it was part of the work of the church—and of the missionary—to recognize and dignify the life and history of the community."[14] The Burt Collection is officially owned by the Episcopal Church in South Dakota, and is part of the David W. Clark Memorial Collection at the W. H. Over Museum at the University of South Dakota in Vermillion.

In April, 1919, the Reverend David W. Clark, the second son of the Reverend Aaron Baker Clark, who served on the Rosebud mission, became Superintending Presbyter of the Crow Creek and Lower Brule missions. David and his wife, Elizabeth, worked closely with the government and native leaders. They established the Crow Creek Museum and started, in 1928, the Crow Creek Dormitory to provide a Christian home for girls attending the Government school.

LOWER BRULE MISSION

In 1872, William Welsh reported of the Lower Brule Indians:

These Indians, estimated at 2,500, are under the control of the Agent of the Yanktonais, and are located on the west bank of the Missouri, extending from the mouth of the White Earth River, up to a point opposite to Crow Creek Agency. The sub-agency buildings are about nine miles from the Agency, and on the opposite bank of the Missouri. A company of United States soldiers is there, principally needed to hold the lawless *whites* in check.[15]

This tribe, and that of the Upper Brules, were so named after a split in the larger tribe; the Upper located north of the Platte river, and the Lower to the south of the Platte. In 1869, they were reported as "perfect Ishmaelites, wandering in small bands thousands of miles over the prairies; are teacherous beyond all other Sioux and commit most of the rascalities which occur in this district."[16]

In the summer of 1872, the Reverend Joshua Cleveland went to Lower Brule, and was joined by Miss Mary J. Leigh, Miss Lizzie Stiteler, and W. S. Hall, who would be teachers. Soon after his arrival at Lower Brule, Cleveland wrote:

On reaching there we found an utterly raw and wild field in which neither the government nor any religious body had yet undertaken aught in the way of civilizing or Christianizing enterprises. No farming or stock raising was attempted by the people, no school had been provided for the children . . . the Lower Brules, about 1500 in number, were camped together in the brush, spending their time wholly in feasting, dancing, the hunt for buffalo, then plenty, and the war path for at that time the Sioux were still in continual warfare with the neighboring tribes. A mission house having been built for us near the mouth of a dry creek about half way between the post and the camp, we began our work without much delay, trying to induce the children to attend services and all to come, on Sundays, to the mission for religious services.[17]

On February 10, 1873, Cleveland reported to the Office of the Indian Commission:

I think I have written you before in regard to the young man whom I have taken into my Mission family. I send this by mail his scalp-lock, one of his ear braids and his necklace; hoping that as they are the first trophies of the Brule Mission, you may be able to make some kind of use of them for our cause.[18]

Sister Lizzie wrote on the same date:

Yesterday (February 9th), we had some twenty-two at Service, quite a good number for wild Indians. One that came was a perfect fright. He had his face painted yellow, green and red; his forehead yellow, cheeks red, and two stripes of green going from each corner of the mouth to the ear.

I am in hopes that it will not be long before I can do more for these poor creatures. It is still considered unsafe for us ladies to visit them alone.[19]

Cleveland, whose Indian name was *Wazihanska,* Tall Pine, and Miss Stiteler were married by Bishop Hare on his visit to Lower Brule in May, 1873.[20] Despite the couple's optimism and hopes for the work of the new mission, in October, Cleveland had to admit, "The prospects are not encouraging for our winter's work. The Indians are quite unsettled in mind and much of the largest portion of them have gone to Spotted Tail's."[21]

In his second annual report, Hare wrote of his decision to temporarily abandon the Lower Brule work:

The Indians among whom this Mission was begun are in constant communication with the wildest Indians of the back country and and were in consequence so often turbulent that the Missionary who had charge of the work among them was removed to a point of greater promise. There is every reason to hope that the Mission may be re-established among the Lower Brules before long, and I expect to send them soon Mr. Walter S. Hall, now a candidate for Holy Orders, who lived among them for some months and who desires very much to return to them.[22]

Hall reopened the work in January of 1875, and Bishop Hare sent with him five hundred dollars for furniture and one thousand dollars for current expenses. The Reverend Heckaliah Burt came from Crow Creek, and the Church of the Savior was built. After Burt's arrival, the Bishop was able to report that the "behavior of the Lower Brules was greatly improved during the last eighteen months. Their desire to better their condition seems sincere.[23] The Reverend Luke C. Walker, a full-blooded Santee, replaced Burt, who was transferred to the even wilder Brules at Spotted Tail's agency in June, 1878.[24] Hare reported that Walker was a natural leader, and "formed a center of moral influence at the agency both among the whites and Indians."[25]

The Reverend Luke C. Walker persevered, and by 1892, the Lower Brule Mission listed eight stations. Agent Dougherty thought highly of Walker and wrote that the Indian missionary "not only preaches but practices, and his well-ordered field gives evidence that his labor with hands as well as brains is not considered by him below his calling."[26]

Mr. Walker was a Minnesota Santee from Birch Coulee. He attended Philadelphia Divinity School, and was ordained deacon by Bishop Clarkson in 1871. He was sent to Yankton Agency where he met Sophie Eymer, the first day school teacher in Yankton, and they were married at Greenwood in 1872. While at Yankton, Walker worked on translations of the Book of Common Prayer for the revisions of the book already published. He was ordained priest in 1876, and in 1878, the Walkers moved to the Old Lower Brule Agency at Oacoma. With his appointment of priest-in-charge at Lower Brule, he became the first of the Dakota priests assigned administrative supervision of reservation work.[27] The Walkers lived to see every Indian on the Crow Creek reservation converted to Christianity.[28]

The Walkers' home, like the Burts' across the river at Fort Thompson, became a center for the community life of the reservation. People came to visit, learn to read, listen to the first victrola, and the people brought their treasures of past Dakota life, for safekeeping. The Walkers, as did the Burts, cherished the Indians gifts and their collection, with the Burts', was left to the Clarks, and is part of the Clark Collection at the University of South Dakota.[29]

In 1920, the Reverend Joseph Dubray was assigned to assist Walker on the Lower Brule. Walker was recuperating from a serious seige of pneumonia, and was urged by Burleson to "rest and let the others take up the work." But the Walkers hesitated to retire and leave Lower Brule, which had been their only home for so long. Finally, Mr. Walker retired in 1921, and moved across the river to Fort Thompson where Sophie died in

1931. After her death, Mr. Walker lived at Fort Lookout where he died in 1933.[30]

In the evening of June 14, 1924, devastating tornados struck both the Crow Creek and Lower Brule reservations, and destroyed six of the ten chapels on the two reserves. The damage was estimated at $6,000 on the Lower Brule, and $3,000 on the Crow Creek. The insurance carried was only about a third of the loss, due to the fact that no insurance company would fully insure the buildings so scattered on the reservations with no fire protection whatsoever. A fund was established to rebuild the chapels, and so prompt was the response from within South Dakota and from the National Church, that only one year later, all of the damaged churches had been restored and five of the six destroyed had been consecrated.[31]

The Reverend David Clark of Crow Creek, and the Reverends Paul H. Barbour and C. B. Blakeslee on the Lower Brule, with the help of Cyril

The Bishop's Chair of the Church of the Holy Comforter, Lower Brule Mission, which was carried by a tornado and deposited undamaged in a corn field a mile away.

Rouillard, Christian Whipple and Robert Dubray, students at Ashley House, did most of the rebuilding.[32]

As was the case in all such storms, unusual things occurred. At the Church of the Holy Comforter, Lower Brule, the Bishop's chair was carried a mile away and deposited undamaged in a cornfield. Holy Name Chapel was lifted bodily from its foundation, carried through a fence, and set down with such a jolt that it exploded, leaving only the floor intact, with the white font in its midst.[33]

When the chapels were rebuilt, they came to serve not only the Indians on the reservation, but also the incoming white settlers. This was an example of a new problem facing the Church in South Dakota: that was an amalgamation of the two races, with the opening of many reservation lands to homesteaders.

Because of the tornados' destruction of agency buildings at Lower Brule, the Government decided to combine the administration of it with Crow Creek, under the Superintendent at Fort Thompson. The Church followed the same plan, and both reservations were assigned to the supervision of the Reverend David W. Clark.[34]

CHEYENNE RIVER MISSION

The delegation of the Executive Committee, with William Welsh, visited in 1872, the agencies placed under the jurisdiction of the Episcopal Church made the following report of the Cheyenne Agency:

We have now reached the uppermost limit of our Indian jurisdiction (so far as the government is concerned) on the river (Missouri). Since leaving Yankton Mission we have been entering the deeper shades of savage life. The dawn of civilization which we saw there, receding as we have moved northward, has been succeeded by the dim twilight at Crow Creek, the duskier shadows among the Brules, and to-day we reach the confines of the black night of barbarism. The Indians living around and visiting the Agency from the interior, are classed as either "Hostiles" or "Friendlies," the former being the wandering nomads of the plain who prefer their independence and a doubtful subsistence procured by hunting, to accepting the white man's food, and thereby, as they understand, becoming his vassals. The effort of the Government at this and other remote frontier posts is to create the appetite for such food as coffee, sugar, and flour, and so make the Indians dependent on our bounty until they are able to receive instruction in tilling the soil.[35]

Bishop Hare thought of the missions in the far areas of the Niobrara Jurisdiction as being similar to the blockhouses of Frontier settlements.

The tribes under "control" of the Cheyenne Agency were the Minnecon-jou, Sans Arc, Two Kettle, and Black Feet Bands of the Teton Lakota (Sioux). Their agent, Major George Randall, described his charges as "wild and roving and it needs but short acquaintance with them to discover their real feeling of hatred for the white race. They are kept quiet only by fear and influence of persons from whom they have received kindness."[36]

Bishop Hare said of the Indians on the Cheyenne:

They (the missionaries) are among tribes who have hardly taken their first lesson in civilization, who are roving and unsettled, and contain within them a considerable element of those who love and glory in lawlessness and violence, and whose contact with the white man has yet been so little with good men, and so frequently with the vicious, that its tendency has been rather to confirm than to shake their conceit that their own, and not the white man's is the better way.[37]

Still there were, by the time of Welsh's 1872 visit, Indian men on the reservation who already realized that the old way of life was doomed, and that Christianity was the path to follow in the white man's world. Charger, who would later be baptized Martin, and his band settled at Little Bend across from Fort Bennett and soon was raising corn and vegetables and built log houses.[38] Near Fort Sully, Charlie Fisherman and Black Thunder began farming, despite the opposition from their family and friends, and also built log houses.[39]

In the summer of 1872, Commander Stanley invited the church to use the post quarters at Fort Sully until mission buildings could be built. In October, the Reverend Henry Swift, whom the Indians called *Putinhinsa,* Red Whiskers, arrived at the fort where he held services and also traveled downstream to the agency to hold services. He lived in a log cabin in Spotted Cloud's camp, and when he was joined by a teacher, Miss Mary J. Leigh, they began a day school and the Indians helped build a boarding school.[40]

In 1874, Hare reported of the work at Cheyenne:

A brave and patient effort is being made to gain an influence over these people. In addition to all usual Missionary work a boarding-school is in operation. The obstacles are great, but I agree with those who are on the ground and feel their brunt, in thinking them not insuperable. Indeed, although the early summer months witnessed an outbreak of the old spirit among them in the starting out of a large war-party against the Rees, the year, as a whole, has been characterized by considerable progress in peaceful pursuits and if not *in,* at least *toward,* the Church and schools.

Give time, wise effort, and God's blessing, and the end we wish is assured.[41]

The wise efforts of Henry Swift was such that in only three years time, "that where white men feared to live, Christian women were able to go among the Indians unmolested."[42]

In 1874, Swift, upon the invitation of the Indians, began St. Paul's Mission at Mackenzie's Point, twenty-five miles from the agency. Hare reported that a house which accommodated the Mission family and fourteen boarding pupils was built, and that plans were underway to build a church.[43]

In June, 1874, Bishop Hare wrote to President Grant and protested the illegality of the government's exploratory expedition, led by General Custer, into the Black Hills. The expedition was in direct violation of the 1868 treaty, and Hare feared that it would provoke an Indian war and "would seriously imperil the existence of the struggling but numerous missions, which encouraged by your (Grant's) policy, the Episcopal Church is nourishing among the Sioux, and endanger the lives of her missionaries."[44]

The next few years saw the Sioux fight to defend their property in a War for the Black Hills, which resulted in their last victory at the Battle of the Little Big Horn, on June 25, 1876. All of the western Lakota tribes were unsettled and hostile to the whites when the government established a treaty commission to negotiate the sale of the Black Hills. Hare declined an invitation to be a part of that commission, but suggested that Samuel Hinman be made a member.[45]

The result of the commission's work was that the Sioux ceded the Black Hills, and as Bishop Hare had predicted to Grant, the work of the Church and her missionaries was endangered. An indirect result of the Indians unrest was the murder of the Reverend R. Archer B. Ffennell, who had come to the Cheyenne Mission only eighteen months before. On September 27, 1876, Ffennell was killed by an Indian who had vowed to take the life of the first white man he saw, in revenge for injury he had suffered from the military.[46]

The Bishop, clergy, and lay helpers of the mission realized that they were surrounded by danger. Years later, the Reverend Henry Swift recalled the perils of the time:

(After) my colleague, the Reverend Archer Ffennell was killed by hostile Dakotas. His mission, St. John's, three miles from the Agency, was temporarily abandoned, until I could reach it from a point twenty-five miles beyond. The country was then swarming with hostiles, and the Agency people, the military, and the friendly Indians, protested against even myself going up to reoccupy St. John's.[47]

Swift, with Bishop Hare, visited the mission at St. John's and he reported, "The people (Indians) fairly thronged us, lamenting over the death of Mr. Ffennell. . . ."[48]

The Cheyenne Agency was placed under the command of the Army, and additional troops brought in because of the restlessness of the Indians. The Reverend and Mrs. Swift resumed work on the Cheyenne River reservation in 1877. In 1880, Swift moved to a new station built at Burnt Face's camp on the Moreau River. In May 1887, Swift transferred to Texas, and he was replaced by the Reverend J. W. Hanford, who served only fifteen months.[49] He was injured after losing control of a mowing machine and bled to death before help could be summoned.[50]

The Reverend Edward Ashley was transferred from the Sisseton Mission, and by 1890, Ashley was in charge of seven mission stations on the Cheyenne.

Ashley remained in charge of the Cheyenne Mission until 1924, when Bishop Burleson assigned the Reverend Joseph Good Teacher as priest-in-charge. Good Teacher, a Santee, had been ordained Deacon by Bishop Hare in 1898, and served at the Yankton Mission until 1913 when, after his ordination to the priesthood, he moved to Cheyenne as an assistant to Ashley. Good Teacher died in 1925, and was succeeded by the Reverend R. P. Frazier.

STANDING ROCK

Seven thousand Indians of the Upper Yanktonais, Lower Yanktonais, Blackfeet, Hunkpapas, Cuthead, Sans Arc, and Oglala were under the charge of the Grand River agency in 1868. In 1871, the agency was moved just north of Oak Creek above the Grand, and again in 1873, moved to a rock plateau, seventy-five feet above the river, to Fort Yates. The permanent reservation became known as Standing Rock, and was under the control of the Roman Catholic Church. Thus, it was not until 1883, that the Episcopal Church became interested in working at Standing Rock. The Reverend Henry Swift, after a visit to the agency, reported to Bishop Hare:

The sentiments of Sitting Bull's people are strong and set for *our church* to build on the Grand River, where they are moving in the spring. The Uncpapas (Hunkpapas) at R. C. Station almost untouched by any influence of the present mission, want us there. The agent told No Heart he was glad we had come and he wanted us to help them. The Roman Priest at the Farm Mission is much exercised and talked angrily with No Heart (He was all sweetness with us). "This is a Roman Catholic Agency. We can prevent them (Episcopalians)." "No," said No Heart, "you cannot. That matter has been decided by the Department." Priest: "We do not fear you." "That," said No Heart, "is no way for a Christian to talk. That is the way bad and fighting men talk to each other, but there is no reason why you should fear us, for we do nothing but try to persuade our people to believe in the faith *(wowaciuye)* and there is no reason why you *should* fear us." Priest: "You do not have the truth. We only have the truth." "No," said No Heart, "you have the crucified one and believe in him as we do. You have his prayers (the mass) and so do we. If ours is not true neither is yours." "Your ministers have wives, that is wrong," said the Priest. No Heart replied, "When God made man he made them male and female, and the woman as wife for the man, and surely we are told He blessed them. He would not have thought woman so bad when he sent his son to be born of one of them." "With that," said No Heart, "the Priest stopped talking." He had not one more word to say. I hope we may have power to work in this field. It is right for the harvest. There is no place on this reserve where we would not be welcome.[51]

In 1885, Bishop Hare wrote in this Thirteenth Annual Report:

A Mission has been begun during the year on the Standing Rock Reserve. . . . A visit made to them by Rev. Mr. Swift in the winter of 1883, followed by a second in November, 1884, in which I accompanied him, brought matters to a head.

An appeal in behalf of these poor people brought the President of the Niobrara League, the Woman's Auxiliary of St. Thomas' Church, New York, and other members of the Niobrara League to our help, and a church with parsonage attached was completed in August. The Church, the gift of Mr. J. J. Astor, is called St. Elizabeth's after her who was the first to salute the Virgin as about to be the mother of the Lord, and in memory of a servant of God who bore the same name in later days. A metallic tablet in the church bears the inscription:

> Let the supplications of Thy servant,
> Elizabeth Hamilton,
> for the poor and needy
> be remembered by Thee,
> O Lord, our God.
> And may Thy mercies be
> multiplied toward all who
> worship Thee, in this place

The church is located on Oak Creek, the site being so chosen that the Mission may become a centre for a settlement of farming Indians.[52]

The work was placed under the charge of the Reverend Edward Ashley from Cheyenne River. In 1890, the Reverend Philip J. Deloria, a deacon, was placed at St. Elizabeth's Church at Oak Creek; at Black Feet, Camp I. Sherman was catechist; Henry Marshall was catechist at Little Oak Station; and catechist Sam Smiley was at Black Horse Creek. In that year, St. Elizabeth's school was built on a bluff overlooking the valleys of the Missouri and Grand Rivers.[53]

At the annual Niobrara Convocation held at Cheyenne River in 1892, Amos Ross and Philip Deloria, Indian deacons, were ordained to the priesthood, and Deloria placed in charge of the Standing Rock Mission where he remained until 1925.

Deloria, whose Dakota name was *Tipi Sapa,* Black Lodge, was to become the best known of all native priests. A former chief of the Yanktons, the story of his conversion has become legend.

The Venerable Edward Ashley, Archdeacon of Niobrara, pioneer missionary who understood the Sioux Indians far better than any other white man. R: The Rev. Philip Deloria, a Yankton chieftain, who became a devoted native priest of the Church. His figure is included in the 98 Saints of the Ages in the National Cathedral, Washington, D.C.

Tipi Sapa was riding by a chapel (at Greenwood) in full war regalia when he heard the congregation singing, "Guide Me Thou Great Jehovah," and he stopped to listen to the words. He did not enter the chapel but rode back later another day to hear the same hymn being sung. Apparently a great impression was made on the young chief. He had understood the words as the hymn was being sung in Dakota. Finally he went to Bishop Hare and stated he wanted to become a Christian. The Bishop told him he must give up his chief's position and cut his hair and become a simple man. *Tipi Sapa* refused to do this, stating he was a powerful chief. He returned later, however, and was baptized.[54]

After his conversion, Philip was sent to Shattuck Military School, Faribault, Minnesota, by Bishop Hare who sensed the young man's leadership potential. At Shattuck, Philip was a special student who concentrated on learning English and mathematics. After his graduation, he returned to Dakota, became a catechist, and then was ordained deacon at St. Stephen's chapel on the Cheyenne River reservation. He was sent to establish St. Elizabeth's school, and after his ordination to the priesthood, became superintending presbyter of the Standing Rock Reservation.[55]

Deloria's daughter, Ella, who became a noted anthropologist and linguist, wrote of her father's influence in the conversion of Gall, Chief of the Hunkpapas:

. . . at the beginning Gall always came to church painted up as for a war council, looking austere and a little frightening. The young clergyman knew he was on trial, he and his message. Gall would sit by the door with his weapons—and would watch every move the minister made in the chancel and take in every word he uttered, with a grimly searching look that was disconcerting. . . . but in the end, he made a great feast with the clergyman his honor guest . . . calling him *misun*, "my younger brother"—a social kinship term, certainly, since Gall was a Teton, while the clergyman was a prince of the Yanktons. . . .[56]

Miss Deloria further reported Gall's words to the young Yankton priest:

What is entirely new to me is that the *Wakan* is actually the father of all men and so he loves even me and wants me to be safe. This man you talk about has made *Wakantanka* very plain to me, whom I only groped for once—in fear. Whereas I once looked about on a mere level with my eyes and saw only my fellow man to do him good, now I know how to look up and see God, my Father, too. It is *wašté* (well).[57]

Gall's daughter, at the 1891 Niobrara Convocation, presented an offering of eight hundred dollars on behalf of the Niobrara branch of the

Womans Auxiliary. Gall was baptized on the fourth of July, 1892.[58] Gall's grandson, Jerome Howard, was senior Lay Reader of the Mobridge Episcopal Prince of Peace Center in the 1950's.[59]

In a letter to George Biller, Jr., Bishop Burleson wrote on May 14, 1925, "It has been rather hard to get Philip to give up, but it is not wise for him to continue. His health is not good. . . ."[60]

After forty years on the Standing Rock, Philip Deloria returned to the Yankton reservation in 1925, and the Church built a home for him at White Swan. In recognition of his devotion, his figure was included among the ninety-eight "Saints of the Ages" in the reredos of the high altar of the National Cathedral in Washington, D. C. He was one of three Americans so honored.

Philip's son, Vine, was ordained deacon in 1913, and to the priesthood in the same year at St. Elizabeth's school, where his family had lived for so many years. Daughters Suzzane, who became a well-known artist under the professional name of Mary Sully, and Ella, returned to the Standing Rock in 1955, and offered their services to St. Elizabeth's School.

ROSEBUD

In a letter, dated November 15, 1870, Whetstone, Dakota Territory, *Sinte Gleska,* Spotted Tail, wrote to William Welsh:

MY FRIEND:

I wish you to send us a missionary, as I find out it will be for the good of my people, and my white relations have recommended it. . . .

I have three villages—one of Ogalalla, say 200 lodges, Black Bear is their chief; the Brule Wanagi (ghost), 150 lodges, Red Leaf is their chief; the Upper Brule, 225 lodges, Spotted Tail is their chief. We wish to have some of our own people to instruct each band, and also an interpreter for each.[61]

Spotted Tail was concerned with the welfare of his people, and in the same letter to Welsh stated: "We would like large garrisons of soldiers kept at Laramie and also on the Missouri River to keep off bad whites and whiskey from our reserve. To us whiskey is death."[62] Welsh, acting on his own, purchased the whiskey ranch and the entire holdings of the trader to remove the temptation from the Indians. He also promised that a missionary and a teacher would be sent to Spotted Tail as soon as they were settled in a permanent location.

Spotted Tail and the Upper Brule tribes were rovers, and thus, their only contact with the whites was with dishonest traders, whiskey sellers and the military. After the signing of the 1868 Treaty, Spotted Tail's Brules were assigned a reservation at the mouth of Whetstone Creek, on the Missouri, eighteen miles from Fort Randall.[63] In 1870, Spotted Tail accepted Chief Wabasha's invitation to visit the Christianized Santee Mission, and was impressed with the Santees' new life, where they had their own wagons and horses, a school, chapel and a hospital. His visit reinforced Spotted Tail's policy of being friendly to the whites. In 1866, Spotted Tail's daughter, *Pw-he-zi-wi*, died, but before her death, she had been convinced that continued fighting with the whites would only lead to disaster for her people. She begged her father to make peace with the whites and bury her in the white, Christian way. Spotted Tail promised, and ever after tried to keep his tribe from warfare with the whites.[64]

Welsh visited the Whetstone agency in 1870, and reported: "The Church has heretofore neglected this people, grown degenerate because brought in contact with a so-called civilization, which, not being restrained by Christianity, sinks in many things far below the most superstitious heathenism."[65] The wife of the agent, Mrs. J. W. Washburn, and Mr. A. Jacobs began a school, sponsored by the Church, for one hundred and fifty Indian children of the Spotted Tail tribes.

The agency was moved twenty miles from its original site, and in 1874, Bishop Hare and Samuel Hinman visited the new location, and Hare wrote, "This is one of the finest opportunities for the establishment of the Church and the preaching of the Gospel that I ever saw."[66] Hare was referring not only to the Indians, but to the many white men who had Indian wives and their half-breed children. "They," Hare wrote, "pleaded for themselves and their children, as if they had been the heaven-taught pitying shepherds, and not the straying sheep. They gave me the names of about a hundred children who would attend the school, if one was opened. The chief need now is living men and women—a Minister and two or three Teachers, male and female—to enter into this field. . . ."[67]

In the spring of 1875, Bishop Hare asked the Reverend and Mrs. Cleveland, Sophie Pendleton, and Mary J. Leigh to undertake the mission at the Spotted Tail Agency. The Bishop also asked Cleveland to care for the Red Cloud group, forty miles farther west.

Cleveland wrote of the location of the Spotted Tail Agency as being in the midst of desolation and isolation, being five days from the nearest railroad and 300 miles east of Yankton.[68] Mr. Cleveland's biographer, Gertrude Young, noted the progress of the new mission:

March 27, 1876: Sunday services well attended. Two singing schools, one in Dakota, one in English, have been kept up.

October 10, 1876: the first day school opened with an average for the first few days of eighty.

February 14, 1877: the school house, built to hold seventy-five, was bursting at the seams. One hundred and fifty-six students were on the rolls.[69]

After the discovery of gold in the Black Hills and the Custer defeat, the government broke up the great Sioux reservation and relocated the Spotted Tail and Red Cloud agencies nearer the Missouri again. Spotted Tail said, "We have been moved five times. I think you had better put the Indians on wheels and then you can run them about whenever you wish."[70] In the new treaty, which Spotted Tail signed on September 23, 1876, was the stipulation that rations would be issued only to those children who regularly attended school.[72] This stipulation would become an important lever for the missionaries to use in persuading the parents to send their children to school.

The new agency on the Missouri lasted only a year, and again, Spotted Tail was moved, this time to a site eighty miles west of Fort Randall where the Rosebud Creek flowed into the south fork of the White River. There the government built a school house, with two rooms which the church was permitted to use. The buildings of the old mission were sold, and the funds used to build the Church of Jesus on the east bank of the Rosebud creek.[72]

The new mission was among a wilder group of Indians which had resisted Christianity and civilization. The new agency was in a most desolate part of the area, and the Indians were unhappy. Cleveland left the territory for a vacation in the East, and on his return, was stationed at St. Paul's school, Yankton Mission. However, many of the Brules, who were devoted to Cleveland, begged the Bishop for his return. Cleveland heeded their pleas and returned, even though he was concerned about the antagonism of Spotted Tail toward the government, and the decrease in attendance at the church and school.[73]

In 1885, the largest missionary enterprise yet undertaken in the Rosebud was the building of St. Mary's school, to replace that which had burned at Santee. Cleveland acted as temporary head of the school, and by the time it had been in operation for two years, it had forty-eight pupils.[74]

Cleveland was transferred to Madison, and the Rosebud Mission was without a priest-in-charge until 1889, when the Reverend Aaron Baker Clark took charge. A. B. Clark was given the name *Sicangu,* Burnt Thigh, which was the Lakota name for the Brule.[75]

In 1891, the first Niobrara Convocation was held on the Rosebud at St. Mary's School and Ephphatha Chapel. A. B. Clark was followed by his eldest son, the Reverend John Booth Clark, *Mato Ska,* White Bear, in 1917. The Reverend Robert Frazier followed in 1927; the Reverend Paul H. Barbour in 1929, who remained until his retirement in 1956.[76]

PINE RIDGE

Red Cloud first heard of Christianity in the Oglala tongue from Father DeSmet, the Jesuit missionary, at the Laramie Council of 1851.[77] Red Cloud was not converted at that time, and during the next years, fought against the United States Army trying to establish forts and a road through the Oglala lands. He signed the 1868 Treaty, but did not settle on the reservation until 1871.

In 1873, the distribution point for rations for the Oglalas had been moved from a point on the Platte River east of Fort Laramie, to Fort Robinson. The mixed bloods, who had been congregating around Fort Laramie since the 1830s, joined in this move, which was upsetting to the Oglalas and Brules.[78] In January and February, 1874, Bishop Hare, at the government's request, visited the Brules and Oglalas as the head of a commission appointed to determine the cause of these Indians' unrest. In his report, Hare wrote that, "Congress made no provision for feeding them at any agency of their own up north and starving men will and must be fed."[79]

Hare and the Commission recommended that the Red Cloud Agency remain at its White River location near Fort Robinson, and advised the presence of troops as a police force to assure order among the Indians and whites alike. At the same time, Hare recommended that a school be started and wrote, "I was on the eve of beginning a School and Mission work . . . when the Government at my request put up a school house; but the disturbed condition of the people and the prospect that the Agency would be removed rendered delay advisable."[80]

During this time, the Reverend William Cleveland had been going each second Sunday to Red Cloud from his station at Spotted Tail's. In September, 1877, "the time seemed to come for immediate action," Hare reported, and sent Luke C. Walker and John Robinson to begin the school and establish a mission. The new missionaries arrived six days after the death of Crazy Horse, and found the Oglalas in a furor over the young chief's death. The mood of the people did not daunt them, and they immediately began the work which Robinson would carry on for twelve years at Pine Ridge.

Robinson had attended a missionary preparation school in the 1860's at St. John's Church, Camden, New Jersey, and was ordained deacon by Bishop Hare at the Yankton Mission in 1874. He was thirty-one years of age when he went to the Oglalas. He followed them to the Missouri when their agency was again moved, and had a school for them. This attempt to relocate the Oglalas failed, and they were returned to the present agency at Pine Ridge in October, 1878.[81]

Bishop Hare visited Pine Ridge and celebrated the first service of Holy Communion, on August 24, 1879.[82] He brought with him two deacons, Heckaliah Burt to be in charge, and P. C. Wolcott to assist.[83]

Burt had six years of experience at Crow Creek, and a year on the Rosebud, but he was never able to reconcile himself to leaving his work among the Yanktonais.

Wolcott "studied all of the time, does not appear interested in the real work and thought Burt and Robinson talked too much about the Indians."[84]

Wolcott's studying enabled him to pass his canonicals, which Burt and Robinson had long neglected, and in December, 1880, he was ordained priest and took charge of the mission. This apparently caused conflict, and may have been one of the reasons for Burt's asking Bishop Hare's permission to return to the Crow Creek, which he did in 1881.

Wolcott did not stay long in charge of Pine Ridge; he moved in July, 1881, to Chariton, Iowa.[85]

On July 4, 1880, the "first fruits" of the missionaries' efforts was presented to Bishop Hare for confirmation: George Sword, Antoine Marshall, Susan Richard, Ellen Tasinatowin, Eliza Morrison, James and Mary Williamson.[86] In the same year, the Church of the Holy Cross was under construction, and was completed for the first service on the fifth Sunday after Epiphany, 1881. Burt wrote of the new church, "It is a perfect gem . . . everything looks so churchly. . . . Behind the altar there is a very rich hanging which Mr. Wolcott brought with him. The color is that of old gold, and with the brasses on the altar and the rich appearance of the altar itself, it looks very pretty indeed."[87]

In 1879, Joseph Marshall joined the Pine Ridge Mission at Wounded

Knee, where he opened a school in a tipi. Marshall was a mixed blood, who had been one of the first students of Miss Mary J. Leigh, who taught the Oglalas. The Reverend Neville Joyner reported that Marshall, "preached well and led many along the holy way to the feet of the Loving Jesus." Marshall married Eliza Morrison, one of the first confirmands, on November 28, 1880, and he was ordained deacon in 1894. He served at Pine Ridge for thirty-eight years.[88]

The Reverend Amos Ross was the next deacon to join the Missionary staff on the Pine Ridge. He was born in 1852, at a Santee winter camp near St. Paul, Minnesota. He moved with his family after the 1862 Minnesota Uprising to Crow Creek, and then to Santee. In 1872, he and John Rouillard went for four months of religious training in Davenport, Iowa, after which he became a catechist, and finally, after long study, a deacon. He married Lucy Gayton, a mixed blood Ponca, in 1877, and she came with him to Pine Ridge.

The Rosses suffered through the cold winter in a half-furnished house at Orphan's Camp at Wounded Knee. Ross named the station, St. Andrew, "because Andrew went and told his brother as the first thing when he discovered Christ, and he hoped those early Christians would do the same."[89]

From 1881 to 1885, the work at Pine Ridge was under the supervision of William Cleveland, who resided at Rosebud. In 1885, William Selwyn, a Yankton Indian, came to teach at White Bird's Camp. In the fall of 1885, the Reverend Charles Smith Cook, a mixed blood Yankton whose foster father was the Reverend Joseph Cook of the Yankton Mission, was assigned to Pine Ridge as Superintending Presbyter. He had graduated from Trinity College, Hartford, in 1881, received an M.A. from Trinity in 1887, and a B.D. from Seabury Divinity School, Faribault, Minnesota, in 1885.[90] He married Jessie Wells in St. Luke's Church, Cambridge, New York, in 1886. Shortly after, he brought his bride to Pine Ridge, their little home burned down to the ground before their very eyes.

Cook encouraged the development of young men's societies in the chapels, and one of the first was the "Man's Faith Society," in Porcupine.[91] The women's work was also organized and one of the earliest active women was Nancy Revenger, who married Robert American Horse, and became loved by all of South Dakota for her example of lay service to the Church.

In 1888, the Niobrara Convocation was held for the first time at the Pine Ridge Agency.[92]

Church of the Holy Fellowship, Pine Ridge Mission, which was used as a hospital for the wounded survivors of the Wounded Knee massacre, Dec. 29, 1890.

From about June, 1890, to about a year later, there were no official acts performed by the Church anywhere on the reservation. The unrest and excited fervor of the Ghost Dance was felt by all of the residents—Indian and white. On December 29, 1890, Big Foot, and his band of Minneconjous, who were fleeing for safety to Pine Ridge, met disaster and death at Wounded Knee.

Thirty-eight of the wounded who survived were brought to Pine Ridge where Cook converted the chapel into a hospital, strewing straw on the floor. Mrs. Cook, Miss Elaine Goodale, and several Indian helpers ministered to the wounded and dying. Bishop Hare arrived a few days later, and was appalled at what he saw:

My visit to Pine Ridge Reserve brought me to a scene which contrasted shockingly with all the signs of progress and peace which have greeted me on my visits for six or eight years past that time will not efface it from my memory. The friendly Indians had all been called in from the ten or twelve farming settlements around their little churches, and were huddled together in tepees of old time just south of the Agency, and on entering the church, two sights presented themselves. On the church floor, instead of the pews on either side of the aisle, two rows of bleeding, groaning, wounded men, women, and children; tending them were two military surgeons and a native physician assisted by the missionary and his helpers, assiduity and tenderness marking all. Above, the Christmas green was still hanging. To one of my moods they seemed a mockery to all my faith and hope; to another they seemed an inspiration still singing, though in a minor key, "Peace, good will to men."[93]

Cook buried thirty soldiers and twenty Indians in the cemetery at Holy Cross. Christian families came forward to adopt the children who survived, but were orphaned.[94]

The strain of the tragic events took their toll on Charles Cook, who had contracted tuberculosis, and said after his first hemorrage, "it was a blow against my future work. . . . I know God sees what is best for me. I look upon this sudden visitation as a warning from on high for a closer and truer walk with God."[95] He died on Good Friday, April 25, 1892.

The Reverend Charles Snavely replaced Cook, and the mission was then divided into two districts. Snavely assumed charge of three-fourths of the area to the west, and Amos Ross was in charge of all the work in the eastern Corn Creek district.

The Reverend Neville Joyner became Superintending Presbyter in 1908, and on his retirement in 1940, the Reverend Frank M. Thorburn, who had been in South Dakota since 1931, succeeded Joyner.

4

/.V.\V.\V.\

Blessings and Adversities

CHURCH PERIODICALS

The *Anpao kin,* Daybreak, was the first church journal to be published in South Dakota. The *Spirit of Missions* reported:

It is proposed to issue each month in the Niobrara Mission, beginning with January, 1876, a newspaper about the size of "The Carrier Dove," to be called in Dakota, *Anpa Kamdeze Cin;* in English, "The Daybreak." Its contents will be partly in Dakota and partly in English. The object of the Dakota paper will be to provide a medium of instruction and inter-communication for the Indians and on the English page to convey to friends of the Mission information regarding its operation. The subscription will be fifty cents in advance.

The Reverend William Joshua Cleveland was its first editor.

The second publication was *The Church News,* which reached Volume 12, No. 3, in 1895, before Bishop Hare found it to be too much of a financial burden and ceased its publication.

The district remained without a newspaper until Bishop Biller felt the need of a means of reaching the people whom he could visit in body only once or twice a year, and the *South Dakota Churchman* began publication in February, 1913. The *Churchman,* as it was and is affectionately called, was the Bishop's Journal, "the light and life of the paper." Its first editor was the Reverend Francis B. Barnett, rector of St. Mary's Church, Mitchell. In June, 1915, Barnett left South Dakota, and the Reverend S. S. Mitchell, rector of Trinity Church, Watertown, became editor.

In December, 1920, the building housing the Watertown Printing and Binding Company, which published the *Churchman,* was destroyed by fire and all *Churchman* records were lost, except for a copy of its mailing

ANPAO.

THE DAY BREAK.

Published by the Niobrara Mission. "WANKANTANHAN ANPAO KIN HIYOUNHIPI." Price, Fifty Cents a Year.

Vol. I. No. 2. FEBRUARY, 1878. Address ANPAO. *Yankton Agency, Dakota.*

WOWAPI UNQUPI.

SANTEE AGENCY, NEB., *Jan.* 17, 1878.

MY DEAR ANPAO:

Nakaha nicaje nawañon qa kohanna wowapi ciçu wacin. Heon awicakehan takuciya wacin sdonyaye kta. Isanyati owasin iyuśkinyan napeniyuzapi, qa honiwaśte kta seca, heon ohinni honiyanpi kta naceca. Qa miś dehan napeciya wacin qa niye on, mitakuyepi, mitakodaku owasin, Ihanktonwan, Titonwan, Sissitonwan, tona ite miksuyapi kin owasin napewicamduza. Eya den taku ota oyagpicaśni, tuka token unyakonpi onśpa cajemdate kta.

tewaśteya ceunkiyapi, qa dowanpi kin ho-waśte, hotanka ko unpi hecen tipi ocowasin wowitan ojudan sececa; qa woyatan unkeyapi kin den Iye sihaoahde ekta hena mañpiya ekta yanke cin Iyeñca iyahde unkecinpi. Christmas iyohakam, St. John Taanpetu en, śiceca unkitawapi kin owasin, takuśniśni, taku on śkatapi, takuwaśtedakapi ko wicunqupi. Wicoñan waśte kin de ohinni den unhapi. Itokaga, New York otonwe kin ekta, winoñinca waśte wan Mrs. Wisner eciyapi, iye takodaku om; qa Germantown, Penna., otonwe ekta, St. Luke, tipi-wakan tonniciye etanhan, den napin ohinni

tanka awicakehan wicayuwaśtepi qa Iye iyoyanpa Tawa kin en sutaya ewicahde kta hecen wacin. Hena misunka owasin napewicamduze. Niś eya, Anpao, napeciyuza. Nitakuye,

SAM'L D. HINMAN, He miye.

OICIMANI.

Eya taku iwokdakapi kta canhan taku ehanna, qaiś dehand, qa eeś taku tokata u kin on iwokdapi ecee. Hecen tukte unna okna keśa eciyatanhan taku nañonpica, qa awacinpica ecee.

Hekta bdoketu kin he en oicimani wanji unyuhapi e he onśpa cajebdatin

---

The Church News.

Vol. VI. SIOUX FALLS, S. DAKOTA, JANUARY, 1890. No. 1.

"It is evident unto all men reading Holy Scripture and Ancient Authors, that from the Apostles' time there have been these Orders of Ministers in Christ's Church,— BISHOPS, PRIESTS and DEACONS. Which Offices were evermore had in such reverend estimation, that no man might presume to execute any of them, except he were first called, tried, examined and known to have such qualities as are requisite for the same; and also by the Public Prayer with Imposition of Hands, were approved and admitted thereunto by lawful authority."—

Missionary District of South Dakota.

Bishop—The Rt. Rev. William Hobart Hare, D. D., Sioux Falls.
Standing Committee—The Rev. John H. Babcock, Mitchell; The Rev. Joseph W. Cook, Greenwood; Mr. R. W. Folds, Sioux Falls; Mr. J. W. Campbell, Huron.
Secretary—The Rev. Walter James Wicks, Springfield.
Treasurer—Mr. Nelson B. Bailey, Sioux Falls.
Registrar—Rev. Jas. Trimble, D. D., Sioux Falls.
Treasurer of the Chapter—Mr. J. S. Lewis, Sioux Falls.
Examining Chaplains—Rev. J. H. Babcock, the Rev. C. S. Cook, the Rev. L. C. Walker, the Rev. A. H. Barrington.

DEANERIES.

NIOBRARA DEANERY.
Rural Dean—The Rev. Ed. Ashley, Fort Bennett.
Secretary—The Rev. C. S. Cook, Pine Ridge Agency.
Treasurer—The Rev. H. Burt, Crow Creek Agency.
EASTERN DEANERY.
Rural Dean—The Rev. James Trimble, D. D., Sioux Falls.
Secretary—The Rev. W. J. Wicks, Springfield.
Treasurer—Mr. R. W. Folds, Sioux Falls.

TRUSTEES

Letters to the Bishop.

The Bishop receives daily from ten to twenty letters, and sometimes, after an absence, fifty to sixty in one lot. Will our correspondents kindly remember this and be plain and explicit in matters of business, and not suppose that mere allusions will of themselves recall matters long past; nor bury items of business, especially not pecuniary matters, among casual remarks or current news.

Woman's Auxiliary.

The Bishop requests the Secretaries of the various societies of women connected with the parishes and missions of the church in South Dakota to send their names and addresses to Mrs. James Trimble, General Secretary, 320 W. 14th

which those who heard them will not soon forget. The services were throughout both chaste and imposing and left an impression, to which the admirable music added not a little, which will prove both lasting and beneficial. In the afternoon of December 12, a good number of the clergy were able to accompany me to Elk Point, where we found waiting us the hearty welcome and cheery presence of the missionary, Rev. J. V. Himes, a man who at 85 years of age preaches the gospel like the youthful Stephen, and fights for the church like the stripling David. We held services in the evening, an account of which will be found elsewhere under the heading "Elk Point." This exceedingly interesting series

SOUTH DAKOTA
CHURCHMAN

PUBLISHED BY THE MISSIONARY DISTRICT OF SOUTH DAKOTA

December, Nineteen Hundred Thirty

IN THIS ISSUE

South Dakota Churchman

list. The Executive Council moved the paper's publication office to Sioux Falls, where it would be under the direct oversight of Bishop Burleson, who became editor.

Burleson was a professional journalist who had edited his college's paper, and after graduation worked for a printing office, before entering seminary. In 1890, he was editor of North Dakota's diocesan paper, *The Sheaf*. As Editorial Secretary for the Board of Missions, he was editor of the missionary magazine, *The Spirit of Missions*. Bishop Burleson was the author of numerous articles and books, and the best known of the latter was *The Conquest of the Continent,* published in 1911.

Bishop Burleson defined the objective of the *South Dakota Churchman* as being:

To reach every family, even in our remotest mission, and the scattered Church-folk of the country side. It is a messenger of religion and life as exemplified in the

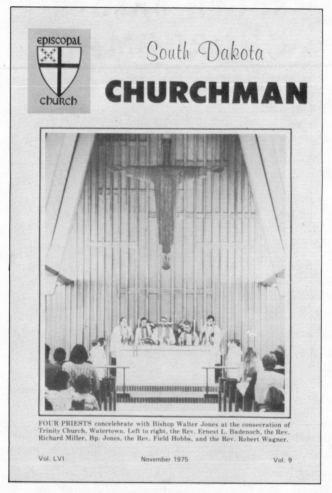

FOUR PRIESTS concelebrate with Bishop Walter Jones at the consecration of Trinity Church, Watertown. Left to right, the Rev. Ernest L. Badenoch, the Rev. Richard Miller, Bp. Jones, the Rev. Field Hobbs, and the Rev. Robert Wagner.

Vol. LVI   November 1975   Vol. 9

South Dakota Churchman

work and service of the Episcopal Church. It should also be a missionary, making known to our own people, and to those favorably disposed to us, the activities which the Church carries on, for the ideals for which she stands.

After Burleson left South Dakota to become Assessor to the Presiding Bishop in 1930, the *Churchman* had three associate editors; Henry Praed, the Reverend Carter Harrison, and Mr. Hal C. Sessions. In 1939, the publication offices were moved to Pierre, back to Sioux Falls in 1942, where it remained until 1976, when once again it moved to Watertown, under the editorship of Mary Barbour Hobbs.

TRINITY HOSPITAL, WINNER

In 1914, the Reverend John Walker began the operation of a four-room hospital, "ordained to be the hope and refuge for the sick and afflicted in a population of 40,000 people covering a territory of nearly seventy miles in any direction."

The parish and entire community of Winner supported Walker's project. Miss Grace Bradley was the first Superintendent, and Dr. Swett was the first doctor.

The hospital functioned under many handicaps. During the winters, women in the community often gave their own bedding for emergency cases which depleted the hospital's supply. Miss Bradley and her successors frequently reached into their own pockets to find money for necessities. In 1917, a brick addition was added to the original frame building.

In November, 1921, the medical facility seemed destined for growth and success with the arrival of Sister Gabrielle and Sister Anne Margaret, nurses from the Episcopal Order of the Sisters of St. Anne, Boston. They were joined by Deaconess Hudson. Unfortunately, the Order decided to withdraw the sisters after six months, and the deaconess also left.

Mrs. Roy C. Hall, who had many years of experience as a missionary nurse in Alaska, joined the staff, and hope flourished again. However, financial support from the community ceased, and the Church could not carry the burden alone. The patient load was curtailed until it was so small

Winner, South Dakota, 1914. L-R: Trinity Hospital, Trinity Church, and cottage of the Rev. John Walker.

Summer Conferences participants at All Saints School.

that the overhead became prohibitive. The Church's only effort at operating a hospital in South Dakota ended on January 1, 1923.

SUMMER CONFERENCE

On June 21 through the 30th, 1921, the first Summer Conference of the Church workers in South Dakota was held at All Saints School. The Reverend E. W. Pigion was chairman of the committee, whose members were Dean Woodruff, the Reverend H. W. Fulweiler, Mrs. Florence Remington, and Miss Mary Peabody, who also served as executive secretary. In addition, there was a camp for boys of high school age or older under the oversight of Bishop Remington.

The morning sessions were devoted to instruction of the Principles of Teaching, Missions, Women's Work, Church History, Social Service, Boys' Work, the Church Service League, and Christian Nature Courses. Each afternoon there was a lecture on some vital topic, and a public meeting in the evening. A special Chaplain had charge of the religious services and instructions and, as the pastor of the conference, was accessible to individuals who desired to ask questions or seek counsel.

The Summer Conferences were a success and well attended by clergy and lay-persons—young and old—from South Dakota and neighboring states. In 1943, Bishop Roberts regretfully cancelled the conferences because of gas and tire rationing, and the general difficulties of travel during the period of World War II.

DAKOTA PRAYER BOOK AND HYMNAL

The Venerable Edward Ashley wrote in his memoirs, ". . . the prayer book is a great missionary of the Church" and translations into the Dakota language of it and of the hymnal became the beloved textbooks of the Indians as they learned to read their own language.

The first translation of parts of the *Book of Common Prayer* was published in 1865, by the Reverend Samuel D. Hinman. Ashley recalled that:

Shortly after Bishop Hare came to the District, the missionaries felt that there should be a translation made of the old prayer book, *The Book of Common Prayer*, 1789. When the proposition was first placed before the Bishop, his opinion was that it was unnecessary for the reason that the Dakota people would soon learn the English language, and in possibly twenty-five years there would be no need of services in the native language at all. The missionaries said the language would be in use after we were all dead and gone, and the Bishop finally consented to the translation. The Reverends S. D. Hinman, J. W. Cook, L. C. Walker, and Daniel Hemans were the committee to work on the translation. Mr. Cook spent

122 *HOLY COMMUNION*

The Decalogue. (68)

God spake these words, and said:
I am the LORD thy God; Thou shalt have none other gods but me.
Lord, have mercy upon us, and incline our hearts to keep this law.

Thou shalt not make to thyself any graven image, nor the likeness of anything that is in heaven above, or in the earth beneath, or in the water under the earth; thou shalt not bow down to them, nor worship them;
Lord, have mercy upon us, and incline our hearts to keep this law.

Thou shalt not take the Name of the LORD thy God in vain;
Lord, have mercy upon us, and incline our hearts to keep this law.

Remember that thou keep holy the Sabbath-day.
Lord, have mercy upon us, and incline our hearts to keep this law.

Honour thy father and thy mother; (69)
Lord, have mercy upon us, and incline our hearts to keep this law.

Thou shalt do no murder.
Lord, have mercy upon us, and incline our hearts to keep this law.

WOTAPI WAKAN

Woahope Wikcemna kin.

Wakantanka wicoie kin dena eye, ça heya; Wakantanka nitawa, Itancan kin he Miye: Mitokan taku wakan tokeca duha kte śni.
Itancan, onśiundapi, qa woope kin de unyuhapi kta e, cante yusunyan miye.

Wakagapi wanjina niçicagin kte śni, nakun wankan maḣpiya ekta, qa ihukuya maka kin en, qa maka kin oḣdateya mini kin mahen, taku hiyeye cin, wanjina oyakagin kte śni. Wicitokab yakipatuje, qa cewicayakiyin kte śni.
Itancan, onśiundapi, qa woope kin de unyuhapi kta e, cante yusunyan miye.

Itancan, Wakantanka nitawa, Caje kin ituya ehin kte śni.
Itancan, onśiundapi, qa woope kin de unyuhapi kta e, cante yusunyan miye.

Anpetu Okiḣpapi kin wakanyan duha kte cin he kiksuya wo.
Itancan, onśiundapi, qa woope kin de unyuhapi kta e, cante yusunyan miye.

Niyate qa nihun wicakduonihan wo.
Itancan, onśiundapi, qa woope kin de unyuhapi kta e, cante yusunyan miye.

Tin-wicaktepi ecanon kte śni.
Itancan, onśiundapi, qa woope kin de unyuhapi kta e, cante yusunyan miye.

The Decalogue in Dakota and English from Niobrara Wocekiye Wowapi, *the Dakota—English service book of selections from the 1929* Book of Common Prayer, *adapted for use in the Niobrara Deanery, 1937 edition.*

some time in New York reading proof and noting corrections. Finally the book was completed and being put into the hands of the helpers and catechists, together with the hymnal. They were found very useful in the evangelistic work among the people. Later in the year of 1875, a great event of the year in the District of Niobrara, was the preparation of a Dakota-English service book consisting of those parts of the prayer book which are most used, and was a revised edition of the old prayer book in Dakota. To this enterprise, Mr. Hinman, Mr. Cook, Mr. Walker, and Mr. Hemans again devoted time and labor of which Bishop Hare said, "All that the Prayer Book is among the members of our Church in the East, that in some respects even more, it is among the Dakotas." We are indebted for the funds to the Girls of Grace Church in New York and to the Niobrara League. The Church at the 1892 General Convention completed an enrichment of the prayer book of 1789 which became the standard book of the Church. The changes were translated in *Anpao* with the hope that the clergy would take these translations, paste them in their service books and use them in the general service of the Church. Many did so, but it was necessary that the service book should be amended to include the corrections completed in 1892. With the coming of Bishop Biller, as Bishop of South Dakota, he appointed a committee, E. Ashley, A. B. Clark, P. J. Deloria, and William Holmes, to revise the service book, but he died before the committee received his approval. When Bishop Burleson came, the matter was referred to him, and he appointed the same committee to work on the corrections of the book. The committee finally made its report to him, which was accepted and approved, and the Bishop authorized the use of it in the Niobrara Deanery. Fortunately, or unfortunately, the General Convention of 1928 again completed an enrichment of the prayer book of 1892, and again there was a necessity for a correction of the Dakota English service book for use in the Deanery.

At the time of the starting of the 1929 Prayer Book, the Reverend Paul Barbour recalled that Ashley said in a clergy meeting, "I wish they'd stop tinkering, and I mean *tinkering,* with the Prayer Book!"

Barbour worked with the Reverends Dallas Shaw and Cyril Rouillard to bring the Dakota Service book up to the 1929 *Book of Common Prayer,* and their effort was first published in 1937, reprinted in 1942 and again in 1967, with slight revisions.

In 1925, Bishop Burleson authorized a new Catechism for use in the Niobrara Deanery. It was modeled somewhat after the Revision of the *Book of Common Prayer,* although simplified and shortened for Indian children.

In 1877, *Hymns in Dakota for Use in the Missionary Jurisdiction of Niobrara* was published, and added to by the Reverend Joseph W. Cook when it was reprinted in 1884. Cook was responsible for the publication in 1902 of *Hymns in Dakota and Hymns in English* corresponding to the Hymnal of the Protestant Episcopal Church. In 1932, the Reverend Wil-

A CATECHISM
CONTAINING INSTRUCTION
.FOR THOSE WHO ARE TO BE CONFIRMED.

———

PREPARED BY DIRECTION OF THE BISHOP
AUTHORIZED FOR USE IN THE
NIOBRARA DEANERY ●
SOUTH DAKOTA

———

WIWICIWANGAPI WAN
Tona Wicayusutapi ecawicakiconpi kte cin
on woonspe kin heca.

———

Bishop kin iye kaȟwicaši qa
South Dakota
Niobrara Deanery en
unpi kta e iyowinwicakiya.

A Catechism

liam J. Cleveland and others published a Dakota Hymnal with tunes and chants.

The Reverend Paul Barbour and others published *Hymns in Dakota and English* in 1946, which was reprinted in 1951 and 1961. The last edition of 1964 was photostatically reprinted bearing the date of 1946, with a printing error, which caused page 127 to precede page 126, instead of following it.

NIOBRARA CONVOCATION

One of the most important events of the missionary work of the Episcopal Church in the United States of America is the annual meeting in South Dakota known as the Niobrara Convocation.

On September 24, 1870, Rt. Rev. Robert H. Clarkson, then Missionary

"Silent Night," in Dakota from **Wakan Cekiye Odowan,** *hymnal for use in the missions among the Dakotas, 1940 edition.*

Bishop of Nebraska and Dakota issued a call to the clergy of the Dakota field for a meeting to be held at the Santee Mission on the fifth day of October, 1870, for the purpose of organizing an Indian Missionary Convocation. Each Chapel was also to be represented by two lay delegates. The Rev. Samuel D. Hinman was appointed by Bishop Clarkson as Dean of the Convocation, and is referred to throughout the meeting as the Rev. Dean.

The Rev. Joseph W. Cook was elected secretary. It is interesting to note that the address delivered by Dean Hinman was in commemoration of the establishment of the Mission among the Santees.

The following are among the resolutions which, adopted by this Convocation, throw light on existing conditions at that time.

1. Resolved, That we ought to cultivate more friendly and brotherly relations with the surrounding Tribes.

2. Resolved, That at home we ought to use our best endeavors to put down evil and idle talking, and to encourage our people to industry and thrift.

3. Resolved, That as our lands are not yet divided nor our patents granted by the President, we know the Church to be the only strong bond that binds us together as a tribe, and keeps our people from wandering and from demoralization.

4. Resolved, That the want of good laws for the government and protection of the Indian, and the non-enforcement of such as do exist, is a great hindrance to the spread of Christianity, and an encouragement to crime and immorality, for the law is a terror to evil doers.

5. Resolved, That the Indian custom of regarding the daughter as belonging to the mother, even after marriage, is destructive of the authority of the husband, and the cause of so much trouble as to almost render Christian marriage impossible among the Indians.

6. Resolved, That the Christian teaching that the husband is the head of the wife should be enforced; and that for the prevention of troubles, young married people should be encouraged, as far as possible, to live in their own homes and not in the families of their parents.

On the morning of October 6, the committee appointed to draft a constitution and by-laws for this Convocation submitted the following:

NAME AND BONDS

This Convocation shall be known by the name and title of The Convocation of the Niobrara; and shall include all the Indian Reservations in the Territory of Dakota and in the Indian Missionary Jurisdiction where Missions of the Church are or shall be hereafter established, together with the Santee Reservation in Nebraska.

MEMBERS

All Clergymen engaged in work among the Indians within the bounds, and all Catechists, shall be entitled to seats. Every Church or Chapel shall be entitled to two lay representatives. Each Band of every Tribe in which there is a Mission shall be entitled to a representative. Provided that no person not a communicant of the Church shall be entitled to vote in this Convocation.

The following resolutions were also adopted:

7. Resolved, That the Rev. Samuel D. Hinman, Dean, and Missionary to the

Camp grounds of the Niobrara Convocation at the Church of the Holy Fellow-ship, Yankton Mission, Greenwood, South Dakota, 1925.

Pawnee Leggins, the Eyapaha *or Herald who rode through the camp to announce the services and meetings at Niobrara Convocation.*

Santee Sioux is hereby nominated to the Bishop for office of Archdeacon of the Archdeaconry of the Niobrara.

8. Resolved, That it is evidently impossible for the Indian Tribes to live any longer as Indians.

9. Resolved, That if they can be saved, it must be by learning the ways and religion of the whites.

10. Resolved, That the Dakota custom of making betrothals without the consent of both parties concerned, is wrong; and that none such should be married by the Clergy of the Mission without diligent inquiry and examination, as to whether the parties are to be so united by their own free will, and by their own desire.

11. Resolved, That so long as the Indians preserve the Tribal relation and live in villages, and hold property in common, it is impossible to civilize them or to firmly establish Christianity among them.

12. Resolved, That although the civil law is a terror to evil doers, yet in our opinion the Christian law of love is far stronger and that most of the dissensions among our people can be healed by kind and Godly advice from the Clergy and Christian people.

From the minutes of the meeting:

After a lengthy debate on the subject of the troubles among Indians arising from wrong notions of the marriage relation, the Rev. Dean offered the following Resolution which was adopted:

13. Resolved, That we request our clergy not to recognize any divorce unless granted for the cause of adultery; and even then not to consent to the marriage of the guilty party.

14. Resolved, That as polygamy is forbidden by the law of Christ, that therefore when any Indian having more than one wife is an applicant for Baptism in the Christian Church, he must first choose the one whom he takes for his wife and be joined to her in holy matrimony.

And at the same time it is the sense of this Convocation that he should as far as he is able continue to support the woman put away, and her children, if she have any, so long as she shall live, unless she shall become the wife of some other man.

15. Resolved, That the thanks of this Convocation are due to the administration of President Grant and the Christian people who have aided him, for the renewed interest taken in the welfare and improvement of the Indians whereby we now receive our annuity intact; and whereby we have the hope that the reform now begun will be carried on until the last abuse shall be swept away.

16. Resolved, That in our opinion among heathen people the custom of the Primitive Church should obtain of meeting for Public Worship only between the rising and setting of the Sun.

17. Resolved, That our thanks are due to Wabasha, Chief of the Santees, for the use of his house for the meetings of the Convocation.

(Note: The resolutions are numbered for convenience only, and do not belong in the original minutes.)

President Calvin Coolidge visited the Niobrara Convocation at Pine Ridge on August 17, 1927. A service of intercession for the President, the country, and the missionary work was held; then the convocation marched out singing a hymn and aligned themselves along the road in front of the Church of the Holy Cross to meet the President, accompanied by Mrs. Coolidge and son, John. The President was presented with a message from the Convocation which was placed in an old beaded and quill worked tobacco pouch given by Moses Shangreau of Pine Ridge. It was presented by native priests, Amos Ross and Philip Deloria. Mrs. Julia Deloria, Mrs. Lucy Ross, and Mrs. Nancy American Horse presented the women's gift of a beaded bag given by Miss Mary Shangreau and containing a pair of moccasins, to Mrs. Coolidge. One verse of "America" was sung in Dakota and then the President and his party left—one minute and fifty seconds after they had arrived.

The Niobrara Convocation grew to be a loved and much looked forward to annual event in South Dakota. Non-Indian Episcopalians and persons from other denominations, as well as government officials and even President Calvin Coolidge visited. The gathering was frequently honored by visitations of numerous Presiding Bishops. Many annual Indian church meetings of other tribes and denominations were modeled after the Niobrara Convocation.

Only three times in its history did the Niobrara Convocation not convene: in 1876, because of Bishop Hare's poor health; in 1901, because of the danger of small-pox contagion; and 1945, because of conditions during World War II when gas and tire rationing and enforced slower speed limits made travel difficult.

CAMP REMINGTON

In July, 1923, Camp Remington opened for the first time. Bishop Burleson had named the camp after Bishop Remington, who first proposed the enterprise and chose the camp's site in the Black Hills. The purpose of the camp was to provide a pleasant and inexpensive place for summer vacations of the clergy and their families, but also for any of the church people who wished to use the facilities. Meals were served in the central building for a dollar a day under the supervision of the camp hostess, the first being Miss Elsie Lampe, of Huron. A small cottage was erected for the bishops, and permission granted for the clergy to build cabins.

In the summer of 1926, the Chapel of the Transfiguration, a log building with only the chancel fully enclosed, was completed. Bishop Burleson and his brother built the foundation. Bishop Roberts and Dean Benedict put on the roof; the altar and other chancel furnishings of white birch were made by Bishop Burleson with clerical help. The bell, which was hung on a pine tree stand near the entrance, was the gift of St. Mary's School, which had been given to the school by Bishop Hare.

CALVARY CATHEDRAL

The Bishop has the cathedral with no congregation of its own, and the rector of the largest Episcopal congregation in the state has no church of his own.

When Bishop Hare selected Sioux Falls as his See city, he found Cal-

Chapel of the Transfiguration, Camp Remington in the Black Hills.

vary Church as a going parish with a small frame house of worship. Mr. John Jacob Astor of New York City gave money for the erection of a Cathedral to be known as St. Augusta's, as a memorial to his wife, Catherine Augusta Astor. When the building was completed, Bishop Hare made arrangements with the Calvary rector and vestry to dispose of their Church and use the new cathedral as their place of worship. Calvary Church continued as an independent parish, choosing its own rector and electing its own vestry. The rector, as is customary, may be nominated by the Bishop and be approved by him, but the Bishop retains the office of rector of the Cathedral Congregation.

In the early days, the work was carried on by Calvary Church in St. Augusta's Cathedral, but time and custom has dropped the name of St. Augusta, and the present generation knows it only as Calvary Cathedral.

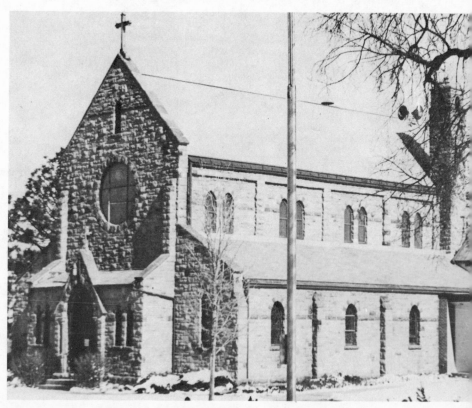

Calvary Cathedral, Sioux Falls, South Dakota.

Bishop Hare and his early traveling equipment.

The complications are only technicalities, and the arrangement is a harmonious one. The Bishop is recognized as the head of Calvary Cathedral. The Dean is Dean of the Cathedral, by appointment of the Bishop, and is rector of the Church by choice of the Vestry.

TRANSPORTATION

Bishop Hare traveled to his far-flung mission stations with a two-horse wagon, a small tent, cooking utensils, and often had to make overnight camps on his rounds. He was usually accompanied by a driver who also served as interpreter. Other early missionaries traveled in the same fashion.

With the advent of public transportation, in the form of stage lines, and later trains, the bishops and missionaries used these unreliable services to visit white parishes or make connections with transportation sent from reservation stations. As late as 1925, Bishop Roberts reported taking the stage from Murdo to White River, where he was met by the Reverend John Clark with an automobile to go to the Rosebud missions.

All of South Dakota's bishops made frequent references in their diaries and correspondence to the difficulties involved in their modes of travel. Services at parishes or mission churches were sometimes missed because of late trains. Often a bishop had to spend a night in drafty depots or were unexpected guests of clergy, lay people—at times non-Episcopalians—because of missed train connections. In November, 1919, Bishop Burleson boarded a sleeper at Mitchell for Sioux Falls at 12:30 A.M. He awoke at 6:30 A.M., to find the train still standing in the Mitchell railroad yard.

The Missouri River, which divides the state, was a formidable challenge which early Episcopalians took in stride. Ferry crossings were at Wheeler, Chamberlain, Pierre, and Running Water. But, when the ferry was missed, many a bishop was rowed across the wide Missouri in small craft. Traffic from Santee to Greenwood and Springfield, from Crow Creek to Lower Brule, was always nonchalantly made in such a way. In the winter, when the Missouri was frozen solid, people walked, rode horseback, used a team and wagon, and later, drove their automobiles across the ice.

Travel with the early automobiles over graveled roads, which rain turned into sticky gumbo in Western South Dakota, was just as unreliable and hazardous as public transportation. Bishop Biller noted in his diary in August, 1915, that the Reverends Paul Barbour and Frank Rhea started the ten-day trip from Sisseton to the Niobrara Convocation at Rosebud, stopping on the way to pick up fellow clergymen, E. F. Siegfriedt of Milbank, and Paul Roberts from Brookings. The roads were in poor condition because of a week of rain, and the group stopped in Sioux Falls, to remove the outer layer of mud, before they proceeded to Rosebud, where they turned up at Convocation with additional layers of mud and their car wired together.

Bishop Burleson's initiation into the dangers of South Dakota travel was in January, 1917. He had caught a ride with a rural mail carrier from Vermillion to Yankton, but six miles out of Yankton, their car was halted by snow drifts and the blizzard which had sprung up. The two men had to walk two miles to a farm where they took shelter from the storm.

Bishop Remington's vehicle was a Buick he christened *Mato Owansin Wašté*, an altogether good bear, after its ability to carry him through snow, mud, and the general bad conditions of South Dakota roads. "Mato" failed him in May, 1922, when it mired down in the mud near Dallas, and the Bishop was forced to spend the night in a haystack. Driving into Peever in May, 1924, Bishop Roberts and the Reverend A. B. Clark escaped injury when a wheel broke off their automobile and rolled down the road in front of them.

Bishop Burleson often thanked Providence that protected bishops, their families, and their missionaries in their hazardous travels.

Unidentified missionaries trying to free their automobile from prairie mud, a frequent hazard of traveling South Dakota Roads in the days before pavement.

THE NIOBRARA CROSS
AND SOUTH DAKOTA SEAL

Certificates of Baptism and Confirmation meant nothing to Indian converts who could not read. Bishop Hare desired to give to those who took upon themselves obligations as Christians some token that would not only mark them as communicants, but also serve as a constant reminder to them of their Christian calling. He, therefore, in 1874, designed a cross to serve this purpose. The oval in the center is his episcopal seal. Around its margin in Latin is inscribed "The Seal of William Hobart Hare, by the grace of God Bishop of Niobrara." The Greek letters on the cross which quarters the oval read, "That they may have life." In each angle of the cross is a tipi surmounted by a small cross. The seal signifies that Christ has come to the Dakotas and gathered them under the protection of the Cross, that they have accepted Him, and their homes have become Christian homes. It was Bishop Hare's custom to give a cross to each Indian candidate he confirmed, just before he made his address to the confirmation class.

Because of the peculiar relationship of the All Saints School girls, whom Bishop Hare confirmed as their immediate pastor and as the head

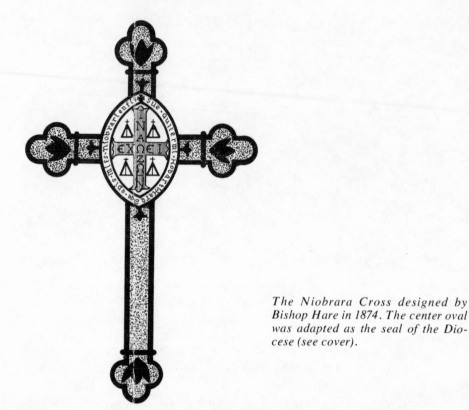

The Niobrara Cross designed by Bishop Hare in 1874. The center oval was adapted as the seal of the Diocese (see cover).

of the school, all girls confirmed at All Saints School were also given the cross.

Over the years, Bishop Hare and his succeeding bishops gave the cross to a few white people who had served the Indians. Non-Indian clergy were given crosses as well as other missionaries in the Niobrara.

In June, 1975, the Niobrara Deanery, by action of the one hundred and third annual Convocation, "in an expression of oneness of God's family and the love of Christ in His Church," voted to share with the whole Church in the Diocese the Niobrara Cross. The fifth annual convention of the Diocese of South Dakota resolved, in October, 1975, that it "exhibit the same love and desire for unity by accepting both this Niobrara Cross and the Christian love this gift represents with thanksgiving."

A new seal of the District of South Dakota was adopted by the 1947 District Convocation. Top center is the mitre, symbol of the Episcopate. The year 1884 is the year when Bishop Hare ceased to be Bishop of Niobrara and became Bishop of South Dakota, which included the white work as well as the Indian. The motto and tipis are taken from the Niobrara Cross.

THE BROTHERHOOD OF ST. ANDREW

The Brotherhood of St. Andrew has always had a strong following in South Dakota, particularly among the Indian men. The first Chapter, No. 53-S, Santee, was chartered at the mission of Our Most Merciful Savior, Santee Agency, in 1886, only three years after the Brotherhood was founded.

The second Chapter was No. 139, chartered at Calvary Cathedral in 1888. The third was No. 471, at the Cheyenne River Agency, St. John's Mission, in 1890.

WOMEN

"No words of mine can adequately tell of the patient, persistent, self-sacrificing work done by the women who love the Church, and to them we owe a great debt," wrote Bishop Hare soon after he came to Niobrara. Later he wrote, ". . . these ladies are an unspeakable blessing to the Jurisdiction. These women come from love, and I think I am thus enabled to do the work which is to be done almost twice as cheaply and more than twice as well as would be possible if they were women who came for pay."

Bishop Hare was speaking of those early women who came as missionaries, but his words are descriptive of all the women who have served the Church, be they sisters of a religious order, Deaconesses, Church Army, clergy wives, and/or thousands of lay women—all had a ministry of love and devotion.

The early women missionaries of Bishop Hare's time faced all of the hardships of pioneer women in a harsh land. Yet, many of them devoted the major part of their lives to the Indians and to South Dakota. A number of them married missionary clergymen, and they and other clergy wives, all of whose names it would be impossible to list, Hare described as "discharging their duties with rare assiduity and cheerfulness . . ."

One of the primary purposes of the missionary women was to work with the Indian women, teaching them sewing, cooking, and housekeeping, along with the word of God. Soon after the Church was established in new missions, there came into existence little bands of Indian women,

Delegation from the Niobrara Deanery to the National Convention of the Brotherhood of St. Andrew, Milwaukee, Wisconsin, 1905.

aided by the white women, to form guilds. They immediately set about saving pennies, or did beadwork, made quilts, and other craftwork, to sell to make money to build a chapel. They not only contributed to the expenses of their own congregations, but also to the native clergy fund, missions in Japan, orphanages in China, the church schools in South Dakota, and innumerable other enterprises.

One year after taking charge of the white field in South Dakota, Hare reported that: "The people have been busy raising money, the Ladies Guilds as usual taking the lead, to build churches." By 1888, the work of the Woman's Auxiliary was well organized, and the Bishop appointed Mrs. Gardiner, wife of the Reverend Frederic Gardiner, Sioux Falls, as General Secretary of the District. Mrs. James Trimble was Hare's next appointment; Miss Mary B. Peabody, also the bishops' secretary for thirty-two years, was General Secretary until 1919.

In his annual address of 1895, Bishop Hare praised the work of the women's guilds, but also cautioned them "to be constantly on their guard and not allow a tempting opportunity to make some money betray them into sacrifice of the sacred cause of concord, modesty, fair dealing and purity. . ." He was referring to certain guilds holding masquerade balls in church halls, and of others raising money by preparing suppers for dances.

In 1911, the Woman's Auxiliary raised $1,000 to assist Bishop Johnson to place a missionary in the newly settled country of the Rosebud. The Reverend John W. Walker, stationed in Winner, became the first on the Church's mission staff to be supported by local funds, and the Reverend W. Blair Roberts was next. In 1915, the fund was named the "Bishop Biller Memorial Fund," and in 1919, its object was changed to be used as part of the salary for one of the Bishops, Burleson and Remington. When W. Blair Roberts became Suffragan, his salary was paid from the fund, and after his election as Bishop of South Dakota, the women voted to continue giving it to him. The fund's purpose and name was again changed in 1956, at the suggestion of Bishop Conrad Gesner, to the Bishop's Sustaining Fund.

The wives of the Bishops Suffragan, Florence Allen Remington in 1919, and Meta Roberts in 1921, were appointed by Bishop Burleson as presidents of the Women Workers. Meta Roberts remained in office after her husband was elected Bishop of South Dakota until 1938, when Mrs. Howard W. Fulweiler, Yankton, was appointed in her place. Mrs. Charles I. Danforth, Yankton, became the first elected president in 1944.

The name of the women's organization changed several times over the

Ellen Everett Hicks Cook, wife of the Rev. Joseph W. Cook of the Yankton Mission in about 1877.

Clergy wives, Mrs. Batiste Lambert and Mrs. Edward Ashley. The latter was known as "Lady Betty."

years. In 1912, it was the Women Workers of the Missionary District of South Dakota, when the women first federated into one body in the State. In 1921, the title of the women's organizations in the United States was changed to the Church Service League, and the South Dakota women adopted the name. In 1936, the name was changed and the constitution revised to become the Woman's Auxiliary. At the annual meeting in September, 1974, a revised constitution and bylaws again changed the title to the South Dakota Episcopal Church Women, and all baptized women of South Dakota were to be considered members.

A number of projects were supported by the women through the years. The United Thank Offering (UTO), formerly known as the United Offering, has been a continuing and vital part of the women's work since the early days. Their offerings returned many times to South Dakota in the form of grants, and with the presence of a number of women missionary workers who were supported by the UTO. The Diocesan Altar Guild was formed in 1939, and the Church Periodical Club, although in operation for

*At Niobrara Convocation at White Horse in 1914. Seated are Mrs. Heckaliah
Burt and Miss Amelia Ives. Standing L-R: Miss Martha Cleveland, Mrs. William
Holmes, Mrs. A. B. Clark, Mrs. Amos Ross, and Mrs. Batiste Lambert. The
other two women and gentleman are unidentified.*

Women's meeting at a District Convocation.

Mrs. Nancy American Horse.

years before, was formally organized in 1924, with Idah Terry Morse, Pierre, as diocesan officer.

The women also supported the Supply Department (later to become the Supply Work), which originated nationally in about 1868, and Bishop Hare's Niobrara Storeroom was part of this project. The purpose of the Supply Department was to assist with clothing for the personal use of missionaries and their families, for needy Indians, and later included the church schools, gifts for women missionaries, and also provided suits for catechists.

A unique project of the women in South Dakota began with a notice in the July, 1920 edition of the *South Dakota Churchman:* "Are you living in a town where there is no Episcopal Church and no regular Church services? Do you feel lonely and wish you might share in the wonderful work the Church is doing?" Mrs. Remington and Mrs. Burleson began a project for these lonely people, which became The Church League of the

Women of the Niobrara Convocation posing in front of their tent with Bishop Burleson (center).

Isolated. South Dakota pioneered in this attempt to serve the isolated, and it was a tremendous success under the direction of Mrs. Dora Vannix. Mrs. Vannix, although suffering from crippling arthritis which confined her to a wheel chair, kept in constant touch with some 500 families throughout the state, and she also conducted a church correspondence school for children. She was totally dedicated to serving the isolated, and much of the effectiveness of the program passed with her when she died in May, 1936.

It was Bishop Hare's custom, which was continued by his successors, to call women delegates to meet at the same time of the Niobrara and District Convocations. The women of the Niobrara Deanery purchased a large tent which was (and is) shipped to the Convocation grounds for their meetings. In 1911, at the Convocation held at St. Elizabeth's Church, Standing Rock, the women delegates presented the following request to the men. "We would like to have the tent for the women's meetings placed near the middle of the (camp) circle, so that we need not walk so far."

Within the tent, the women and children gathered and the Bishop used to preside at the meeting when the offerings and gifts of the missions were presented. The delegate placed either cash or check before the Bishop, with a printed blank filled in with the amount or objects her particular guild had sent. The Bishop counted the money to see if it tallied with the blank, and then read aloud the amount or what the gifts were.

The members of the 1912 District Convocation recorded that, "the Church Women of the Missionary District of South Dakota have always been present at the annual Convocations and are eligible as delegates to Convocation and this custom has certainly been no detriment to the church, to the women themselves nor to the men of the church."

In 1951, Bishop Roberts presented the Women's Auxiliary with a gold cross in appreciation of the women's work. The cross is worn by the presiding president and passed on to succeeding presidents. In 1955, the women formed a Conference Center Committee to refurbish corridors and bedrooms of the main building at All Saints School, which was to be used as the Conference Center of the district.

Bishop Gesner noted the contributions of women to church work saying that he "has never discounted the value of nor recommended that women discontinue money raising activities in behalf of the church . . . since that activity is the outpouring of a personal devotion to the Church."

YOUTH

Up until 1939, the work of the Church among the young people had been an individual parish and mission undertaking without any statewide organization. Various organizations, other than Sunday Schools, attempted to meet the needs of the young: the Young People's Fellowship, Daughters of the King, Acolyte Guilds, Junior Auxiliary, Girls Friendly Society, and in some cases, no formal organizations at all.

In 1939, the Reverend Joseph Ewing was appointed by the Bishop as the District Young People's Advisor, and the work with the youth was reorganized to bring it in line with the League for Young Churchmen. South Dakota was following the national movement, which sought to answer the need for a united expression among all the young people of the Church between the ages of fourteen and twenty-five.

In South Dakota, the League was divided into five districts for the purpose of meeting together. Each district elected a chairman and secretary, and an adult advisor was appointed by the Bishop.

In 1946, the first of several Young People's Summer Conferences was held at Yankton College, and later expanded to include clergy conferences. Classes in Church History, Church Doctrine, acolyte training,

Campers on cleanup detail at Thunderhead Episcopal Camp in the Black Hills.

junior altar guild, and choir were offered, and there was time allotted for recreation and fellowship. The day began with the service of Holy Communion and ended with Evening Prayer.

Another project, but not aimed at South Dakota youngsters, was work camps, "an adventure and an opportunity for service in the Sioux Indian country." The camps were sponsored by the National Commission for Work Camps in the Episcopal Church and the Missionary District of South Dakota. College students, usually from the East, paid for the opportunity to build and repair community centers and chapels, teach vacation schools, and direct recreation programs on the reservations during the summer. The campers also attended the Niobrara Convocation, and their summer's experience culminated with a visit to the Black Hills and Camp Remington.

The project for young people which has generated the most enthusiastic support, including physical labor as well as fund raising efforts, was the establishment of the Thunderhead Episcopal Camp (TEC) in the Black Hills in 1965.

The Diocesan offices located in Dexter House at All Saints School.

White Robes. Front L-R: _____, *Luke C. Walker, Bishop Hare; Center:* _____, _____, *J. W. Cook,* _____, _____, _____; *Back: Heckaliah Burt, David Tatiyopa, Issac Tuttle,* _____.

DIOCESAN OFFICE

After Bishop Burleson closed his home in Sioux Falls in 1928, he moved into Dexter House at All Saints School. He used a little corner room on the ground floor for his office, which overlooked a big porch. It was decided to transform the porch into the diocesan offices, which would be more accessible to the Bishops and Executive Secretary. The move would also increase the income of All Saints by paying the school the rent which had been used to lease offices in downtown Sioux Falls. It would also amount to a considerable savings of district funds. The second floor of the porch was glassed in to become a sunroom for Bishop Burleson and a private bath was installed.

WHITE ROBES

In 1938, Jacob White Eyes, a churchman on the Pine Ridge, recalled a story told by his father about Red Cloud and Spotted Tail, prominent leaders of the Oglalas and Brule tribes, who went to Washington, D.C. to see the President of the United States, U. S. Grant.

My father was invited to go. They shook hands with the President, who said: 'Red Cloud and Spotted Tail, the reason I called you here is to ask permission on behalf of some people called missionaries who want to go out and work among you.' The President then named the Roman Catholics, Presbyterians, and Episcopalians and said: 'Now, Red Cloud and Spotted Tail, pick one of these three and give them your permission and that will be the group to tell the Gospel to you people.' Spotted Tail said to Red Cloud, 'All right, cousin, we the Rosebuds will accept the one you choose.' Red Cloud replied, 'No, now cousin, let's have you pick one and that will be the one accepted by the Oglalas.' And so Spotted Tail said, 'All right then, we'll take the wearers of the white.' So Red Cloud said, 'Fine, we will take the wearers of the white too.'

The wearers of the white were also known as "white robes," as opposed to the "black robes" of the Roman Catholic Jesuit missionaries.

5

⋀⋀⋀⋀

Learning for Life

Where the Church went, so did education. In order to obtain converts, the missionaries had to first educate the Indians, not only in religion, but in language, which was needed for the transference of ideas.

Education for the white settlers of Dakota came with territorial days. Dr. Malancthon Hoyt, the first Episcopal clergyman and his family to reside in the territory, built Dakota Hall in 1862, in back of St. John's Church in Yankton.[1]

Shortly after the missions were established at Santee in 1866, and Ponca in 1871, the Reverends Samuel Hinman and J. Owen Dorsey took Indian children into their homes. In 1870, the Reverend Joseph Cook arrived at Yankton and started a school which was held in the church.

Bishop Hare, after his arrival in 1873, inaugurated the boarding schools for the first time in Dakota Territory. He saw that the Indian children became domestically docile after living for a while in a missionary's home, and that there was improvement in their "isolation from heathen influences and residence with Christian people."[2] Hare felt that the Indian parents did not control their children, "They have the conceit that they develop better if left to themselves. . . . Indian children are not fonder of school than white children are . . . and it is almost impossible to secure their regular attendance at day schools. . . ."[3]

Bishop Hare further justified the establishment of boarding schools by the failure of the government's attempts at training the Indians. He believed that the Church had the responsibility to not only Christianize the Indians, but train them in practical ways to better prepare for their future—whatever that would be.

Suppose these people to be designed by Providence to be hewers of wood and drawers of water. Our duty is to fit them for that lot. Suppose that they are to be merged in our more numerous race. Our duty is to fit them for that absorption by intermarriage, and so arrest the present various intermingling. Suppose that they are to die out. Our duty is to prepare them for their departure. Our duty is the plainer, because the treatment which will fit these people for any one of these lots will fit them for either of the others.[4]

The boarding schools would teach trade skills as well as educational skills, civilized habits and Christian training. Hare hoped that the children thus educated would, in adulthood, form the nuclei of congregations. The schools would be the first homes and starting points of the Gospel.

In December 1873, five picked boys (the number limited because of the shortage of bedding and clothing), were the first students of St. Paul's School at the Yankton Agency. St. Paul's, directly under the Bishop's supervision, operated under a self-serving basis. The boys cared for themselves and their house. Each had weekly assigned housekeeping duties. The dormitory squad made beds and cleaned the dorm; the table squad set the tables and washed dishes; the outdoor squad ran errands, milked the cows, and carried wood. All of the boys worked in the garden and kept up the school grounds.

The boys finished their chores by 10:00 A.M., and then had two hours of school. After lunch, they finished the outdoor work and then resumed classes from 3:00 to 5:00 P.M. After the first year, the enrollment at St.

St. Paul's School at Yankton Mission.

Paul's was from thirty-five to forty boys, and they came from all of the reservation missions.

St. Paul's became typical of what the other boarding schools would become:

> . . . plain and practical and not calculated to engender fastidious tastes and habits which would make the pupils unhappy in and unfitted for the lowly and hard life to which their people are called; as the Indians are not accustomed to labor, the school training should be such as would not only cultivate their intellect, but also develop their physical functions and teach them to do well the common acts of daily humble life, such as sewing, sweeping, etc.[5]

Educating the young Indians was a difficult and strenuous process. The Episcopal church schools had many of the same problems that other denominational and government boarding schools had. None of the educational institutions truly understood the traditional freedom that the Dakota granted their young, and that the Indians' education had been by precept and example.[6]

There were clashes between the old and new values. The intricacies of the Dakota kinship system and its duties, which held the tribes together, complicated matters for the young in schools. Its pull was strong and often won out.[7]

The missionary teachers found it difficult to discipline children unused to any type of discipline. Vacations were also problems, for once the students left school, they returned when they thought it was time, and not when the calendar said it was. The white teachers were frustrated by the Indians' strange concept of time and duty.

Linguistic peculiarities also played havoc with a Dakota child in school:

> "You won't do that again, will you?" asked a teacher correcting a child. "Yes," answers the child. "Well of all perversity," thought the teacher and perhaps punished the child. But the trouble was that in Dakota you say "yes" to a question like that, when in English you mean "no." English says, "No (I will not)." Dakota says, "Yes (you are right that I will not)."[8]

Still, progress was made. Miraculous progress, when the fact is considered that these children were only the beginnings of tribal settlement on reservations and whose parents were often counted with the "Hostiles." At St. Paul's by 1881, many of the boys were ready to continue their education beyond the elementary level, and a new department was begun. These young men wished to prepare themselves as teachers or for the ministry, and under the new program, they acquired sufficient education to qualify as deacons and teachers on the reservations.[9]

In 1874, quarters were built for the sisters, from Bishop Potter's Memorial House in Philadelphia, who were working at the Yankton Mission. In conjunction with the new building, Emmanuel Hall for girls was started. It had an average of fifteen to seventeen girls in attendance, and became the center for all women's work connected with the Yankton Mission.

The girls learned to read and write, but emphasis was placed on the female accomplishments of cooking, sewing, housework, and nursing, which would prepare them to be "better" wives and mothers than their own mothers had been. The brighter girls were trained to be teachers of the younger ones, and the older women of the mission had, once a week, an afternoon class in home economics. These older Indian women, under the supervision of the sisters, helped with the clothing received by the Niobrara store room, which Bishop Hare established as a central storage and distribution area for the rummage sent from the East in the missionary barrels.

Emmanuel Hall soon became too small. The old log chapel built by Paul Mazakute was used as the wash house, and Bishop Hare complained of the inadequacies of a necessary facility: "Now that our family has become so large, the single privy put at first in the wood shed is entirely inadequate, especially as there are two sexes in the house."[10] Emmanuel Hall was converted to the residence of the Yankton assistant to the Reverend Joseph Cook, Philip Deloria.

"I'm glad to say," wrote Bishop Hare in his first annual report of 1873, "that the need of special effort for the elevation of Indian females . . . will soon be met. The Executive Committee have approved my plan for opening at the Santee Mission an Industrial School for girls. . . ."[11] The Industrial School for girls was named St. Mary's, and was housed in part of the mission building at Santee. There were about thirteen girls in attendance the first year, ranging from age nine to fifteen, and by 1877, it was a model of order, neatness and good management.[12]

In February, 1884, St. Mary's at Santee was destroyed by fire, but the girls finished the school year across the river in the building vacated by Hope School. Bishop Hare decided to rebuild St. Mary's on the Rosebud reservation because, "the Santees were well provided with schools and the tribe small, the fifteen thousand souls on the Pine Ridge and Rosebud Reserves, for whom we had not provided one boarding school, had claims which ought to prevail."[13]

The new St. Mary's was built in 1885 on Antelope Creek for both boys

St. Mary's School and Ephphatha Chapel on the Rosebud Reservation.

Hope School, Springfield, Dakota Territory. This building, erected in 1884, became the site of St. Mary's School in 1923.

and girls with an average attendance of forty-five. The academic program included reading, writing, arithmetic and geography, but the greatest emphasis was still on domestic skills. St. Mary's girls retained their training after leaving the school, and Bishop Hare proudly stated, "one can pick out a St. Mary's girl wherever she goes in the Indian country by the kind of home she keeps."[14]

St. Mary's was again destroyed by fire in August, 1910, but classes continued in a barracks until the new building, this time of cement block, was ready the next year.

The School continued to grow in its service to the Indian people. Bishop Burleson gave St. Mary's credit for the establishment of the strong Christian communities which grew among the Indians on the Rosebud.

On April 24, 1922, the Reverend John B. Clark sent Bishop Burleson a telegram: "St. Mary's Main Building Burned People Save Chapel. Cause Unknown Letter Follows."[15] In his followup letter, Clark reported on the disaster:

We have been unable to get any real theory as to the cause of the fire. It apparently started near the front of the building and near the big furnace.

Some of the girls were taken to the Boarding School; others were taken by parents who were nearby.[16]

Clark conducted an investigation and found that two girls, students of the school, set the fire. The oldest, fourteen, was sent to Reform school.

St. Mary's moved again in 1923, to Hope School, across the river from its original home at Santee, and the historic building, with its lovely chapel, saw thirty-seven years of girls pass through its halls before new facilities replaced it in 1960. During the years in Springfield, the enrollment of the school expanded to include Indian girls not only from the Dakotas, but Nebraska, Iowa, Wisconsin, Minnesota, Michigan, Wyoming, Idaho, Ohio, and California; with thirteen or more tribal groups.[17]

In connection with the work at St. Mary's in Springfield, there was established in 1924, "a systematic effort" toward the better training of candidates for Holy orders from the Indian field. One of the buildings on the school grounds was the dormitory for young men, and was called Ashley House; so named after Archdeacon Edward Ashley. Five or six men were in residence and had the opportunity of completing high school at St. Mary's and attending the State Normal school located in Springfield. Bishop Burleson said of Ashley House: "It is no easy matter for the best of us to understand theological English, and to one whose mother tongue is the Dakota, the difficulties involved in attendance at the average seminary with a class of college trained white men were insuperable. . . . I consider Ashley House one of our most interesting and helpful experiments.''[18]

Theological instruction was taught by Dr. John Burleson, with the assistance of the Reverend William Holmes and Archdeacon Ashley, who, with the Reverends Lester Bradner and William Holmes, translated and compiled in 1915 the original series of lessons for study by Dakota candidates for Holy Orders.

There were no residents in 1928, but the program continued with the Reverend Paul H. Barbour conducting classes by correspondence. In 1929, William Holmes' grandson, Harold S. Jones, lived at Ashley House while attending college at the Normal School. The resident program at

The Rev. Paul H. Barbour and wife Margaret. Father Barbour was Warden of Ashley House, Springfield from 1928-30. He continued the Ashley House courses by correspondence after he moved to the Rosebud Mission.

Ashley House ended in 1930, when Barbour was transferred to the Rosebud Mission, taking Ashley House with him. He continued the correspondence courses until his retirement in 1956. The program ended in about 1960.

Springfield was also the site of Hope School, which took the place of the Crow Creek Agency Boarding School, begun in 1874, and directed by the Church until 1879, when the government assumed control.[19] Bishop Hare then put into operation a plan which he had long considered: "beginning a Boarding School for Indian children outside the Indian country, where they would be removed from the wild ways and lethargy of their own people, and be surrounded by the civilization and energy of the white man, and yet not be cut off from occasional intercourse with their parents. . . ."[20]

Springfield was selected as the site because it was ideally located between Yankton and Santee reservations and there was an Episcopal Church, Ascension, already well established in the town. An old inn was bought and the school opened in the fall of 1879.[21]

The citizens of Springfield were impressed with the school and the town donated a block of land and $900 towards the erection of a new school building. Other funds and supplies were donated by eastern parishes, and in the fall of 1884, a new chalkstone building, on a high plateau overlooking the Missouri River, was opened.

Hope School was the only one of Bishop Hare's boarding schools which had a contract with the United States Government. The contract was made, at Hare's request, by the Government with J. S. Lewis, Treasurer of the Chapter of Calvary Cathedral. Lewis was to turn over to Hare, as president of Hope School, all money received under the contract. Unfortunately, Lewis "had brought himself by the use of strong drink into a condition which rendered him incompetent to attend to business," and appropriated to his own use over two thousand dollars of Hope School's funds.[22]

Bishop Hare, upon learning of the misuse of funds, immediately notified the Commissioner of Indian Affairs that Lewis was no longer Treasurer and not to send him future vouchers. Through some mix-up in governmental communication, Lewis received $2,430 more, which he promptly cashed, and then he disappeared.[23]

This unscrupulous and criminal action doomed the school. It was now deep in debt from which Bishop Hare could not extract it. Reluctantly, the school was closed as a Church project. The government contracted for the building and operated a government boarding school for a time. However, the Church retained title, and thus, it was reopened as St. Mary's.

Hope School (and later St. Mary's), was successful because of its distance from the reservation homes of its students and the influence and distractions of family and Indian customs. Those boarding schools established on the reservations did not fare as well. Many of the Indians were still hostile to the whites, and the missionary teachers faced many difficulties.

At St. Paul's, there were problems with parents: "Some half or wholly hostile; others so friendly that they made themselves a nuisance by sitting about with loaded rifles on their knees to guard the teachers against possible attacks. . . ."[24]

On the Cheyenne River reservation, the Reverend Henry Swift had started a day school in 1872, and in 1873, in a two-story building provided by the government. It was named St. John's and opened as a boarding school in 1874. Ten to thirteen boys and girls attended the school, which was located within the midst of hostile Indians, and had more than its share of Indian interference.

The parents and relations of our boarding school children were a great source of annoyance to us. They considered the fact of our having the children living with us sufficient claim on us for indefinite supplies of clothing and food; and a refusal to accede to their exhorbitant demands was followed, usually, by the carrying off of one of the children, and a troublesome chase after him. We were much harassed by the hostiles, who invaded us at all hours of the day and night, though never offering to do any violence, and by officious kindness of friendly Indians, who, considering us in great peril, paraded around the house through the night, and often kept us up late in the evening, sitting with conspiciously loaded rifles on their knees and entertaining us with prophecies of possible catastrophe.[25]

In 1876, because of the Indian animosity against the whites, as the result of the encroachment into the Black Hills and the murder of the Reverend R. Archer Ffennell, St. John's and all work of missions on the Cheyenne was closed. Swift returned and reopened the school in 1877, but attendence dropped.

In September, 1878, St. John's was given new life, and developed into one of the best girls boarding schools on the reservations with the arrival of Mr. and Mrs. J. F. Kinney. "Mr. and Mrs. Kinney," wrote Captain Schwan, the agent on the Cheyenne, "displayed from the very outset

St. John's William Welsh Memorial School for girls, Cheyenne River Mission, 1889

St. Elizabeth's School, Standing Rock Reservation.

great tact, fidelity, firmness, and perserverance, qualities absolutely required in the successful prosecution of the peculiarly difficult task assumed by them. The progress of the pupils was, in consequence, very marked and gratifying, and the general apearance and conditions of the grounds adjacent to the school-house were greatly improved."[26]

In 1888, a new school building was erected as a memorial to William Welsh who did so much for the Dakota Episcopal missions. The school, renamed St. John's William Welsh Memorial School, resembled that of a Cape Cod New England home, and even had a widow's walk around its chimney. Its main floor had sitting and dining rooms for the missionary family, and similar accommodations for the girls, plus sewing rooms, a large kitchen, storage rooms, porches, and halls.[27]

Only three years after the opening of the new school, St. John's began its decline when the agency was moved forty-five miles north. In 1902, the government no longer made appropriations for Indian education in sectarian schools, ". . . henceforth this was taken to mean that any Indian child attending a mission boarding school should *ipso facto* forfeit its rights to the rations issued to its tribe."[28]

Bishop Hare, unable to raise more than enough funds for only one year's budget, was forced to sell at a great loss not only St. John's, but also St. Paul's at Yankton. The lack of government appropriations also prevented the opening of a school in Rapid City, St. Augusta's, which was named for Mrs. Astor, who had left funds for the new school in her will.[29] It would ever after be a bitter thorn to Bishop Hare that the Roman Catholic Schools were able to continue their operations, and even received some tribal funds.[30]

Bishop Hare had to now concentrate the church's educational efforts at the two surviving schools, St. Mary's and St. Elizabeth's, on the Standing Rock reservation.

Chief Gall of the Hunkpapas on the Standing Rock reservation had asked Bishop Hare for a school similar to St. John's at Cheyenne.[31] Bishop Hare complied, and St. Elizabeth's was built in 1890, with Miss Mary S. Francis in charge until 1907. In 1894, Miss Priscilla Bridge came to assist Miss Francis. Deaconess Baker was another principal in 1925, and during the time when Mrs. Mary McKibbon was principal, the school developed into a high school. Many native lay and ordained ministers for the Standing Rock Mission and other reservations received training at St. Elizabeth's.

The church bell at St. Elizabeth's was the gift of the Sunday School of St. Peter's Church, German Town, Pennsylvania. It was shipped up the

Missouri River by boat, and near Chamberlain, it was lost overboard. Years later it was discovered in low water and finally reached St. Elizabeth's, after it was identified by the inscription engraved on it.[32]

St. Elizabeth's opened at an inopportune time. Bishop Hare had not taken advantage of the government aid available to duly accredited parties for the education of Indian children at so much per capita. Most of the support of the mission schools had come from church funds and private donations. Only when a deduction was made in the church's appropriations for Indian work did Bishop Hare request assistance from the government, but he was turned down. However, Bishop Hare was confident that funds would come from somewhere to operate St. Elizabeth's.

In the winter of 1897, St. Elizabeth's school was destroyed by fire. The financial situation was so critical that there was at first doubt if the school could be rebuilt. However, the Indians of the mission on the Standing Rock immediately set about raising money, which added to the insurance, enabled the school to be rebuilt.

In 1939, fire again brought disaster to the school when the girls' dormitory burned. Forty-three girls and their housemother fled to safety in the night with a temperature of thirty-six degrees below zero.[33] The loss far exceeded the insurance, but Bishop Roberts, the Reverend John B.

Bishop Hare Home on left in 1961.

The Crow Creek Dormitory.

Clark, and Miss Mary McKibbon, principal, worked to raise a fire-proof replacement costing $40,000.[34] The new building was dedicated by Bishop Roberts on May 21, 1940.

When Miss Ella Deloria became principal in 1955, she designed a new boys' dormitory, which would be the final addition to the school's plant. It was dedicated by Bishop Gesner on May 11, 1958.[35]

During the depression years, classes at St. Elizabeth's school were discontinued, and it became St. Elizabeth's Mission Home, which boarded students attending the public school at Wakpala. In 1967, the home was discontinued and the buildings closed until 1973, when the Dakota Leadership Program established its residential program. The school was renamed St. Elizabeth's Training Center where young men could study to be catechists, helpers, and for Holy Orders.[36] In 1974, the residential program ceased, and St. Elizabeth's was again vacant.

Also vacant was Ephphatha Chapel at the old site of St. Mary's school near Mission, South Dakota. In 1927, Bishop Burleson initiated a "great enterprise," with the building on the site of a school for older Indian boys. The first contribution to the boys school, known as Hare Industrial School, was from Mrs. Rebecca Hobbs Holmes, wife of the Reverend William Holmes.[37]

Hare School (Industrial was dropped), was under the Reverend Robert

P. Frazier, who was then Junior Archdeacon of Niobrara, and Carl Sacre was the first principal. The school's emphasis was on shop work, farming, and animal care, besides academic classes. Class work ceased in 1932, and the school became a dormitory for boys attending public school in Mission.[38]

In 1936, the dormitory was closed for lack of funds until 1942, when the National Youth Administration rented the property and operated a resident center for Indian girls from isolated reservation villages until 1944.

In 1946, the Church reopened the buildings as a boarding home, with John Artichoker as principal. Artichoker was responsible for the general mental, physical and spiritual welfare of the boys, in addition to the maintenance and improvements of the school plant. The school had a herd of cattle and a garden which the boys helped care for. Emily Artichoker, wife of the principal, was the general manager, and made the school home-like, attractive and well kept. She planned the meals, served as a banker for the boys, and was affectionately regarded by them as their schoolmother.

Many of the boys who attended Hare School, or later lived in the home, went on to become catechists, helpers, and were ordained priests, and one, Harold S. Jones was elected Suffragan Bishop of South Dakota.

In 1963, the name was officially changed from Bishop Hare School to Bishop Hare Mission Home. The Reverend Noah Brokenleg, himself a former student, assumed direction of the Home in 1964. The Ephphatha Chapel was renamed the Reverend James Driving Hawk Memorial Chapel, in memory of a young priest who was also a product of Hare School. In 1974, the Reverend David G. Devore became the Home's director.

Another Boarding Home was established for girls attending the government school on the Crow Creek reservation in 1928, under the direction of the Reverend and Mrs. David Clark. It continued until 1936.

One of Bishop Hare's first thoughts upon the enlargement of his Mission District to include the white settlements in Dakota, was the importance of beginning at least one Church School for white children, and thus, providing for the education of at least the daughters of the Church in the rapidly developing Territory.

Bishop Hare had long been embarrassed that there was no such provision for the education of the children of the faithful missionaries among the Indians, in their isolated stations. In 1884, he wrote:

All Saints School,
SIOUX FALLS, S. D.

Boarding & Day School
For Young Ladies and Children, under the immediate supervision of the Rt. Rev.
W. H. HARE, D. D.

Address, Miss Helen S. Peabody, Principal,

ALL SAINTS SCHOOL, SIOUX FALLS, S. D.

...Great Advantages at Low Rates.

SO GREAT has been the progress of educational science during the past thirty years, so radical the change in public opinion regarding subjects for school study and methods of instructions, that the system of today is well named the "New Education." In order to meet the ever increasing demands of this new education the course of study in this school has been revised, the basis of revision being the "Report of the Committee of Ten." The course as revised covers a period beginning with the kindergarten and ending two years beyond the ordinary high school. There is more work in practical English, reading, composition, etc.; more laboratory work in natural science, and as much manual training as practicable.

In making up the faculty of the school no effort is spared in securing teachers whose natural gifts, supplemented by careful training and thorough culture, fit them for the grave responsibilities which must ever rest upon the teacher of the young.

A picture and information about All Saints School appeared in every issue of The Church News.

111

Helen S. Peabody,
first principal of All Saints School.

Bishop Hare made his home at All Saints School and the students were his family.

Three days had not elapsed after I was assigned to the Episcopal charge of the South-eastern part of Dakota, before the telegraph brought me from more than one town offers of land and money to aid in such an enterprise, and a dear friend and tried contributor to my work in years past no sooner heard of the enlargement of my field than she marked the event by handing me $1,000 (as she said), "toward laying corner-stone of such a School." Another gave me $2,500 to erect a Memorial Chapel, and a third bade me set my mind at rest regarding contributions from the city where he lived, and expect $5,000. Several other smaller gifts have been received.

The people of Sioux Falls have subscribed $10,000 in cash and land. Enough has thus been secured to begin the work, and the project has taken definite shape.

The School will be located at Sioux Falls on a beautiful and commanding site, a five-acre tract, the gift of Artemas Gale, Esq., of that town.

It will be constructed in the most substantial manner of the celebrated Sioux Falls Jasper, from foundation stone to turret.

It will be called "All-Saints' School," in a deep sense of how many sons God has already conducted through the ordeal of life and brought to glory under the leadership of the Captain of our salvation; in the thankful remembrance of the treasure He has stored up in this world for our use in the good examples of His servants, who, having finished their course in faith, now rest from their labors; and in hope that through their examples, goodness may be made to seem to the young, who shall be educated within the wall of All-Saints' School, thoroughly human, attractive, practicable, and near at hand.

The motto of the School, suggested by my friend, the Rev. W. J. Harris, D.D., will be "From Glory to Glory," in the hope that the pupils will reach in the school attainments of mind and heart, which will be a "glory" to their youth, and that these attainments will mature into *characters* which will be the "glory" of their after life, and will finally make them to be numbered with All Saints in "glory everlasting" hereafter.[39]

The school, intended for the daughters of Hare's missionaries, and for other white girls to whom a Church Boarding School of the first order, near their homes, could impart the influences which otherwise they must go far to seek, embodied some of his most cherished ideals. As it was his wish in the Indian boarding schools to prepare the young to carry back to their home some of the underlying principles of Christian civilization, so he felt that each of the more privileged girls of his own race, who should fall under the influence of such a good school as he meant All Saints to be, might bear to her own surroundings through life something of cultivation and character, which could best be molded and guided through daily contact with the highest standards of living.[40]

All Saints was Bishop Hare's personal home, and for the rest of his life the students and staff were his family. Upon his death, Bishop Hare was buried next to Calvary Cathedral, but in 1951, with the permission of the state of South Dakota, his body was moved to the grounds of All Saints.

All Saints, since its founding, had been the care and responsibility of the bishops. In 1922, Bishop Burleson determined that this policy was no longer desirable. The Chapter of Calvary Cathedral, at Burleson's request, authorized the bishop to appoint a Board of Directors, consisting of six persons, with the Bishop as chairman and the Suffragan Bishop as vice-chairman, plus one person elected by the alumnae of the school. In 1926, the Executive Council was made the Board of Directors, thus moving the school's management under the District's administrative body.[41]

In September, 1922, a Junior College Department was established, where girls may be thoroughly trained in the work of the freshman year, combined with the home and cultural advantages for which All Saints was so well known. The Junior College ceased in 1928. From 1951, when the boarding school was discontinued, All Saints has operated as a Day School for boys and girls in Sioux Falls from kindergarten through the eighth grade.

6

⋏⋏⋏⋏

Swift Bird–Good Timber

"The beginning of our history among the white people of South Dakota was emphatically a day of small things," wrote the Reverend Edward Ashley in his history of the first forty years of the Church in South Dakota.[1] The first use of *The Book of Common Prayer* in the territory was in the summer of 1860, when the Right Reverend Joseph C. Talbot, Missionary Bishop of the Northwest, held services among the settlers from Sioux City to Fort Randall, on the Missouri River.[2] Bishop Talbot was accompanied by the Reverend Doctor Melancthon Hoyt, who would continue traveling the river until he moved to Yankton in 1862.

The Protestant Episcopal Church of the United States realized by 1868 that it had a duty to the Indians within its boundaries. Bishop Whipple of Minnesota had pleaded, since the Sioux Uprising of 1862, and the Santees' subsequent removal to Dakota Territory, that the Church provide for them and the wilder tribes to the west. In the General Convention of 1868, some attempt was made to provide for the Indians' spiritual needs, but the ending of the Civil War with its problems of reconstruction intervened. In that year, a missionary jurisdiction among the Indian tribes was constituted and placed under the charge of Bishop Clarkson of Nebraska. In 1871, the jurisdiction was named Niobrara, after the river which flowed between what would become the states of South Dakota and Nebraska. But Bishop Clarkson, because of the vast expanse of the new district, could give it but scant attention, and resigned its charge in 1872. He did retain supervision of the white settlers moving into the area.

The House of Bishops next elected Bishop Whipple, but he could not leave his work in Minnesota. Whipple, on All Saints Day, 1872, nominated William Hobart Hare, the young secretary of the foreign committee of the Board of Missions, as Bishop of the Missionary Jurisdiction of Niobrara.

This action of the Church was the first and only instance of a racial episcopate. Hare, consecrated on January 9, 1873, became the bishop for a race of people rather than for a particular place. The House of Bishops passed a resolution stating that the Missionary Bishop of Niobrara be authorized to take charge of such work among the Indians, east of the Rocky Mountains, as may be transferred to his oversight by the Bishops within whose jurisdiction such work may lie.[3]

Thus began the episcopate of a man that would bring change to not only the Dakota Indians, but to the citizens of the new state of South Dakota.

William Hobart Hare was born in Princeton, New Jersey, on May 17, 1838, to the Reverend Doctor George Emlen Hare and Elizabeth Catherine Hobart. Elizabeth was the daughter of the Right Reverend John Henry Hobart, the third Bishop of New York.[4] On October 30, 1861, William married Mary Amory Howe, the daughter of the Reverend Doctor Howe, but the happy marriage ended with Mary's death of a pulmonary disease on January 7, 1866, leaving Hare with a three-year-old son, Hobart.[5]

Upon his election as Bishop of Niobrara, Hare wrote: "The news of the election was utterly unexpected, and fell upon me like a thunderbolt from a clear sky."[6] His first thought was to decline, because he had thought that his vocation would be that of Secretary and General Agent for the Foreign Work. "My heart had become knit with the brave standard bearers of the Church in heathen lands, and tears filled my eyes as I thought of seeming to desert the army in the field. . . . Moreover, a domestic tie of tender sacredness bound me to my home."[7]

Hare's decision to accept the episcopate was regretted by his many friends in the East. A man of scholarly tastes, finesse and cultivation, they felt his place was in the centers of learning and education, not in the destitute and dangerous west among hostile Indians.[8]

Hare arrived in May, 1873, to his new jurisdiction of 80,000 square miles, over which separate bands of Indians were scattered, and found the church's work established in nine mission stations and two sub-stations.[9]

"The Indians sometimes call me *Zitkana Duzahan,* Swift Bird, from the rapidity with which I travel," Hare wrote to a friends in 1889.[10] Hare, in his first six months, made the rounds twice of Santee, Yankton, Crow Creek, Lower Brule, and Cheyenne—over three hundred miles of uninhabited country. Very early in his travels he learned to carry only the bare

Rt. Rev. Robert H. Clarkson, Missionary Bishop of Nebraska and Dakota.

Rt. Rev. William Hobart Hare

necessities "in a land where porters and cabs do not abound, much luggage is a weariness to the flesh."[11]

Hare soon determined that the Indian race had to be trained to be self-supporting in order to have independent control over their lives. He felt that their position as wards was disastrous. Even though he gave the Indians many gifts and met their desperate needs, he tried to "teach them to be self-respecting, independent, and responsible; to give, as they were able, and to look forward to a still larger exercise of that which, to the Indian, is joy and not grief—the pleasure of bestowing."[12]

He carried out his philosophy by establishing boarding schools to teach the children and through them their parents, and secondly, by raising up teachers from among the Indians themselves. He felt that only by the aid of its own people could a race be effectively evangelized, and chose men who became first helpers, then catechists, and after training, deacons and priests. The native clergy became the backbone of Hare's work among the Indians.[13]

In 1883, the House of Bishops re-established the boundaries of North and South Dakota as separate missionary districts. South Dakota included the Indian district of Niobrara, but now the work among the white people of South Dakota increasingly demanded the time and care of Bishop Hare. In his first report to the convention of 1883, Hare said:

"From the first I have struggled against the notion that we are missionaries to Indians alone and not missionaries to *all men*. I have pressed the study of the English language in our schools, and however imperfect my efforts, the aim of them has been *to break down the middle wall of partition between whites and Indians and to seek not the welfare of one class or race,* but the *common good."* [14]

By 1883, the work in the white field had made some progress, primarily because of the efforts of Melancthon Hoyt.

Hoyt, who was appointed General Missionary to Dakota by Bishop Clarkson, had built a log house on the corner of Linne and Fourth Streets in Yankton, where services were held and living quarters established for his family of ten children. [15] This building, known as St. John's Church, was also used by the House of Representatives of the first territorial legislature when Yankton was the capitol of Dakota Territory. As the town of Yankton grew, St. John's was abandoned and a new parish was created in 1864, under the name of Christ Church. The new building, affectionately called "The Little Brown Church," served the parish until 1880, when again Yankton's growth necessitated a move from the center of the city and the construction of a new building.

Christ Church became known as the "Mother Church of the Dakotas," and from this center, Hoyt traveled to establish churches among the settlers in southeastern Dakota. While at Yankton, Hoyt was also instrumental in organizing St. John's Masonic Lodge, No. 1, the first Masonic Lodge in what would become South Dakota. [16]

Vermillion was one of the settlements visited by Bishop Talbot and Hoyt in 1860, and the congregations organized in 1864, but work was delayed on that church until the site of the territorial capitol was selected. [17] At Elk Point, twenty-two miles up-river from Sioux City, Hoyt found a small group interested in the Church. In all of the new settlements, Hoyt found that there were few Episcopal communicants, but large congregations, because other denominations had not yet come to the territory. [18]

The first annual convocation of the Protestant Episcopal Church assembled in Dakota Hall, Yankton, on Friday, September 23, 1870. Present were the Right Reverend Robert H. Clarkson, the Reverends Samuel D. Hinman, Joseph W. Cook, Yankton mission; P. B. Morrison, Vermillion, and Melancthon Hoyt, Yankton. The territory of Dakota was organized for missionary work by the appointment of the Reverend Doctor Hoyt as Dean. The counties of Yankton, Bon Homme, Lincoln, and

The Rev. Melancthon Hoyt.

The Mother Church of the Dakotas, Christ Church, Yankton.

Minnehaha were set off as the Yankton district, under Dean Hoyt; Union and Clay counties as Vermillion district, under Morrison, and the Indian reservations were formed into a separate convocation under Hinman as Dean.

With the growth of the work of Dr. Hoyt, the Reverend J. V. Himes arrived in Elk Point in 1879, at the age of seventy-five, and served until his death in 1895.[19]

In 1872, under Hoyt's direction, a small church building was erected at Swan Lake, and in 1876, Hoyt organized Good Samaritan at Turner. Dr. Hoyt made bimonthly visits to Swan Lake and Turner until January, 1881, when Deacon M. S. Robinson was assigned by Bishop Clarkson. In 1883, The Chicago and Northwestern Railroad established the town of Hurley, and most of the buildings and businesses at Swan Lake and Turner were moved to the new town. In May, 1883, Grace Church was organized as a parish in Hurley.[20]

"Melancthon Hoyt," wrote Ashley, "itinerated with great system, regularity, and promptness and the amount of his work is simply surprising. He was never at rest, always on the way to some appointment, always seeking out places where he could preach the gospel and plant the Church."[21] In 1881, Hoyt went to Huron to be the first rector of Grace Church. From Huron, Hoyt drove to Watertown with a span of Indian ponies, Cap and Punch, which were known all over the Territory as well as Hoyt was. Trinity Church, Watertown, was organized in 1881, under Hoyt's direction, and the building was built and paid for by 1882, with the Reverend C. H. Fulforth as first rector.

In 1871, Hoyt held the first service in Firesteel, later to become St. Mary's, Mitchell, and also organized congregations at Eden in 1879, Canton, 1876, and Parker in 1871.

Hoyt was again given charge of the Hurley parish in 1884, until he was transferred to St. Andrew's, Scotland, in 1886, where he began the building of the church. After his death on January 2, 1888, Bishop Hare proposed that St. Andrew's be Hoyt's memorial church.[22]

"Then," wrote Ashley, "there was Father (John) Morris who traveled up and down the James River Valley from Scotland to Firesteel. He was actively engaged in looking up Church people and giving them services in Miner, Sanborn, Jerauld, Davison, and Hutchinson counties."[23]

John Morris was one of the early settlers in Firesteel and had a family of grown sons and daughters when he was appointed lay reader, then ordained deacon and priest. He had a regular circuit which took him to all of the settlements between Firesteel, Yankton, and Carthage.[24] He was responsible for establishing congregations of Trinity, Howard, in 1882, and St. Andrew's in Scotland in 1888.

The Reverend J. M. McBride began his ministry in the Territory in 1870. He journeyed for more than twenty years over the eastern and northern part, and in 1884, moved to Pierre to become the first rector of the congregation which would become Trinity parish. In 1886, he held services in the county courthouse, a skating rink, and until as Bishop Hare reported: "Through some generous aid of the Society of the Double Temple of New York and a loan from the Church Building Society, the people of Pierre under the ministry of the Reverend J. M. McBride, have been able to erect a commodious church, the basement of which has been fitted up and made ready for divine services."[25] Later in 1887, McBride was rector of St. Mark's, Aberdeen, and from there established Christ Church, Gettysburg, in 1888.[26]

In the western part of the Territory, the Black Hills, after the discovery of gold, was fast filling with miners and other high-living, reckless, spirited adventurers. Close on their heels came the businessmen, who sought their fortunes not in mining, but in supplying the needs of the free-spending miners. When the businessmen brought their wives and families, permanent settlements were established and the Black Hills boomed.

The first Episcopal service in the Black Hills was conducted by Seth Bullock, Deadwood's first sheriff, in August, 1876. Bullock borrowed a *Book of Common Prayer* and read the Burial Office for Preacher H. W. Smith, an itinerant Methodist minister who had been killed by Indians.[27]

The first Episcopal Church service held by an ordained minister in the Black Hills, was in the new village of Rapid City, by the Reverend Edward Ashley in 1878, while he was there as a witness before the Federal Court. The following is Ashley's account of that service:

Realizing that I was to be in Rapid City over Sunday, the thought occurred to me that the place being a new one and there being no services of any kind held there, I might arrange for a service Sunday evening. Court was held over a saloon. I went to the janitor, asked if I might use the court room and he said, "Sure." I wrote out notices for a service and tacked one at the foot of the stairs leading up to the Court room, and one outside of the hotel door, stating that services would be Sunday evening at seven o'clock, and giving the first lines of the hymns to be sung, and that the service would be according to the Episcopal form. Sunday evening, just before the time for the service, I went to the court room, and the janitor was nailing candle holders to the walls. This was before the day of kerosene oil or electricity. I was grateful for the interest of the janitor. I saw also that someone had interested themselves to take an organ to the hall although I had not arranged for any choir. At the end of the court room two small parts had been partitioned off for jury rooms. I thought one of them would be a suitable place for me to robe in. At first there was only the janitor and myself, and it was then fifteen minutes after seven, and I thought no one was coming to the service, but about five minutes later there was a tramp, tramp up the stairs and soon the hall was full of people. I went into the room to put on my vestments, and started up the aisle toward the judge's bench, whereupon the people who had been interested enough to come, started up the hymn, "Hold the Fort for I am Coming!" It had not been mentioned in the notices for the service. At first I was a little bit non-plussed, but then decided if the good people desired to sing this, let them do it. During the singing of the hymn, I reached my place, and began the service. This was the first Episcopal service held in Rapid City. At that time Rapid City was just one short street with a few buildings on either side and on one side was the hotel, such as it was, some offices, the store and a saloon.[28]

The first organized Episcopal service was conducted by Mr. Goddard, a layman, in Deadwood at the Langrishe Theater in 1877, and was attended by about one hundred men and three women.[29]

In 1878, the Reverend E. K. Lessell arrived in Dakota and was appointed missionary to the Black Hills. Lessell was sent to open up the missionary field in the Black Hills and headquartered in Deadwood, "where saloons ran twenty-four hours a day, where there were gambling dens and opium joints in great number."[30] Lead, he found, although a smaller city, had its share of "dives and services were held wherever there was a place provided. Sometimes it was on the second floor of a poolroom where the click of the billiard balls punctuated the service.[31]

Lessell was ill almost all of the time of his ministry, and in the spring of 1879, physicians warned him that his days were numbered. He left the Black Hills for his home in New Haven, Connecticut, where his wife and children were living. He died there in January, 1880.[32]

In 1880, Bishop Hare noted in his annual report, that he had made two visits to the Black Hills during the past year, spending two Sundays there on his first visit and four on his second. He understood the difficulties of establishing the Church in a frontier setting. "The population is made up chiefly of young men who have come to make their fortunes, and of those who have been driven there by the necessity of retrieving theirs. The work of the resident population is to get out the rich mineral, transfer it to others at the centres of capital rather than to keep it for themselves. Old Church habits do not exist. No church building, no Church services remind the new-comers of things divine and eternal."[33]

In October, 1880, the House of Bishops, during the session of the General Convention, changed the boundaries of the Missionary District of Niobrara, by adding to it all of that part of Dakota which lies north of the 40th parallel, and south and west of the Missouri River.[34] This brought the Black Hills under Hare's jurisdiction, and was in accordance with his wishes.

The Reverend George C. Pennell, S.T.D., was placed in charge of the missions in the Black Hills in 1880, and through his efforts, St. John's, Deadwood, was organized. On September 12, 1880, Bishop Hare laid the cornerstone and St. John's first service was held on Easter Sunday, April 17, 1881.[35]

Pennell also worked with the fledgling mission of Christ Church, Lead, but because many church families left, the mission was temporarily discontinued. Pennell's time in the Black Hills was cut short by his sudden death in May, 1882, and the Black Hills remained without pastoral care for several years, with only occasional visits from Bishop Hare.

When the boundaries of the Missionary jurisdiction of Niobrara were changed in 1883, to that which would be the new state of South Dakota, Bishop Hare now had official charge of the white field. He reported on its status in 1884:

The years 1881, 1882, 1883 were years of extravagant growth in South Dakota. (The) railroads opened up thousands upon thousands of acres of farming land of astonishing fertility, and over them settlers poured into the country with a rapidity which has perhaps never been equalled.

Towns sprang up everywhere as if by magic.

The change wrought has been marvellous. The wilderness has been changed into a garden.

But the feverish excitement is over. In the towns it is discovered that everything has been overdone. . . . The supply is waiting for the demand to catch up and men feel that they can fit themselves to the situation only by the most prudent economy. Lots for churches must now be bought where once they were freely given.

Not withstanding all drawbacks, however, no words can express the splendid opportunity which I find here for the planting of the Church. . . . Here clergymen can find a noble field for work if they be men who seek for souls and not for place; men who will seek though they not be sought; men who hanker not to work before man's eye on church superstructure if only they can lay beneath *God's* eye the hidden but enduring foundation.[36]

Hare went on to report the status of the established congregations and those just beginning:

WATERTOWN:
Trinity Church, Rev. A. H. Barrington, Rector
The town is marked by one of the prettiest of our churches in Dakota and by the presence of several laymen who give the Church their active personal support. I hail with satisfaction the fact that here the people are taking steps towards securing a rector.

ELK POINT AND VERMILLION:
St. Andrew's Church, Elk Point, Rev. J. V. Himes, Missionary
St. Paul's Church, Vermillion, Rev. J. V. Himes
We have neat and pretty churches, in everything complete, in both these towns, thanks to the indefatigable labors of the Rev. Himes, who, though in his 80th year, is one of the most active of the Church's Missionaries. I am hoping to secure a clergyman to take charge of Vermillion which is the seat of the Territorial college.

CANTON, PARKER AND EDEN:
Church of the Holy Innocents, Canton
St. Thomas' Church, Eden
We have a neat and comfortable church in each of these towns.
Church of the Good Samaritan, Parker
We have no church building here. Services are held in the Presbyterian Church. These three points were in the charge of the Rev. J. O. Babin till January 1st, when he resigned. I expect to assign Mr. W. J. Wicks to the charge of them on his Ordination, which is expected to take place in July.

MITCHELL AND TOWNS ADJACENT:
St. Mary's Church, Rev. C. C. Harris, Rector and Missionary in adjacent towns.
The Church in this important town had dwindled almost to nothing when the present Rector took charge in November, 1883, and special hindrances besides the religious lukewarmness, which we lament generally, have interfered with its recovery. The last few months have witnesed many tokens of returning vigor.
Alexandria, (Communicants, 22)
Mr. Charles S. Cook, a candidate for Orders, has done efficient work as resident Lay-reader during his vacation.
Plankinton, (Communicants, 5)
Chamberlain, (Communicants, 19)
In none of these towns have we as yet church buildings, and Services have been held in halls or in churches kindly loaned to us by other religious bodies.

SIOUX FALLS AND TOWNS ADJACENT:
Calvary Church, Rev. J. M. McBride, Rector
Mr. McBride has succeeded in recovering this church from great depression and putting it in a condition full of promise. I have determined to make this town and parish my home and the seat of our general Church institutions. The Rev. Mr. McBride has resigned the rectorship in order to plant the Church in the important town of Pierre, and the Rev. Wm. J. Harris, D.D., has accepted an invitation to take charge of the church and to assist me in organizing the central work.

DELL RAPIDS:

The Church owns here, through the activity of the Ladies' Guild, a lot of ground and a small frame building which serves for the time as a chapel. Services have been held several times by the Rev. Mr. McBride.

VALLEY SPRINGS:

We have no building here, but there are a few who love the Church, and Services have been given them several times by Rev. Mr. McBride.

HURON AND TOWNS ADJACENT:

Grace Church, Huron, Rev. Melancthon Hoyt, D.D., Rector and Honorary Dean of South Dakota

Dr. Hoyt has been in Orders for over fifty years, and for over forty-nine years he has been in Indiana, Michigan, Iowa and Dakota, a pioneer Missionary under our General Missionary Society. He is now in his 76th year. Years before railroads were known in Dakota he travelled over its plains in his buggy, preaching the Gospel and planting Missions. There is hardly a church or Mission in South Dakota which does not owe its organization to him. He had just resigned this parish at Huron that he may find a less exacting field, and one nearer his children, the comparative rest and the succor which the infirmities of age demand.

Huron is one of the most important points in South Dakota. Were only the right man at hand to take charge of the work the prospect of the Church there would be exceptionally good.

The parish has enjoyed the services of T. J. Nicholl, ESQ., who has given valuable assistance to the Rector as a Lay-reader. Would God we had more such laymen!

Iroquois, (Communicants, 7)

We have no church building here, but occasional Services have been held by the Rev. Dr. Hoyt and by Mr. Nicholl.

SPRINGFIELD MISSION (Population, 500):

Church of the Ascension, Mr. W. J. Wicks, Catechist

The services have been maintained as best we could by the Rev. Mr. Fowler and myself. An interesting Sunday-school has been conducted under the superintendence of Mrs. Knapp, Principal of Hope School.

ABERDEEN:

St. Mark's Church

We have a regular organization here, but no church building. Aberdeen is a vigorous town of about two thousand people, where at any time during eighteen months past we might have had a strong congregation, had we had a suitable clergyman on the ground. The people have been busy raising money, the Ladies' Guild, as usual, taking the lead, and will soon set about putting up a church.

GROTON:
Trinity Church
We have only a few Church people here, but they are earnest workers, and have raised, chiefly among friends at the East, $12,000, with which they have erected a very pretty church. One of their number, Mr. William J. Brewster, has zealously conducted Services as Lay-reader, and the people have regularly assembled for the worship of Almighty God.

HURLEY:
Grace Church
We have a comfortable church and rectory here, representing the buildings which used to be at Swan Lake and Turner, towns now deserted. The Rev. Mr. S. Robinson, Deacon, resigned his charge here after successful efforts to get the church and rectory ready for use and was succeeded by the Rev. Dr. Hoyt.

PIERRE:
This is an important town at the terminus of the C. & N. W. R. R. on the Missouri River—a point which we should have occupied two or three years ago. Our Church people there have all along been anxious that steps should be taken without delay to provide the town with Services and to build a church, and though they have had no minister and but little encouragement of any kind, the good women have raised for this purpose $300. At my suggestion, however, they have turned this money over to the Rectory Fund, and this money with other contributions from the people, and with borrowed money, is putting up a comfortable parsonage to which Mr. McBride expects to soon remove from Sioux Falls, and to begin holding regular services.

MORRISTOWN:
St. Thomas' Church, Rev. John Morris, Missionary

BLACK HILLS MISSION
St. John's Church, Deadwood, vacant
Since the death of the Rev. Dr. Pennell in May, 1882, this important district has been left entirely destitute of the ministrations of the Church.

Hare counted parishes as self-supporting if they paid their rector a salary of $800 a year and furnished a house. "There is," he wrote in 1884, "but one church in the district which has attained this distinction: Christ Church, Yankton. . . . I am happy to record that Calvary Church, Sioux Falls, will claim this honor for the year beginning September 1st."[37]

"There has been a great revival of Church interest in the beautiful and promising section of South Dakota known as the Black Hills," wrote Hare in 1887. "Zealous congregations now worship regularly every Sunday, led by Mr. George Garbett (sic) Ware, a candidate for Holy Orders, at Rapid City, and under the Rev. R. M. Doherty at Lead City."[38]

Mr. Ware came from England in 1886, and filed on a homestead near Farmingdale. He was ordained deacon in the newly completed Emmanuel Chapel, Rapid City, on December 20th, 1888. He was ordained priest at Emmanuel on June 1, 1890, and the next year, Bishop Hare named him rural dean of the newly created Black Hills Deanery, which consisted of missions at Rapid City, Deadwood, Lead, Sturgis, Hot Springs and "other points" of Spearfish and Belle Fourche. Ware was named Archdeacon for the Black Hills in 1895.

In his Sixteenth Annual Report of 1888, Bishop Hare reminded the Missionary Board and the National Church that he was loaded with two burdens: the Indian work, which had assumed large proportions, and a population of whites, which was equal to that of any missionary district in the country. His special plea was for financial assistance in establishing the work in the white field, which was "laden with all the burdens which our forefathers carried when they occupied the Atlantic seaboard. They (white people) are the sons and daughters, mothers and sisters of people at the East. Help us to found and build up here in our new home those institutions which purify society, sweeten the household, enlighten the conscience and smoothe the pillow of sickness and of death."[39]

Bishop Hare had selected Sioux Falls as his See City. There he organized and incorporated a board of trustees, The Chapter of Calvary Cathedral, composed of representatives clergy and laymen of the district. To this board he transferred title to property which came to him as Bishop from the Bishop of Nebraska, and all future property acquisitions of the new district. He began a fund for the endowment of the episcopate; organized the work in the white field into the Eastern Deanery, which included the Black Hills, and the District of Niobrara became the Niobrara Deanery. Each deanery held its own annual convocation with a triennial meeting of the whole district.[40]

A gift of $1,000 "to lay the corner-stone of a girls' school" from Mrs. John Jacob Astor, permitted Hare to establish a school for the daughters of his missionaries and for other white girls, and thus, provide for the education of the daughters of the Church in the rapidly developing district.[41] There, at All Saints School in Sioux Falls, Bishop Hare made his home.

Soon after South Dakota's admission to statehood in 1889, the state became known nationwide as the place which required only ninety days residence before the granting of a divorce. Sioux Falls, the Bishop's See city, became a "Divorce Colony," and Hare was ashamed that such conditions should exist in a town where he was asking people to send their young daughters to be educated.

Hare's view and subsequent efforts to have the divorce law changed received much criticism from within the state. He was accused of religious sensationalism as he worked to gain the cooperation of other denominations. In 1892, there was organized at Sioux Falls the State Association of Clergymen, for the purpose of securing a change in the state's divorce laws. Bishop Hare was the head of the association, and he objected openly and seriously to the haste with which divorces and remarriages occurred. Through Hare's efforts, a law was passed to lengthen the period of residency to six months, and improved the requirements regarding summons.[42]

Bishop Hare was also opposed to the proposed prohibition bill before the 1890 legislature. His opposition, and that of the Episcopal Church, was based upon the restrictions placed upon the use of wine at the sacrament. He declared "that the proposed bill would make a criminal of every Episcopal or Catholic in the state who used fermented wine at the communion table."[43]

Bishop Hare also felt that the prohibitionists were intolerant, domineering, and self-righteous, and that their high-handed tactics of forcing the bill upon the state was objectionable.

In 1895, Hare reported that "The year was signalized by the assembling of a number of clergy with the Bishop to mark by suitable services and words of congratulations the completion by the Reverend J. W. Cook of twenty-five years of service in the Niobrara missionary field." He also listed members of the Mission Corps, clerical and lay, male and female, who had been in the field for ten to twenty-five years.[44]

Name	Date Entered
Ashley	May 9, 1874
Burt	Sept. 24, 1872
Cook	May 9, 1870
Deloria	1874
Robinson	Aug. 22, 1871
Ross	1877
Saul	(about) 1882
Tatiyopa	(about) 1876
Walker	(about) 1872
Cleveland	Oct. 8, 1872
Himes	(came to the district at age 75 and died at ninety years in 1895)

Name	Date Entered
Wicks	1882
Miss Amelia Ives	Aug. 27, 1872
Miss M. Z. Graves	Aug. 27, 1872
Miss Mary S. Francis	Aug. 21, 1880
Mrs. J. H. Johnstone	1883
Miss H. S. Peabody	1885

In his personal relationships with his missionaries, Hare was at times arbitrary. He had the "inveterate habit of believing and expecting the best of people," and his expectations were high, which at times led to conflict and disagreement with his subordinates.[45] In the drawn out controversy with Samuel Hinman, Hare firmly believed that it was his right as Bishop to have only those whom he wanted in his diocese; however, Joseph Cook thought Hare had acted rashly and had transgressed Hinman's rights.[46]

Often during his episcopate, Hare reminded the clergy of their roles and responsibilities. "You are faithfully to feed that portion of the flock entrusted to you, not as a man pleaser, but as continually bearing in mind that you are accountable unto us here and to the Chief Bishop and Sovereign Judge of (the) hereafter."[47]

Edward Ashley recalled that:

In the earlier part of Bishop Hare's Episcopate he was known as an Evangelical Low Churchman. As such he was opposed to ritual of any kind and to colored stoles or colored altar cloths. Each missionary was supposed to wear a long surplice with a black stole. I well remember at the time of the laying of the corner stone at St. Mark's Church, Aberdeen, the Bishop announced to the clergy that ordinarily a black stole was usually prescribed in South Dakota, but that on this occasion those disposed to do so might wear white stoles. Most of his clergy, especially those of the Niobrara Deanery might be classed as High Churchmen, and gradually they adopted the use of the colored stoles and colored altar cloths for the seasons of the Christian Church, and in some places the use of Eucharistic lights was adopted. As the years went by Bishop Hare became more liberal.[48]

In September, 1895, Bishop Hare addressed a letter to the clergy and laity of South Dakota:

I came back from long journeys early last summer very much exhausted. My system has failed to rally and I am advised by my physicians that serious consequences can be averted only by entire rest and absence from my field of work.[49]

He was at last giving in to the physical frailities which had plagued him since his first years in Niobrara. In 1874, he wrote to a friend:

I am face to face with the necessity of leaving the Indian work. . . . A year ago I received a warning from my physician at the East that I had made a mistake in entering upon my present life. The physician at Fort Randall tells me that he discovered a year ago that I could not live in this climate; if I were a soldier he would discharge me at once. . . . Dr. Mitchell writes me that I am running an immense risk and that it is imperative and a duty that I should leave and seek a gentler life as soon as I can do so consistently with duty.[50]

But he did not leave, and suffered his physical ailments with silent resignation, with only occasional vacations from his work to renew his strength. He left South Dakota in October, 1895, and was absent until April, 1896, but needed further rest and sailed for Europe in July, returning in September. Upon his return, he plunged again into his work and reported in November, 1897, that he had in "twenty days preached twenty times, held sixteen confirmations in which I confirmed seventy candidates, have driven two hundred miles by wagon and traveled eight hundred and sixty-seven miles by rail, and slept in thirteen different beds."[51]

In between his trips, he returned to his home at All Saints School "always weary, often exhausted, sometimes ill," and still insisted that he not be given preferential treatment.[52]

In 1903, a malignant growth appeared on his face, and in 1904 the defective blood circulation caused from a narrowing of the mitral orifice of his heart, took a new form which again necessitated complete rest and medical treatment.

He returned to South Dakota in December, 1905, when he wrote to his sister: "I have frequently suffered so much pain that I had to think up a good story and tell it and laugh to keep myself from crying."[53] In April, 1907, he wrote from Atlantic City: "I wish you to know that the surgical operation which will cost me the loss of my right eye-ball and then probably bring relief from pain and more power to work, or ?—has my full approval."[54]

The radical surgery was done, giving Hare temporary relief from the pain, but not stopping the cancer's growth. Still in June, 1908, he gave the convocation address in Sioux Falls, and received a framed expression of gratitude and appreciation in recognition of his seventieth birthday, which was signed by over a thousand clergy and laity both white and Indian of South Dakota.

Soon he had to return to Atlantic City for more treatment and wrote: "My suffering is intense and constant. . . . I have lived in South Dakota and have been one of its people for thirty-six years. I wish to rest in its soil, and in their midst."[55]

When word reached South Dakota that Bishop Hare was dying, many of his beloved Indians made a pilgrimage to Sioux Falls where they gathered at All Saints School. There they kept an all-night vigil, praying and singing, until they had word of his death on October 23, 1909.[56]

On April 20, 1910, a memorial service was held for Bishop Hare which was attended by men and women, white and Indian, from all parts of the state. It was decided that a memorial to Bishop Hare be established and in some way be connected to All Saints School. A fund was established, and the first contributions were made by the Indians who sent with their subscriptions a letter to Bishop Johnson:

DEAR BISHOP:
One of the old customs of the Indians that whenever a Father dies his children while shedding their tears, rubbing with their hands to the body and say, Oh! Father, father. Now although we do not touch or rub his body with our hands, but remember him lovingly and many of us come together to attend this great memorial services to our late Bishop Hare who has been a true loving Father to us by his wise counsel and exhortations; and through his untiring efforts many of us now become Christians and follow the progress of civilization. . . .[57]

In 1904, Bishop Hare, after coming to terms with the nature of his illness, wrote to the Secretary of the Board of Missions: "It is quite manifest that I shall need relief before long in South Dakota either by a division of the field or by the appointment of a coadjutor. . . ."[58]

When Hare's needs were known, the General Convention of 1904 passed a new law to specifically meet that need. On June 5, 1905, Frederick Foote Johnson, then General Missionary in Western Massachusetts, was elected by the House of Bishops as assistant to Bishop Hare. Hare wrote of the younger man: "I have found a man like-minded who will naturally care for your state. . . . Bishop J. proves all that I could wish, both personally and officially."[59]

Johnson did not have the right of succession, but was elected Bishop of South Dakota in 1910. In his annual report of 1910, Johnson said:

. . . The Niobrara Field is no longer distinctively Indian. It is rapidly overrun by white folk. The problem is, how shall the Church take care of Whites and Indians in one field? Heretofore they have been in separate fields. Now the fences have well-nigh disappeared, and this within the last three years. How shall the Church take care of the two peoples so that the potentialities of each may best be realized? The need which this question first of all reveals is the need for more men. Where are they?[60]

Only a few months later, in 1911, Johnson was elected coadjutor of the

Diocese of Missouri which he felt constrained to accept. He became Bishop of Missouri in 1923.[61]

At a special meeting, the House of Bishops elected Bishop Rowe of Alaska, to replace Johnson in South Dakota. Rowe declined, feeling bound to remain in Alaska. In the spring of 1912, the House of Bishops next elected the Reverend George Biller, Jr., who had been Dean of Calvary Cathedral.

George Biller, Jr., had been born in London, England, on February 25, 1874. He began his missionary work in the United States in the Choctaw Nation, Indian Territory, Oklahoma. He was Dean of Calvary Cathedral from 1908, until his consecration as the third Bishop of South Dakota on September 18, 1912.

Biller began his work after there had been no bishop in residence for eighteen months. He immediately began visitation of the field of 163 missions and seeing the extreme need of the Indians for missionaries and financial assistance, Biller found it necessary to make frequent trips East to secure this support.

At the 1913 Annual Convocation of the Missionary District of South Dakota, a resolution was passed in which the delegates petitioned the General Convention of the Protestant Episcopal Church in the United States to adopt a canon or canons, to provide for the election of a suffragan bishop for work in missionary districts, and that a suffragan bishop be elected and consecrated for South Dakota.

In his first annual address to the 1913 Convocation, Biller spoke of the need for a Suffragan Bishop in South Dakota:

Since Bishop Johnson was elected to assist Hare, the field has developed rapidly until today there are 166 stations, more than half of which are off the railroad, scattered over an area of 80,000 square miles—by far the largest Missionary District of the American Church and is larger than all but nine of the Dioceses, five of which have a second bishop and all of which are small in area and with excellent traveling facilities. Problem complicated in South Dakota because of the 166 stations, 100 are Indian.[62]

Bishop Biller died suddenly at St. Mary's School, Rosebud Mission, on October 22, 1915, while on a confirmation trip. His constitution was unable to stand the strain he forced upon himself in overseeing the large district, and his death from heart failure was brought on by overwork.

While the district waited for another Bishop, the Presiding Bishop, Daniel S. Tuttle, assumed personal charge of South Dakota, visiting frequently himself and also sending Bishop Johnson to help with the district.

Rt. Rev. Frederick Foote Johnson, Bishop of South Dakota, 1910-1911.

Rt. Rev. George Biller, Jr., Bishop of South Dakota, 1912-1915.

Rt. Rev. Hugh Latimer Burleson, Bishop of South Dakota, 1916-1931.

In 1916, the annual convocation again petitioned the General Convention for assistance for the Bishop of South Dakota, noting ". . . there is no question that the death of Bishop Biller was largely caused by overwork in faithfully trying to discharge the duties of the District."[63]

At the General Convention in St. Louis, October, 1916, Hugh Latimer Burleson, editorial secretary of the Board of Missions, was elected the fourth Missionary Bishop of South Dakota. For the second time, the Church sent a secretary of the Board of Missions to the state.

Hugh L. Burleson was born at Northfield, Minnesota, on April 25, 1865, to the Reverend Solomon Stevens Burleson and Abigail Pomeroy Burleson. Bishop Burleson was the fouth child of nine, and attended grammer school at Racine, Wisconsin, where he also graduated from Racine College in 1887. He graduated from the General Theological Seminary, New York City, in 1893, and was ordained deacon on June 24, 1893, at the Hobart Church, Oneida Indian reservation, Wisconsin, where his father was then missionary. His contact with the Oneidas during his vacations had endeared him to them, and on the same afternoon of his ordination, they formally adopted him into the Oneida Nation and gave him the name, *Galahodt,* Good Timber.[64]

He served for a year as assistant of the Church of the Holy Communion, New York City, and there was ordained priest on April 4, 1894. A few days later, he married Helen S. Ely of New York, and the young couple left immediately to Waupaca, Wisconsin, where Burleson served as rector until 1898. He then accepted a call to act as assistant at St. Luke's Church, Rochester, New York, the ancestral home of his wife's family. Two years later in 1900, Burleson accepted a call to become dean at Gethsemane Cathedral, Fargo, North Dakota. In 1909, he answered an emergency call from the Missions House in New York to temporarily take the place of a secretary who had to be absent for a few months. He became Editorial Secretary under Presiding Bishop Lloyd, and editor of the *Spirit of Missions*.[65]

When Burleson heard of his election as Bishop of South Dakota, he said it was "a missionary call to which a missionary's son could not say no."[66] He was consecrated in the Cathedral of St. John the Divine, New York City, on December 14, 1916, and took up his work in South Dakota in January, 1917.

In his first annual address to the Convocation held at St. Mark's, Aberdeen, on June 3, 1917, Burleson solemnly accepted his charge and said: "I know of no missionary district which presents so conspicuous and unique an opportunity and responsibility. Here the old and the new are found together; domestic and foreign missions dwell side by side; the prairie and the mountains meet one another."[67]

Burleson felt that the time was right for a real advance in the missionary work among the white people. He felt that the country west of the river should have immediate attention, and hoped to make a "real" deanery of the Black Hills, which had so long existed on paper.

In May, 1917, Burleson visited Pierre for the first time and was shown the capitol by Judge Gates. "I was struck," he reported, "by the fact that excellent oil portraits of the two Roman Catholic prelates, who have presided over the eastern part of the state, appear on its walls . . . and I was chagrined that the portrait of the bishop who really made history in South Dakota, and who stands pre-eminent as an ecclesiastical figure in all the years of its statehood, nowhere appeared."[68] Burleson immediately set to work to correct this absence, and on January 15, 1919, an oil painting of Bishop Hare, the gift of the Church in South Dakota, was presented to the State and given to the care of the State Historical Society.

Bishop Burleson surveyed the district and created the office of Archdeacon of Niobrara, and appointed the Reverend Edward Ashley to that position. Ashley had served as Rural Dean under Bishop Hare and General Missionary under Bishop Biller.

Burleson attended his first Niobrara Convocation at the Church of the Inestimable Gift, Corn Creek. The October, 1917, *Churchman* reported on that visit:

> The delegates and visitors from the chapels and stations of the ten reservations had pitched their tents for the three day meeting. The home of the genial Dakota priest, Amos Ross, was the only permanent dwelling in the circle. As darkness began to close in, an anxious questioning arose: "Where is our new Bishop; why does he not come?" When suddenly, in a dense cloud of dust the Episcopal Cadillac plunged down through the gulch and up onto the plain to the gate of the Mission House. Amos Ross went forward, joyfully, to greet the Bishop and his party. The the glad news of the Bishop's arrival spread through the camp."[69]

Burleson held his first ordination at the 1917 Niobrara Convocation when two young Indian men were ordained deacon; Charles King, who had been a catechist, and Henry Whipple, who had completed studying. The Bishop confirmed ninety-six persons, many of them adults, at that same time.

In Bishop Burleson's first year in South Dakota, the report of parishes, missions and clergy included the following list:[70]

PLACES WHERE SERVICES ARE OCCASIONALLY HELD

Bonesteel	Rev. W. B. Roberts
Burke (2)	Rev. W. B. Roberts
Britton (8)	Rev. W. B. Roberts
Carter (3)	
Colome (7)	Rev. W. B. Roberts
Crow Peak	Rev. A. E. Cash
Fairfax (6)	Rev. W. B. Roberts
Gregory (3)	Rev. W. B. Roberts
Herrick (6)	Rev. W. B. Roberts
Keystone (5)	
Martin	
McIntosh (3)	
Philip (6)	
Wilmot (4)	
DeGray	
Dupree (6)	General Missionary
Andover	
Canton	General Missionary

Marvin (3)
Terraville
Wood (1)   Rev. W. B. Roberts
White River   Rev. J. B. Clark

The name of the Reverend W. B. Roberts appears in eight different places on this 1917 list. The communities in which he held services reflected the opening of the Rosebud reservation to white settlement. The first services in this new area of the white field were held by the Reverend A. B. Clark, Superintending Presbyter of the Rosebud Mission.

When Bishop Johnson had contacted Roberts about coming to work in South Dakota after the young man graduated from Berkeley Divinity School, Roberts responded, "Send me anywhere you please; no place is too rough or raw for me."[71]

Roberts arrived, a newly ordained deacon, to start work among the white people in Gregory and Tripp counties in July, 1908, and found a bed in a bunk house in Dallas.

Dallas was the main point in which homesteaders filed their claims. Roberts had to hold services in many different buildings which happened to be avilable on Sunday, but managed to have regular services. One Sunday service was held outside on an open lot, and in order to insure a good attendance, Roberts secured the services of a band which had been hired to advertise lot sales in Dallas. He gave them copies of "Onward Christian Soldier," and a sign which read, "Come to Church." The band played the hymn and carried the sign up and down main street a couple times, and gathered a fair sized congregation.[72]

In 1910, Roberts announced his approaching marriage to Miss Meta K. Jackson of Middletown, Connecticut. Bishop Johnson and the Dallas congregation raised funds to build Roberts and his bride a rectory east of the Church of the Incarnation, which had been consecrated in 1909.

The only other town besides Dallas where a permanent mission was established in Gregory county was at St. Andrew's, Bonesteel, which was organized in 1921. Dallas, Bonesteel, and All Saints, Ponca Creek, are presently (in 1976) combined in the Gregory County Mission.

There were in 1917, in addition to the Rosebud counties, many organized and unorganized missions in western South Dakota which Bishop Burleson felt he could not adequately minister to without assistance.

In November, Bishop Burleson happily announced that William Proctor Remington, rector of St. Paul's, Minneapolis, had been elected Suf-

Rt. Rev. William Procter Remington, Suffragan Bishop of South Dakota, 1918-1922.

fragan Bishop of South Dakota. Remington was consecrated on January 10, 1918, in Minneapolis, and that same night left for Camp McPherson, Atlanta, Georgia, to serve as Chaplain of the University of Minnesota Base Hospital, Unit 26.[73]

World War I not only prevented the new suffragan bishop from taking up the work in South Dakota, but also made it difficult for Bishop Burleson to secure needed clergy for the state. Burleson wrote in 1918:

[I] deplore the unrest of the clergy who were abandoning posts where they ought to stay, and leaving churches where great spiritual loss was certain, in order to throw themselves into army work.[74]

The fact that the clergy in the West remained brought accusations from Easterners of indifference to the War. Burleson replied: "We are as deeply interested as you are, but not so much excited; we are back of this war to the limit, but we do not grow hysterical over it."[75]

In October, 1918, Burleson noted that South Dakota was both sad and glad as it heard that the Government had called into service, as Chaplain Lieutenant, the Reverend W. Blair Roberts, Dean of the Rosebud Deanery, who received his commission towards the end of August, reported at Camp Dodge on the 26th, and was on his way to Europe the first week in September.[76]

In November, 1918, *The Churchman* noted:

The distressing news reaches us of the influenza conditions in Pine Ridge and Rosebud. The number of cases has been large and there have been many deaths. The missionaries have been overburdened with work and care. The influenza epidemic also became of such proportion to establish a quarantine to halt public gatherings such as Sunday school and church services.

It wasn't until Ash Wednesday, 1919, that the Suffragan Bishop took up his residence and work in South Dakota. Rapid City was selected as the strategic center from which Remington would "prosecute the missionary work."[77] The reasons for the choice were: first, that the people of the Black Hills had long felt isolated from the life of the Church and that they might take new interest if they had a resident Bishop; and second, was that Rapid City had been growing rapidly, was the railroad center of western South Dakota and would become the distributing center for that area. Remington purchased his own home which the Archdeacon's wife, Elizabeth Ashley, named "Bishopgate." The name had a double significance since Rapid City was considered the "Gateway to the Hills," and the Remington home became an open door to the clergy and their wives and to the people of the community.[78]

In June, 1920, the organizational meeting of the Executive Council of the Episcopal Church in South Dakota was held at the home of Bishop Burleson in Sioux Falls. Mr. J. M. Miller was elected Executive Secretary.

Both Bishops, Burleson and Remington, had an interest and were in touch with all parts of the work in South Dakota, but each had a specific area of responsibility.[79]

Bishop Burleson had charge of:
1. White and Indian Convocations
2. Meetings of the Executive Council
3. Oversight of the Departments of Finance, Publicity and Religious Education
4. Oversight of Indian Missions
5. Oversight of the white parishes east of the Missouri River

Native Clergy in 1915. Front L-R: Stephen King, Herbert Welsh, P. J. Deloria, David Tatiyopa; Back: Luke Walker, Batiste Lambert, William Holmes, Dallas Shaw.

Historic St. John's Church which was established in the gold-mining frontier town of Deadwood, Dakota Territory.

6. Direction of Candidates for Ministry and Ordination to Ministry
7. Calling of Clergy
8. Oversight of Institutions
9. Visitations, as arranged.

Bishop Remington had the responsibility of:
1. Assisting at Convocations
2. Charge of all Deanery Meetings
3. Oversight of the Departments of
   Missions, Social Service, Stewardship and Service
4. Oversight of all white Missions
5. Oversight of all white parishes
   west of the Missouri River and Pierre
6. Visitations, as arranged.

Both bishops loved the Black Hills, and their diaries make frequent references to excursions and camping trips in the Dakota mountains. Burleson noted, in 1925:

(The) remarkable proposal for improving the Black Hills by changing the Needles into something different . . . some of our influential South Dakotans have proposed that portion of the Needles be created into something similar to the gigantic statue of Robert E. Lee at Stone Mountain, Georgia.

Just why these wonderful perfections of nature would be turned into stone Washingtons, Lincolns, and Grants, is not very clearly shown. . . . The only argument we have heard in favor of this "improvement" is that it will excite the interest of tourists. No doubt this is true. Other exhibitions of bad taste have done so in the past, but is it worth the price?[80]

Remington, because of his closer proximity to the Hills, often sounded like an advertising brochure when he wrote of the grand scenery, the stately pines and awesome granite shapes of the Needles. "I am determined," he wrote in September, 1922, "to make all of our clergy, their families and congregations enjoy with us the beauties of western South Dakota."[81]

Before he and his wife Florence left to attend the General Convention in Portland, Oregon, Bishop Remington began negotiations with the Federal Government to lease a number of acres in the Black Hills in behalf of the Church in South Dakota. He dreamed of the construction of a central log cabin to be used as a chapel and recreation hall for the campers of "prairie dwelling clergy and their families who would then have the chance to look up into the Hills, whence cometh their help and they will be refreshed."[82]

After the 1922 General Convention, Bishop Burleson reported, "This

Convention has brought to us a great and unexpected change. We have lost the Suffragan who we loved and gained another whom we also love."[83]

The House of Bishops elected Remington as Bishop of Eastern Oregon on their first ballot. Burleson was dismayed, and after the election, he pleaded for the immediate election of a suffragan for South Dakota, so that the work would not suffer in the usual delay of choosing another. The House of Bishops agreed to suspend its rules, and proceeded to the immediate nomination and election of the Reverend W. Blair Roberts.

Bishop Burleson was pleased with the results of the Convention's action, and telegraphed the news to the new Suffragan saying, "Everyone here happy in the choice." When the news reached South Dakota, the *Churchman* reported that Burleson's telegram expressed the feelings of the whole district.[84]

The record of Bishop Burleson's years in South Dakota was one of wise administration, far-seeing statesmanship, and affectionate guidance for the Church and the people of South Dakota. In 1918, at Burleson's wish, the Annual Convocation passed a Canon which established new deanery boundaries:

> *Niobrara Deanery*—Archdeacon Edward Ashley, Aberdeen. Included all Indian work.
> *Northern Deanery*—Rural Dean F. B. Bartlett, Aberdeen.
> *Central Deanery*—Rural Dean C. A. Weed, Mitchell.
> *Southern Deanery*—Rural Dean E. F. Siegredt, Yankton.
> *Deanery of the Rosebud*—Rural Dean W. B. Roberts, Dallas.
> *Deanery of the Black Hills*—Rural Dean A. E. Cash, Spearfish.[85]

Burleson's time in South Dakota were years of increasing toil, but he was rewarded by increasing results. His wife, Helen, was unfortunately unable to share all of those years with him. In 1924, she suffered a nervous breakdown which necessitated her placement in a sanitarium. She died on February 6, 1928.[86]

In the 1928 meeting of the General Convention in Washington, Presiding Bishop Murray appointed Bishop Burleson as his assistant, with the title of "Assessor." During the next three years, Burleson served as assistant to three presiding bishops in succession. It was a trying experience, but Burleson's presence gave continuity to the administration of the national Church.

President Franklin D. Roosevelt paused in a tour of drought stricken states to attend the Sunday morning service at Emmanuel Church, Rapid City on Aug. 30, 1936. L-R: The Emmanuel choir; the rector, the Reverend E. Jerome Pipes; President Roosevelt with son, James, daughter-in-law, Barbara, and son, John.

In 1931, there was a strong sentiment at the General Convention in favor of electing Burleson as Presiding Bishop. But the fact that he had been a Missionary Bishop and not a Diocesan, led many to question the legality of such an election. Burleson neither desired nor sought the office, and was pleased with the election of Bishop Perry, and again accepted the position as assistant to the new presiding bishop, stating: "If I can only do the work for the Church for which I am fitted I do not care who has the honors."[87]

As assistant to the presiding bishops, and with the increasing load placed upon him, Burleson had to resign his work in South Dakota. However, he returned as often as he could to visit and rest in his beloved cabin at Camp Remington, which he considered the only real home he ever had. There it was, in the beautiful Black Hills, that Bishop Burleson died in the evening of July 30, 1933.[88]

7

/\./\./\./\

Yesterday

In 1908, W. Blair Roberts, "a tall rawboned youth, fired with a zeal to spread the gospel of Christ, came out of the east to our newly opened Rosebud country—a young man with big hands, big feet, and a heart as big as all South Dakota."[1] Peter Beaulieu, early resident of the Rosebud and Roberts' friend, described the new South Dakota frontier as "wild and wooly—indians, cowboys, cattle rustlers, gamblers, homesteaders, lawyers, doctors, merchants, adventurers, fortune seekers—as motley a crowd as ever found its way to any western frontier. He [Roberts] commanded the respect of all classes of people, even the most lawless and ungodly."[2]

Roberts' election as Suffragan of South Dakota in 1922 had the unanimous approval of the district, a fact which Bishop Burleson found to be unprecedented where a local man was chosen as bishop. Burleson thought that Roberts disproved the notion prevalent at the time that a man who went into the mission field was forever lost to sight. "He," Burleson said of Roberts, "disappeared into the new Rosebud country, identified himself utterly with its life, gave no thought to his own advancement, and was the person most astounded when told that he had been chosen as suffragan bishop of this district."[3]

In 1930, Roberts was elected Bishop of Harrisburg, Pennsylvania, but immediately declined because he believed that his work in South Dakota was more important. "Sometimes," editorialized the *Churchman* in its report of Roberts' election and refusal, "something will have to be written on the presumption of eastern dioceses in thinking that everyone at work west of the Mississippi is just crazy to get a job back east."[4]

Bishop Burleson was spending most of his time on the business of the

*The Rt. Rev. W. Blair
Roberts, fifth Bishop of
South Dakota, 1931-1954.*

national church, and Roberts had, by 1930, assumed the major portion of
the work of the Bishop of South Dakota. In that year, the Niobrara
Council was organized, along the general lines of the Executive Council,
to handle the problems peculiar to the Indian field. It was a supplement to
the Executive Council, with its members composed of the Bishops, Arch-
deacons, the Executive Secretary, the Superintending Presbyters, and
the Wardens of the Indian Schools. In its first year, the Niobrara Council
sent a petition to the U.S. Senate opposing the proposed bill which would
legalize the use of peyote for sacramental use by the Native American
Church. They also sent a petition to the Secretary of the Interior and the
Commissioner of Indian Affairs to curb Indian dancing, and the practice
of old-time customs which were considered detrimental to the Indians
progress.[5]

Burleson resigned as Bishop of South Dakota in 1931, saying, "I felt
that I ought to step completely aside and give to Bishop Roberts the
opportunity of carrying on the work. . . . He has been elected as your

Bishop (on September 29, 1931), and we are assured of the appointment of a Suffragan at an early date."[6]

However, the state of the nation's economy was felt very strongly in the Church, as it was in every other branch of life. For the first time since the Nationwide Campaign was originated in 1919, South Dakota failed in 1931 to pay its pledge. South Dakota's condition was general throughout the Church. The National Council had a shortage of nearly a million dollars, and had to make drastic reductions in the running expenses of the Church. Cuts were made in all missionary salaries. South Dakota's appropriations from the National Council were reduced by $12,000, which included a ten percent cut on all missionary salaries.[7] Because of the heavily burdened missionary budget, Bishop Roberts withdrew the request for a suffragan in South Dakota.

World War II also had an affect on the Church's economy and, as the other great war had done, brought about a shortage of clergy because many of them were enlisting as chaplains. In 1944, there were only nine resident priests in the white field in South Dakota. Bishop Roberts had to curtail travel, cancel meetings, or move them to more centrally located places in the state because of the war-time restrictions on travel.

When the Army came to South Dakota cities and towns, the Churches responded to the needs of soldiers and civilians who came with it. The Army Technical School was established at Sioux Falls, and Calvary Cathedral opened its doors to meet the spiritual and social needs of the many Episcopalians at the new camp. A Service Men's Club was provided in a guild room, and on Sundays, one of the Women's Auxiliary committees served Sunday dinners for the service men who attended morning worship.

Emmanuel Church in Rapid City turned its parish house into a Welcome Center for the service men and families of the construction workers at the Air Base. St. Paul's, Brookings, invited soldiers in training at State College to lunch and a social hour after Sunday services. At the Ammunition Storage Center, Provo, the Reverend Frank Thorburn held a monthly service of Holy Communion for Episcopalians stationed there.

In 1943, the Indian work of North and South Dakota was consolidated under the supervision of the Bishop of South Dakota.[8] North Dakota was handicapped because of its widely scattered chapels, lack of numerical strength, and shortage of trained native workers. There was no change in jurisdiction lines or finances. The Reverend John B. Clark, Superintending Presbyter of the Standing Rock reservation, was named Superintend-

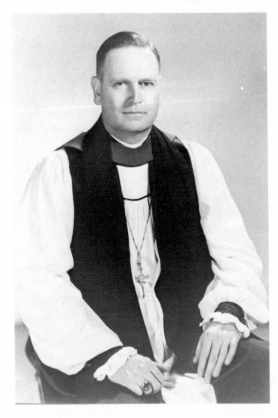

The Rt. Rev. Conrad H. Gesner, sixth Bishop of South Dakota, 1954-1970.

ing Presbyter of the North Dakota field, and the Reverend Sidney Bearsheart, who had been priest in charge of the Santee mission, was sent to Cannon Ball, North Dakota, as priest in charge of the work there. Bishop Roberts and Bishop Atwill of North Dakota shared official visitations for confirmations in the Indian field, and Atwill made a number of official visitations to parishes and missions in the white field of South Dakota to offset the additional load on Bishop Roberts.

Clark supervised the North Dakota Indian field and that of the South Dakota portion of the Standing Rock reservation from his residence at Mobridge. However, the distance and remoteness from the other North Dakota reservations made his work extremely difficult. Clark recommended that the Diocese of North Dakota resume the responsibility for its Indian communicants, which it did in 1951.[9]

In 1945, Bishop Roberts notified the Presiding Bishop that he was going to ask for a Bishop Coadjutor. "It is physically impossible for me any longer to cover the entire field and preparation should be made for the time when I must relinquish the work. . . . This Indian work is different from that of any other Diocese or District in the Church on account of its size and extent. Any Bishop taking it over should have at least a few years of working experience before assuming the entire responsibility."[10]

Conrad Herbert Gesner was elected by the House of Bishops on May 2, 1945. Gesner was the godson of Bishop Burleson, and on one of Burleson's visits to South Dakota students at General Theological Seminary, he invited Gesner to join the group while he was there. "The result of his gentle persuasion led me to be transferred and become a Candidate for the Missionary District of South Dakota and to be ordained deacon by Bishop Burleson in the parish of All Souls, Waterbury, Connecticut, where my father was rector."[11]

Gesner's first South Dakota charge was of St. Peter's Mission, Sioux Falls, and he was Canon Missionary of Calvary Cathedral with two rural congregations at Hurley and Parker. After two years, he moved to Trinity Church, Pierre, where he served from 1929 to 1933. He then was rector of the Church of St. John the Evangelist, St. Paul, Minnesota, until his election as Coadjutor of South Dakota.

In his first address to the District Convocation of 1945, Gesner said:

The Church in South Dakota has been a suckling child of Mother Church. Our maturity will be found in the readiness now to aid the Mother and to lift from her some more of the burden of our support. Dependency may be all right for infants and children, but in prime of life there must be vigor and substantial contribution to family support.

We have been in the Church work here a good many years. We are as old as many a neighbor. I propose therefore:

A program for Youth; A program for Missionary endeavor; A program for making known our District's own All Saints School; A program for the attainment of the stature of ecclesiastical manhood. We are the Church in South Dakota but we must declare that Bishop Hare's infant Church has now grown to maturity.[12]

Gesner's special responsibilities were to be the mission Churches of the District and the supervision of Church institutions, with All Saints School being a chief responsibility.

In 1948, Bishop Roberts reported:

One of our big problems in South Dakota is that of Indians who have moved off the reservation into towns and cities in order to find work. This has become more acute in recent years. . . . The problem is both religious and social, for it is not easy for our Dakota people to take their place in the life of their white brethren.

They tend to become a separated group, and this through no fault of their own . . . steps have been taken which, we trust, will eventually bridge the chasm between these two races and mould these brethren into our common life. In Winner through the leadership of the Rev. Bruce W. Swain and consecrated church men and women, the Indians have been organized into religious societies. Services are held regularly in homes and in Trinity Church.

In Rapid City the problem is greater than in any other place. It is estimated that over 3,000 Indians moved here finding work in various fields of industry . . . comparatively few of these people attend Emmanuel Church.

The Home Missions Council has been much exercised over these conditions and in January, 1948, I assigned the Rev. Levi M. Roulliard to the task of working among non-reservation Indians. He will contact Indians not only in Rapid City, Huron, Sioux Falls, and other cities and towns.[13]

Mr. Wilbert D. Swain retired as Executive Secretary of the District on June 30, 1950, after twenty-four years at that post. Those years were difficult ones, for they included the years of financial depression, followed by the period of drought and dirt storms, which almost ruined the state economically, and caused the greatest proportionate loss in population of any state in the union. Following that, there came the years of World War II, when the entire District of South Dakota struggled to keep the work alive with almost one-fourth of the active clergy gone off to war service; this was the highest proportion of any Diocese in the Church. Swain had no bed of roses in the hard and exacting work he was called to do for the District, trying to make financial ends meet, trying to use limited means to the utmost, and trying to keep the clergy supplied with cars. His work included about everything except that which Priests and Bishops alone are empowered to do.

Mrs. William Limpo joined the staff of the Executive Office on a part-time basis early in July, 1950. Bishop Gesner recalled that he was fortunate indeed to have the able assistance of Connie Limpo as financial secretary, a position which she held until 1975. "Twenty-six years of adding and subtracting, scrounging and giving; God bless her as He has blessed us in her. . . ."[14]

Bishop Roberts retired in 1954, at age seventy-two, in the home in Sioux Falls which the District had presented to him and Mrs. Roberts on the twenty-fifth anniversary of his consecration. He remained active in his retirement and through his efforts a new parish, the Church of the Good Shepherd, was established in Sioux Falls. Bishop Roberts died in 1965, after giving fifty-seven years of his life to South Dakota.

Conrad H. Gesner succeeded Roberts in 1954, as Bishop of the Missionary District of South Dakota. The following is Bishop Gesner's recollections of the years of his episcopate:

I inherited a fine group of Missionary Clergy and we were joined by newcomers to our ranks. A new parish known as the Church of the Good Shepherd, Sioux Falls, emerged from the notable missionary endeavor of the retired Bishop W. Blair Roberts. The one time St. Peter's Mission gave way to a brand new mission known as the Church of the Holy Apostles which continued to serve the eastern portion of Sioux Falls.

South Dakota's relations with the National Church remained particularly gratifying. Three Presiding Bishops, Henry Knox Sherrill, Arthur Lichtenberger, and John E. Hines, all honored our Niobrara Deanery with a visit at the Niobrara Convocation during their period in office. New rectories were constructed, and a series of new church buildings came to replace chapels and churches of reservations and in towns. Our clergy rolls increased and we were able to put Church Army personnel to work at points where we had had no resident ministry before.

The native clergy were a source of strength in the Niobrara Deanery, and younger Indian men were in seminary training for the priesthood. The graduates brought further invigoration to the entire District.

Two administrative assistants in succession, Gordon R. Plowe, now a clergyman, and the Reverend Walter H. Jones, proved of mighty assistance to the progress of the Church's programs.

I was permitted opportunities to share in the joys of Camp Remington, and to take part in the origination of the Thunderhead Episcopal Camp (in 1965).

With the approach of the time for my retirement and with the consent of the Executive Council and the House of Bishops, the Right Reverend Lyman C. Ogilby, resigned Bishop of the Philippines, was elected Coadjutor of South Dakota in 1964. He came for a period of something over two years. Then desiring to have South Dakota make the choice of its own Bishop, he stepped aside. He was Bishop-in-charge at the Convocation which elected the Reverend Walter H. Jones (in 1970).[15]

South Dakota, by the action of the General Convention, became a Diocese in 1971, and elected its first Suffragan Bishop, Harold S. Jones, the same year. The Diocese now had two Bishops Jones, and affectionately came to differentiate between them as Bishop Walter and Bishop Harold. Bishop Harold was the first native South Dakotan to be elected a bishop, and the first American Indian bishop in the Episcopal Church.

The work of the Episcopal Church in South Dakota began with Bishop Harold's ancestors, the Santee. The structure of the Church for both Indians and non-Indians were built by Bishop Hare, and reinforced and expanded by those who came after. Bishop Hare still speaks to us in the legacy of his writings, and his words are relevant to a survey of the past one hundred and seventeen years:

The Rt. Rev. Lyman C. Ogilby, Bishop Coadjutor, 1964-1970.

The Rt. Rev. Harold S. Jones, Suffragan Bishop of South Dakota, 1971-1976 (retired).

Bishop Hare's final resting place on the campus of All Saints School. Marker reads:

William Hobart Hare
First Bishop of South Dakota
1838-1909
Feed My Sheep

This period has been one of many difficulties, and I have many shortcomings to lament; but on reviewing it I give thanks to Him Who, having Himself gone over the open country, and through the towns, preaching the Gospel of the Kingdom, deigns to call us men to share His work.

I find it hard to believe now that this is the country of which in earlier years I truthfully wrote and spoke as a hopeless desert.

Thanks be to God . . .[16]

Notes

Chapter 1, GOD IS WAKANTANKA

1. Malan, Vernon D., Jesser, Clinton J., *Dakota Indian Religion,* Bulletin 473, Rural Sociology Department, South Dakota State College, Feb., 1959, p. 31.

2. Whipple, Rt. Rev. Henry Benjamin, *Lights and Shadows of a Long Episcopate,* The Macmillan Company, New York, 1899, p. 186.

3. Macgregor, Gordon, *Warrriors Without Weapons,* University of Chicago Press, Chicago, 1946, p. 92.

4. Deloria, Ella, *Speaking of Indians,* Friendship Press, New York, 1944, pp. 98–99.

5. *Indian Tribes and Missions,* Church Missions Publishing Co., Hartford, 1926, p. 28.

6. Kingsbury, George, *A History of Dakota Territory,* S.J. Clarke Company, Chicago, 1915, Vol. I, p. 783–784.

7. *First Annual Report,* Indian Commision of the Protestant Episcopal Church, Bible House, New York, 1872, p. 4.

8. *Ibid.*

9. *Ibid.*

10. *Ibid.,* p. 3.

11. *Ibid.,* p. 4.

12. *Ibid.*

13. *Ibid.,* p. 5.

14. Hare, Rt. Rev. William H., *Annual Reports of the Missionary Bishop of Niobrara, 1873–1893,* Bible House, New York, 1874, pp. 1–2.

15. *Ibid.*

16. Hare letter to Mr. H. Bohlen, Nov. 21, 1872, Hare papers, South Dakota Protestant Episcopal Church Diocesan Archives, (hereafter referred to as Diocesan Archives).

17. Hare, *loc. cit.*

18. *Ibid.*

19. Marrs, James David, Sr., *Grant's "Quaker" Policy and the Bishop of Niobrara,* unpublished Master's Thesis, Department of History, University of South Dakota, 1970, pp. 10–11.

20. *Ibid.*

21. *Ibid.*

22. Gilkerson, Peggy, *Missionary Rivalries Among the Santee Sioux,* unpublished Master's Thesis, Department of History, Harvard University, 1961, p. 39.

23. *Ibid.,* p. 40.

154

24. *Ibid.*

25. *A Month Among the Indian Missions,* American Church Press, New York, 1872, (no page numbers).

26. Gilkerson, *op. cit.,* p. 20.

27. Howe, Dewolfe M. A., *Life and Labors of Bishop Hare,* Sturgis and Walton, New York, 1912, p. 214.

28. Macgregor, *op. cit.,* pp. 92–96.

29. Howe, *Loc. cit.,* p. 296.

30. Malan, etc., *op. cit.,* p. 47.

31. Howe, *Loc. cit.,* p. 243.

32. *Church News,* Sioux Falls, April, 1891, p. 1.

33. *Ibid.*

34. Malan, etc., *op. cit.,* pp. 47–48.

35. Macgregor, *op. cit.,* p. 100.

36. *Ibid.*

37. Young, Gertrude S., "Correspondence of a Niobrara Archdeacon," *Historical Magazine,* Protestant Episcopal Church, Vol. XXXII, March, 1963, pp. 13–15.

38. Thorburn, Rev. Frank, "Peyote Cult, Yuwipi, Back-sliders," paper written for S. D. Church history project, Feb. 1975.

39. Macgregor, *op. cit.,* p. 99.

40. *Loc. cit.*

41. *Loc. cit.,* p. 102.

42. "A Brief History of the Brotherhood of Christian Unity," pamphlet, no publisher, no date, no page numbers.

43. *Ibid.*

44. *Ibid.*

45. *Ibid.*

46. *Ibid.*

47. Deloria, the Ven. Vine V., letter to author, Sept. 23, 1975.

Chapter 2, LOWER MISSOURI AND EASTERN DAKOTA

1. Whipple, Rt. Rev. Henry Benjamin, *Lights and Shadows of a Long Episcopate,* Macmillan Company, New York, 1900, p. 27.

2. Meyer, Roy, *History of the Santee Sioux,* University of Oklahoma Press, Norman, 1967, p. 138.

3. Gilkerson, Peggy, *Missionary Rivalries Among the Santee Sioux,* unpublished Master's Thesis, Department of History, Harvard University, March 31, 1961, p. 4.

4. Meyer, *loc. cit.,* p. 137.

5. Whipple, *op. cit.,* p. 133.

6. Gilkerson, *op. cit.,* p. 8.

7. Meyer, *op. cit.,* p. 146.

8. Heard, Issac V. D., *History of the Sioux War and Massacres of 1862 and 1863,* Harper and Brothers, New York, 1863, p. 295.

9. Meyer, *loc. cit.*

10. *Annual Report of the Board of Missions, 1869,* Protestant Episcopal Church, (no publisher), p. 94.

11. "*Chronology of the Episcopal Church's Indian Mission Work, 1860–1878,*" Diocesan Archives, no page numbers.

12. Girton, Polly W., *The Protestant Episcopal Indian Missions of Dakota Territory,* unpublished Master's Thesis, University of South Dakota, August, 1960, pp. 17–18.

13. *Ibid.,* p. 18.

14. Chronology, *op. cit.*

15. *Ibid.*

16. Welsh, William, *Semi-Official Report,* letter to Hon. J. D. Cox, 1870, (no publisher), p. 16.

17. Girton, *op. cit.,* p. 19.

18. Hare, Rt. Rev. W. H., *Annual Reports of the Missionary Bishop of Niobrara, 1873–1893,* Bible House, New York, 1873, p. 6.

19. Clarkson, Rt. Rev. Robert, *Letter to Spirit of Missions,* Vol. XXVI, 1871, p. 430.

20. *The Last Words to His Friends of the Rev. Paul Mazakute,* Dakota League of Massachusetts, 1874, p. 18.

21. Chronology, *op. cit.*

22. Girton, *op. cit.,* p. 22.

23. *First Annual Report of the Indian Commission,* Bible House, New York, 1872, pp. 10–11.

24. *Ibid.,* p. 2.

25. Meyer, *op. cit.,* p. 179.

26. "The Church and the Indians," *Indian Pamphlets,* 1876, (no publisher), p. 1.

27. Howe, Dewolfe M. A., *Life and Labors of Bishop Hare,* Sturgis and Walton Co., New York, p. 163.

28. Gilkerson, *op. cit.,* p. 20.

29. Office of Indian Affairs, (O.A.I.), Special File 269.

30. Gilkerson, *loc. cit.,* p. 165.

31. O.A.I., *loc. cit.*

32. Howe, *op. cit.*

33. *Ibid.*

34. *Ibid.,* p. 166.

35. *Ibid.,* p. 167.

36. Hare papers, Houghton Library, Harvard University, call no. 58-11, Hare statement.

37. *Ibid.,* Hinman statement.

38. Ashley, Rev. Edward, papers, Diocesan Archives.

39. Hyde, George E., *A Sioux Chronicle,* University of Oklahoma Press, Norman, 1956, p. 114.

40. *Ibid.*

41. Hyde, *loc. cit.* Criticism of Hinman not only came from Hare, but also in the 1878 editions of the Niobrara, Nebraska, *Pioneer,* and the 1877–1884 editions of the Yankton newspaper.

42. *Ibid.,* p. 143.

43. *Ibid.,* p. 139.

44. Ashley, *op. cit.*

45. Gilkerson, *op. cit.,* p. 56.

46. Hare papers, *op. cit.*

47. *Ibid.*

48. Hare, *op. cit.,* 1893, p. 1.

49. Hare, *op. cit.,* 1895, p. 5.

50. Meyer, *op. cit.,* p. 242.

51. *Ibid.,* p. 243.

52. *Ibid.*

53. *Ibid.*

54. Riggs, Stephen, *Mary and I: Forty Years Among the Sioux,* Blakely, Brown and Marsh, Chicago, 1880, p. 266.

55. Meyer, *op. cit.,* p. 244.

56. *Ibid.,* p. 245.

57. Girton, *op. cit.,* p. 34.

58. Cook, the Rev. Joseph, *Diary,* May 1875–Feb. 1902, Diocesan Archives.

59. Girton, *loc. cit.,* p. 36.

60. Howe, *op. cit.,* pp. 182–183.

61. Girton, *loc. cit.,* p. 36.

62. *Ibid.*

63. Young, Gertrude S., *William Joshua Cleveland,* South Dakota State College, Brookings, (no date), p. 24.

64. *Ibid.,* p. 26.

65. Johnson, Rt. Rev. Frederick F., *Annual Report, 1910,* (no page numbers).

66. Meyer, *op. cit.,* p. 202.

67. *Ibid.*

68. *Ibid.*

69. Sisseton File, English Translation, Diocesan Archives.

70. Hare, *op. cit.,* 1882, p. 3.

71. *Ibid.*

72. Ashley, *op. cit.*

73. Ashley, Rev. Edward, letter to Bishop Hare, March 28, 1884, Hare papers, Diocesan Archives.

74. *South Dakota Churchman,* April 1931, p. 5.

75. Barbour, D.D., The Rev. Paul H., letter to author, Feb. 24, 1975.

76. Robinson, Doane, *History of the Sioux or Dakota Indians,* Ross and Haines edition, Minneapolis, 1956, p. 20.

77. Jennewein, J. Leonard, Boorman, Jane, *Dakota Panorama,* Dakota Territory Centennial Commission, Brevet Press edition, Sioux Falls, 1973, p. 170.

78. Cook, the Rev. J. W., "Historical Sketch of the Growth of the Church in the Indian Field of South Dakota," *Journals,* Missionary District of South Dakota, 1898–1902, (1898), p. 69.

79. *Ibid.,* pp. 69–71.

80. Woodruff, K. Brent, "Episcopal Missions to the Dakotas," *South Dakota Historical Collections,* (SDHC), Pierre, Vol. XXVII, p. 561.

81. Cook, *loc. cit.,* pp. 69–71.

82. *Ibid.,* p. 71.

83. *Ibid.,* p. 72

84. *Ibid.,* p. 73.

85. *Ibid.,* p. 77.

86. *Ibid.,* p. 78.

87. *Ibid.,* pp. 78–79.

88. Chronology, *op. cit.*

89. *Loc. cit.*

90. *Ibid.,* pp. 83–84.

91. Chronology, *op. cit.*

92. *Ibid.*

93. *Ibid.*

94. Cook, *op. cit.,* p. 94.

95. Welsh, William, *Sioux and Ponca Indian Reports,* M'Calla and Stavely Printers, Philadelphia, 1870. p. 19.

96. Girton, *op. cit.,* p. 46.

97. *Ibid.,* p. 45.

98. Welsh, *op. cit.*, p. 20.

99. Welsh, William, *Our Mission to the Poncas,* (no publisher, no date), p. 3. Dorsey's work with the Ponca language in so short a time was amazing as there were five thousand words in the monograph he prepared and three thousand verbs. His work was registered with the U.S. Bureau of Ethnology.

100. *Ibid.*

101. Chronology, *op. cit.*

102. Welsh, *op. cit.*

103. *A Month Among,* etc., *op. cit.*

104. *Ibid.*

105. Hare, *op. cit.*, 1876, p. 8.

106. *Ibid.*

107. Tibbles, Thomas H., *The Ponca Chiefs: An Account of the Trial of Standing Bear,* University of Nebraska Press, Lincoln, 1972, p. 5.

108. Girton, *op. cit.*

109. Hare, *op. cit.*, 1876, p. 9.

110. Tibbles, *op. cit.*, p. xii.

111. Girton, *op. cit.*, p. 50.

112. *Ibid.*

Chapter 3, UPPER MISSOURI AND WESTERN DAKOTAS

1. Robinson, Doane, *History of the Dakota or Sioux Indians,* Ross and Haines edition, Minneapolis, 1967, p. 292.

2. Welsh, William, *Sioux and Ponca Reports,* M'Calla and Stavely Printers, Philadelphia, 1872, p. 11.

3. *A Month Among the Indian Missions,* American Church Press, New York, 1872, (no page numbers).

4. The David W. Clark Memorial Collection, mimeographed biographies, W. H. Over Museum, University of South Dakota, Vermillion, (no page numbers).

5. Chronology of the Episcopal Church's Indian Mission Work, 1860–1878, Diocesan Archives, (no page numbers).

6. Girton, Polly, *The Protestant Episcopal Indian Missions of Dakota Territory,* unpublished Master's Thesis, University of South Dakota, Vermillion, August, 1960, pp. 40–41.

7. Hare, Rt. Rev. William Hobart, *Annual Reports of the Missionary Bishop of Niobrara, 1873–1893,* Bible House, New York, 1875, p. 9.

8. Clark collection, *op. cit.*

9. Hare, *loc. cit.*, 1883, p. 6.

10. Hyde, George E., *A Sioux Chronicle,* University of Oklahoma Press, Norman, Okla., 1956, p. 129.

11. Clark Collection, *op. cit.*

12. *South Dakota (S. D.) Churchman,* Dec. 1914, p. 6.

13. *Ibid.*

14. Clark Collection, *op. cit.*

15. Welsh, *op. cit.*, p. 6.

16. Robinson, *op. cit.*, p. 392.

17. Young, Gertrude S., *William Joshua Cleveland,* 1845–1910, South Dakota State College, Brookings, (no date), p. 10.

18. *The Church and the Indians,* Office of the Indian Commission, Bible House, New York, 1873, p. 5.

19. *Ibid.*, pp. 5–6.

20. Young, *op. cit.*, p. 10.
21. *Ibid.*
22. Hare, *op. cit.*, 1874, p. 10.
23. Hare, *op. cit.*, 1877, p. 10.
24. Chronology, *op. cit.*
25. *Annual Report of the Board of Indian Commissioners,* Government Printing Office, Washington, D.C., 1879, p. 55.
26. Hare, *op. cit.*, 1882, pp. 30–31.
27. Clark Collection, *op. cit.*
28. *S. D. Churchman, op. cit.*, June 1931, p. 45.
29. *Ibid.*
30. *Ibid.*
31. *S. D. Churchman,* May 1924, pp. 5–7.
32. *S. D. Churchman,* Oct. 1924, pp. 6–7.
33. *Ibid.*
34. *S. D. Churchman,* Sept. 1924, p. 4.
35. *A Month Among,* etc., *op. cit.*
36. Robinson, Will, SDHC, Vol. XXVIII, p. 402.
37. Hare, *op. cit.*, 1873, p. 12.
38. "Biography of Martin Charger," SDHC, Vol. XXII, p. 17.
39. *A Month Among,* etc., *op. cit.*
40. Chronology, *op. cit.*
41. Hare, *op. cit.*, 1874, p. 10.
42. Girton, *op. cit.*, p. 66.
43. Hare, *op. cit.*, 1875, p. 11.
44. Howe, M. A. Dewolfe, *The Life and Labors of Bishop Hare,* Sturgis and Walton Co., New York, 1912, pp. 124–130.
45. *Ibid.*, p. 130.
46. *Ibid.*, p. 132.
47. *Ibid.*, p. 133.
48. *Ibid.*, pp. 133–134.
49. Chronology, *op. cit.*
50. *Reports of the Niobrara League,* American Church Press, New York, 1877–1900, p. 18.
51. Swift, Rev. Henry, letter to Bishop Hare, Feb. 27, 1884, Hare papers, Diocesan Archives.
52. Hare, *op. cit.*, 1885, pp. 4–5.
53. *Indian Tribes and Missions,* Church Missions Publishing Co., New York, 1926, p. 29.
54. Deloria File, Diocesan Archives.
55. *Ibid.*
56. Deloria, Ella, *Speaking of Indians,* Friendship Press, New York, 1944, p. 100.
57. *Ibid.*, pp. 100–101.
58. Howe, *op. cit.*, p. 231.
59. *Mobridge Tribune,* Mobridge, S.D., Vol. LI, No. 39, May 9, 1958.
60. Burleson, Rt. Rev. H. L., letter to George Biller, Jr., May 14, 1925, Diocesan Archives.
61. Welsh, *op. cit.*, 1870, p. 17.
62. *Ibid.*
63. Robinson, Doane, *op. cit.*, p. 354.
64. Kingsbury, George, *Dakota Territory,* Vol. I., pp. 770–771.

65. Welsh, *op. cit.*, p. 15.

66. Hare, *op. cit.*, 1874, p. 19.

67. *Ibid.*, p. 20

68. Young, *op. cit.*, p. 12.

69. *Ibid.*, pp. 13–14.

70. Robinson, Doane, *op. cit.*, p. 440.

71. Kingsbury, *op. cit.*, p. 808.

72. Girton, *op. cit.*, p. 56.

73. Young, *op. cit.*, pp. 16–17.

74. *Ibid.*, pp. 18–19.

75. "100 Years on the Rosebud," unpublished manuscript, anonymous, Rosebud file, Diocesan Archives, p. 2.

76. *Ibid.*

77. Robinson, Doane, "Education of Red Cloud," SDHC, 1924, Vol. VXII, p. 162.

78. *Early History of the Pine Ridge Missions,* 1876–1892, unpublished, anonymous, no date, Pine Ridge file, Diocesan Archives, p. 2.

79. Hare, letter to Commissioner of Indian Affairs, 1874, Hare papers, Diocesan Archives.

80. Hare, *op. cit.*, 1877, p. 11.

81. *Early History,* etc., *op. cit.*, p. 6.

82. *Ibid.*, p. 7.

83. *Ibid.*

84. *Ibid.*, p. 8.

85. *Ibid.*

86. *Ibid.*

87. *Ibid.*, p. 10.

88. *Ibid.*, p. 12.

89. *Ibid.*, p. 13.

90. *Ibid.*, p. 15.

91. *Ibid.*

92. *Ibid.*, p. 20.

93. Howe, *op. cit.*, p. 240.

94. *Loc. cit.*, p. 22.

95. *Ibid.*, p. 23.

Chapter 5, LEARNING FOR LIFE

1. Parker, Donald D., *Founding the Church in South Dakota,* History Department, South Dakota State College, Brookings, 1962, pp. 37–39.

2. Hare, Rt. Rev. W. H., *Annual Reports of the Missionary Bishop of Niobrara, 1873–1893,* Bible House, New York, 1873, p. 10.

3. *Ibid.*

4. *Ibid.*, p. 15. The author was unable to find the names of St. Paul's first students.

5. *Annual Report of the Board of Indian Commissioners,* Government Printing Office, Washington, D.C., 1880, p. 114.

6. Deloria, Ella, *Speaking of Indians,* New York, 1944, p. 63.

7. *Ibid.*, p. 117.

8. *Ibid.*

9. Girton, Polly, *Protestant Episcopal Indian Missions of Dakota Territory,* unpublished Master's Thesis, University of South Dakota, 1960, p. 82.

10. Hare, Bishop, letter to Robert Rogers, Dec. 30, 1874, Hare papers, Diocesan Archives.

11. Hare, *op. cit.,* 1873, p. 7.

12. *The Bugle,* Centennial edition, St. Mary's Episcopal School, Springfield, June 1973, p. 2.

13. *Ibid.*

14. "St. Mary's Episcopal School for Indian Girls," school circular, (no date, no page numbers).

15. Clark, the Rev. A. B., to Bishop Burleson, Apr. 24, 1922, Burleson papers, Diocesan Archives.

16. Clark, the Rev. A. B., to Bishop Burleson, Apr. 24, 1922, Burleson papers, Diocesan Archives.

17. St. Mary's, *op. cit.*

18. *South Dakota (S. D.) Churchman,* June 1924, p. 11.

19. "Hope School, Springfield, S. D.," school circular, 1885.

20. *Ibid.*

21. *Ibid.*

22. Bishop Hare letter to (name illegible), Nov. 25, 1892, Hare papers, Diocesan Archives.

23. *Ibid.*

24. Howe, M. A. Dewolfe, *Life and Labors of Bishop Hare,* Sturgis and Walton Co., New York, 1911, pp. 107–108.

25. *Indian Missions,* Pamphlet No. 329, Bible House, New York, (no date, no page numbers).

26. *Ibid.*

27. Girton, *op. cit.,* p. 90.

28. Howe, *op. cit.,* p. 280.

29. Hare, *op. cit.,* 1890, p. 4.

30. *Loc. cit.*

31. *Mobridge Tribune,* May 8, 1958.

32. *Ibid.*

33. *Ibid.*

34. *Ibid.*

35. *Ibid.*

36. Dakota Leadership Program, Brochure, Apr. 1975.

37. *S. D. Churchman,* Jan. 1942, p. 4.

38. "Bishop Hare School for Dakota Boys," Mission, S. D., school circular—this was the source of all information about Hare school, as no records were available.

39. *Journals,* Missionary District of South Dakota, 1889, p. 24.

40. Howe, *op. cit.,* pp. 220–221.

41. *S. D. Churchman,* June 1926, p. 5.

Chapter 6, SWIFT BIRD—GOOD TIMBER

1. Ashley, the Ven. Edward, "The Episcopal Church in South Dakota," original manuscript, Ashley papers, Diocesan Archives, (no date, no page numbers). Ashley apparently began a history of the Church's work in Dakota Territory and South Dakota, but never completed it. The manuscript (parts were later printed in the *Churchman),* his diaries, memoirs, and correspondence are in the Diocesan Archives collections.

2. "Chronology of the Episcopal Church's Indian Mission Work in South Dakota, 1860–1878," Diocesan Archives.

3. Woodruff, Brent K.,"The Episcopal Mission to the Dakotas, 1860–1898," SDHC, 1934, p. 593.

4. Howe, Dewolfe M. A., *The Life and Labors of Bishop Hare*, Sturgis and Walton Co., New York, 1912, pp. 6–7.

5. *Ibid.*, pp. 13 and 21.

6. *Ibid.*, pp. 30–33.

7. *Ibid.*, p. 32.

8. Burleson, Rt. Rev. H. L., "How Our Church Came to Dakota," pamphlet, Young Churchmen Co., Milwaukee, (no date, no page numbers).

9. *Ibid.*

10. *The Church News*, May, 1889, (no page numbers).

11. *Swift Bird, The Indians' Bishop*, Church Missions Publishing Co., Hartford, 1915, pp. 15–16.

12. Burleson, Rt. Rev., *op cit.*

13. *Ibid.*

14. *Swift Bird, op. cit.*, p. 42.

15. "History of Christ Church, Yankton," unpublished by parish of Christ Church, (no date, no page numbers).

16. *The First 100 Years*, Grand Lodge A.F. & A.M., South Dakota, 1974, Centennial Committee, p. 2.

17. *St. Paul's Episcopal Church History*, St. Paul's Church, Vermillion, (no date), p. 19.

18. *Ibid.*

19. Ashley, *op. cit.*

20. "Historical Sketch of Grace Church, Hurley," *S. D. Churchman*, April 1945, pp. 3–5.

21. Ashley, *op. cit.*

22. Hurley, *loc. cit.*

23. Ashley, *loc. cit.*

24. *1875–1950 Seventy-fifth Anniversary St. Mary's Church, Mitchell*, St. Mary's Church, Mitchell, (no page numbers).

25. "Trinity Church, Pierre," unpublished parish history, p. 2.

26. "History of Christ Church, Gettysburg," unpublished parish history, (no page numbers).

27. "Historic St. John's Episcopal Church, 1876–1976," unpublished St. John's, Deadwood, p. 1.

28. Ashley, *op. cit.*

29. *Loc. cit.*

30. Hare, *op. cit.*, 1878, p. 1.

31. Klock, Irma H., "Christ Church, Episcopal, Lead," unpublished parish history, 1975, p. 2.

32. Hare, *loc. cit.*, p. 1.

33. Hare, *op. cit.*, 1880, p. 1.

34. Hare, *op. cit.*, 1881, p. 1.

35. "St. John's," *op. cit.*, p. 2.

36. Hare, *op. cit.*, 1884, pp. 8–10.

37. *Ibid.*, p. 7.

38. *Ibid.*, Hare, *op. cit.*, 1887, p. 4.

39. Hare, *op. cit.*, 1888, p. 1.

40. Hare, *op. cit.*, 1884, p. 2.

41. *Ibid.*, p. 10.

42. Smith, George Martin, *South Dakota*, Vol. III, S. J. Clarke Publishing, Chicago, 1915, p. 768.

43. *Ibid.,* p. 970.

44. Hare, *op. cit.,* 1895, p. ii.

45. *Swift Bird, op. cit.,* p. 37.

46. Cook, the Rev. Joseph, *Diary,* May 1875–Feb. 1902, (no page numbers).

47. *Church News,* Oct. 1895.

48. Ashley, *op. cit.*

49. *Church News,* Sept. 1895.

50. Howe, *op. cit.,* p. 141.

51. *Ibid.,* p. 381.

52. *Ibid.*

53. *Ibid.,* p. 383.

54. *Ibid.,* p. 394.

55. *Ibid.,* pp. 400–401.

56. Pageant Script of the first 50 years in South Dakota, Diocesan Archives, (no page numbers).

57. *Journals,* Missionary District of South Dakota, 1910, p. 82.

58. Howe, *op. cit.,* p. 390.

59. *Ibid.,* p. 393.

60. Journals, *op. cit.,* p. 88.

61. Rehkopf, The Ven. Charles F., "The Episcopate of Bishop Johnson," reprint from *The Bulletin of the Missouri Historical Society,* April 1963, p. 232.

62. *Journals, op. cit.,* 1909–1913, p. 42.

63. *Ibid.,* 1916, p. 60.

64. Burleson, the Rev. John K., "Hugh L. Burleson—A Biography," *S. D. Churchman,* July–August, 1933, p. 3.

65. *Ibid.*

66. *Ibid.*

67. *Journals, op. cit.,* 1917, p. 21.

68. *Ibid.,* p. 35.

69. *S. D. Churchman,* Oct. 1917, pp. 15–17.

70. *Journals, op. cit.,* p. 20.

71. *Journals, op. cit.,* 1910, p. 92.

72. Roberts, Rt. Rev. W. Blair, "A History of the Churches of the Rosebud," unpublished, Diocesan Archives, (no page numbers).

73. *S. D. Churchman,* Feb. 1918, p. 6.

74. *Ibid.,* p. 4.

75. *Ibid.*

76. *S. D. Churchman,* Oct. 1918, p. 1.

77. *S. D. Churchman,* June 1920, p. 7.

78. *Ibid.,* p. 8.

79. *S. D. Churchman,* April 1921, p. 1.

80. *S. D. Churchman,* Sept. 1922, p. 1.

81. *Ibid.*

82. *Ibid.*

83. *S. D. Churchman,* Oct. 1922, p. 5.

84. *Ibid.,* p. 7.

85. *S. D. Churchman,* July 1918, p. 17.

86. Burleson papers, Diocesan Archives.

87. Burleson, Rev. John K., *op. cit.*

88. *Ibid.*

Chapter 7, YESTERDAY

1. Beaulieu, Peter O., letter to Robert Fayerharm, October 14, 1947, W. Blair Roberts file, Diocesan Archives.

2. *Ibid.*

3. *Journals,* Missionary District of South Dakota, 1923, p. 16.

4. *S. D. Churchman,* Dec. 1930, p. 7.

5. *S. D. Churchman,* June 1930, p. 12.

6. *S. D. Churchman,* Oct. 1931, p. 5.

7. *S. D. Churchman,* June 1932, p. 5.

8. *S. D. Churchman,* June 1943, p. 5.

9. Wilkens, Robert P. and Wyman H., *God Giveth the Increase,* North Dakota Institute for Regional Studies, Fargo, 1959, p. 165.

10. *S. D. Churchman,* Jan. 1945, p. 3.

11. Gesner, Rt. Rev. Conrad H., unpublished autobiographical sketch to author, April 1, 1975, p. 1.

12. *S. D. Churchman,* Sept. 1945, p. 10.

13. *S. D. Churchman,* May 1948, p. 7.

14. *S. D. Churchman,* Dec. 1975, p. 8.

15. Gesner, *op. cit.,* pp. 2–5.

16. Hare, *Annual Reports,* 1882, p. 1; 1883, p. 15.

/\/\.\/\/\.\
.\/.\.\/\.\/.\

Bishops

Robert H. Clarkson
    Missionary Jurisdiction of Dakota   1868–1883
    Missionary Jurisdiction of Niobrara   1863–1873
William Hobart Hare
    Missionary Jurisdiction of Niobrara   1873–1883
    Missionary District of South Dakota   1883–1909
Frederick Foote Johnson
    Assistant Bishop   1905–1909
    Missionary District of South Dakota   1909–1911
George Biller, Jr.
    Missionary District of South Dakota   1912–1915
Hugh L. Burleson
    Missionary District of South Dakota   1916–1931
William P. Remington
    Bishop Suffragan   1918–1922
W. Blair Roberts
    Bishop Suffragan   1922–1931
    Missionary District of South Dakota   1931–1954
Conrad H. Gesner
    Bishop Coadjutor   1945–1954
    Missionary District of South Dakota   1954–1970
Lyman C. Ogilby
    Bishop Coadjutor   1964–1970
Harold S. Jones
    Bishop Suffragan   1971–1976
Walter H. Jones
    District and Diocese of South Dakota   1970–

.∧.∧.∧.∧.

Clergy, Parish, Mission Histories

Selected listings of parishes, missions, institutions, clergy, and officers of the Jurisdiction of Dakota, Niobrara, District and Diocese of South Dakota. A complete year by year listing can be found in the Diocesan Office, Sioux Falls, South Dakota.

MISSIONARY JURISDICTION OF DAKOTA
1871

The Right Reverend Robert H. Clarkson, Bishop.
The Rev. Melancthon Hoyt, D. D., Dean, Rector of Christ Church, Yankton.
The Rev. Peter B. Morrison, Missionary at Vermillion and parts adjacent.
The Rev. W. H. H. Ross, Missionary in the Sioux Valley, P.O. Sioux Falls.
The Rev. J. J. Townsend, Head Master of Dakota Hall and Missionary, P.O., Yankton.
The Rev. John F. Fish, D. D., U.S. Chaplain, Ft. Randall.
The Rev. Hiram Stone, U.S. Chaplain, Ft. Dakota.
The Rev. John Woart, U.S. Chaplain at Fort Abercrombie.

THE STANDING COMMITTEE OF DAKOTA.
The Rev. M. Hoyt, D. D., *President*.
The Rev. P. B. Morrison, *Secretary*.
Mr. M. A. Hoyt.
Mr. H. C. Burr.

INDIAN MISSIONARY JURISDICTION
1871

The Right Reverend R. H. Clarkson, D. D., Bishop.
The Rev. Samuel D. Hinman, Arch Deacon, Rector of the Church of the Merciful Saviour, Santee Mission.
The Rev. Joseph W. Cooke, Dean, Rector of the Church of the Holy Fellowship, Yankton Mission.
The Rev. J. Owen Dorsey, Deacon, Missionary to the Ponca Indians.
The Rev. Daniel Hemans (Indian), Deacon, Missionary among the Yankton Indians.
The Rev. Paul Mazakute, Rector of the Church of the Holy Name, Yankton Indians.
The Rev. Philip Johnston (Indian), Deacon, Missionary at St. Matthew's Chapel, Yankton Indians.
The Rev. Christian Taopi (Indian), Deacon, Missionary among the Santee Indians.
The Rev. Luke C. Walker (Indian), Deacon, Missionary among the Santee Indians.

166

STANDING COMMITTEE OF THE INDIAN MISSIONARY JURISDICTION.
The Rev. Samuel D. Hinman,
Mr. Henry Gregory,
The Rev. Joseph W. Cooke,
Mr. Alexander Pepe.

MISSIONARY JURISDICATION OF NIOBRARA
1873

Santee Mission
Samuel D. Hinman, *Presbyter*
Our Most Merciful Savior, Samuel D. Hinman
Blessed Redeemer, Paul Mazakute, *Presbyter*
Holy Faith, Daniel Hemans, *Deacon*
Ponka Agency, J. Owen Dorsey, *Presbyter*
Yankton Mission
Joseph W. Cook, *Presbyter*
Cathedral of the Holy Fellowship, The Bishop
                                Joseph W. Cook
                                John Gasman (agent, non-parochial priest)
                                Luke C. Walker, Deacon
Lower Brule Mission
William J. Cleveland, *Presbyter*
Yanktonnais (Crow Creek) Mission
Heckaliah Burt, *Deacon*
Cheyenne River Mission
Henry Swift, *Presbyter*
Spotted Tail's and Red Cloud's Bands
visited by S. D. Hinman
St. Paul's School
Mrs. M. E. Duigan

1884
PARISHES, MISSIONS, AND CLERGY.
with number of communicants.

WESTERN, OR NIOBRARA, DEANERY.
———

CHEYENNE RIVER MISSION, H. Swift. (P. O., Scranton, Walworth Co., Dak.)
St. John's Chapel, Striped Cloud's, (54).
St. Paul's Chapel, Mackenzie's Point, (38).
St. Stephen's, Moreau, (103).
LOWER BRULE MISSION, Luke C. Walker. (P. O., Lower Brule Agency, Dak.)
Church of the Saviour, the Agency, (42).
St. Alban's Station, Standing Cloud's.
St. Luke's Station, Little Pheasant's.
OGALALA OR PINE RIDGE MISSION, W. J. Cleveland. (P. O., Rosebud Agency.)
Holy Cross Church, Pine Ridge Agency, (38), John Robinson.
St. Andrew's Station, Orphan's Camp, (10).
St. Barnabas' Station, Medicine Root Creek, (25).
St. Philip's Station, Red Dog Camp, (5).

ROSEBUD, OR UPPER BRULE, MISSION, W. J. Cleveland. (P. O., Rosebud Agency, Dak.)
Church of Jesus, Margaret Memorial, (81).
St. Luke's Chapel, Good Voice's Camp. (15).
SANTEE MISSION, W. W. Fowler. (P. O. Santee Agency, Neb.)
Church of our Merciful Saviour, (80).
Chapel of our Blessed Redeemer, Bazille Creek, (80), Amos Ross.
Chapel of the Holy Faith, Wabashaw Village, (44).
St. Mary's, Flandreau, Dak., (25).
SISSETON MISSION, Edward Ashley. (P. O., Sisseton Agency, Dak.)
St. Mary's, the Agency, (28).
St. Luke's Station, North End.
St. John Baptist's Station, Lake Traverse.
YANKTON MISSION, J. W. Cook. (P. O., Greenwood, Dak.)
Church of the Holy Fellowship, Yankton Agency, (102).
Chapel of the Holy Name, Choteau Creek, (50), Isaac H. Tuttle.
Chapel of St. Philip the Deacon, White Swan, (29), Philip J. Deloria.
YANKTONNAIS MISSION, H. Burt. (P. O., Crow Creek, Dak.)
St. Thomas', the Agency, (2).
Christ Church, Upper Camp, (21).
Chapel of St. John Baptist, Lower Camp, (28), David Tatiyopa.

EASTERN DEANERY.
———

ABERDEEN, *St. Mark's* (18).
ALEXANDRIA, *Grace* (22), Charles C. Harris.
CANTON, *Holy Innocents'* (20), Walter J. Wicks.
CHAMBERLAIN, *St. Andrew's* (19), Charles C. Harris.
DEADWOOD, *St. John's* (20).
DELL RAPIDS, *Gethsemane* (17), Cathedral Clergy.
EDEN, *St. Thomas'* (9), Walter J. Wicks.
ELK POINT, *St. Andrew's* (18), Joshua V. Himes.
GROTON, *Trinity* (8).
HOWARD, John Morris.
HURLEY, *Grace* (25), Melancthon Hoyt, D. D.
HURON, *Grace* (42), Frederick Humphrey.
MITCHELL, *St. Mary's* (41), Charles C. Harris.
MORRISTON, *St. Thomas'* (14), John Morris.
PARKER, *Good Samaritan* (15), Walter J. Wicks.
PIERRE, *Trinity* (20), James M. McBride.
PLANKINTON, Charles C. Harris.
SIOUX FALLS, *Calvary Cathedral* (73), the Bishop; William J. Harris, D. D., *Dean.*
SCOTLAND, *St. Andrew's* (10), John Morris.
SPRINGFIELD, *Ascension* (21), the Bishop.
VALLEY SPRINGS (6), Cathedral Clergy.
VERMILLION, *St. Paul's* (10), Joshua V. Himes.
WATERTOWN, *Trinity* (26), A. H. Barrington.
YANKTON, *Christ* (108), Charles P. Dorset.

INSTITUTIONS.

WESTERN DEANERY.

ST. PAUL'S SCHOOL (for boys), Yankton Agency,—the Rev. W. E. Jacob, *Principal.*

ST. MARY'S SCHOOL (for girls), Santee Agency, Neb., (temporarily at Springfield, Dak.),— Mrs. J. H. Johnstone, *Principal.*

ST. JOHN'S SCHOOL (for girls), Cheyenne Agency,—Mr. J. F. Kinney, Jr., *Principal.*

HOPE SCHOOL (for boys and girls), Springfield,—Mrs. E. E. Knapp, *Principal.*

EASTERN DEANERY.

ALL-SAINTS' SCHOOL, Sioux Falls.—Building in process of erection,—intended to be ready for use September, 1885.

OFFICERS OF THE DISTRICT, 1884-5.

Bishop.

The Rt. Rev. William Hobart Hare, D. D.,—Sioux Falls, Dak.

Honorary Dean.

The Rev. Melancthon Hoyt, D. D.,—Hurley.

Dean of the Cathedral.

The Rev. William J. Harris, D. D.,—Sioux Falls.

Standing Committee.

The Rev. William J. Harris, D. D.,—Sioux Falls.

The Rev. Joseph W. Cook,—Greenwood.

Mr. George W. Lewis,—Sioux Falls.

Mr. T. W. Noyes,—Sioux Falls.

Secretary.

The Rev. Walter J. Wicks,—Canton.

Registrar.

Mr. John S. Lewis,—Sioux Falls.

Treasurer.

Mr. R. W. Folds,—Sioux Falls.

Chancellor. (Vacant.)

Examining Chaplains.

The Rev. H. Swift,—Scranton, Walworth Co.

The Rev. L. C. Walker,—Lower Brule Agency.

The Rev. M. Hoyt, D. D.,—Hurley.

The Rev. Charles C. Harris,—Mitchell.

OFFICERS OF THE DEANERIES, 1884-5.

WESTERN, OR NIOBRARA, DEANERY, (INDIAN FIELD.)

Rural Dean.

The Rev. William J. Cleveland,—Rosebud Agency.

Secretary.

The Rev. Edward Ashley.—Sisseton Agency.

Treasurer.

The Rev. H. Burt,—Crow Creek Agency.

Rural Dean.
The Rev. William J. Harris, D. D.,—Sioux Falls.
Secretary.
The Rev. Walter J. Wicks,—Canton.
Treasurer.
Mr. John S. Lewis,—Sioux Falls.

CANDIDATES FOR HOLY ORDERS.

SEPTEMBER, 1884

WESTERN DEANERY.

Charles S. Cook.
George W. Paypay.
Joseph C. Taylor.
F. M. Weddell, (Postulant.)

SUMMARY OF STATISTICS.

	Western Deanry	Eastern Deanery	The District
Number of Clergy	14	13	27
Parishes and Missions	26	21	47
Baptism—Infants	362	37	399
Baptism—Adults	158	21	179
Baptism—Total	520	58	578
Confirmed	83	24	106
Communicants	823	447	1270
Sunday School Scholars		324	324
Contributions	$1,514.81	$5,644.36	$7,156.17

1910
LIST OF PARISHES AND MISSIONS

NIOBRARA DEANERY.
(Corrected to September 1st, 1910.)

CHEYENNE RIVER MISSION—Rev. E. Ashley.
St. John's Church (25) and residence, Agency. Helper, Jas. Crowfeather.
Calvary (49) Helper, Samuel Smiley.
St. Stephen's (26) Helper, Edward W. Face.
Ascension (69) Catechist, Andrew White Face.
St. Mary's (55) Deacon, Rev. J. Wahoyapi; Catechist, Thos. F. Bear.
Emanuel (67) Deacon, Rev. Eugene St. Bull.
St. Thomas' (92) Helper, Henry Y. Face.
St. Luke's (29) Catechist, Louis Egna.
St. Andrew's (55) Helper Louis Tahe.
St. James (54) Helper, Luke Kanpeske.

St. Mark's (39) Helper, Louis Tahe.

St. Paul's (52) Catechist, William Lee.

St. Barnabas' (38) Helper, Chas. Gabe.

FLANDREAU MISSION—Rev. Robert Doherty, D. D.

St. Mary's Church (28), Catechist, William Jones; Helper, Zenas Graham.

LOWER BRULE MISSION—Rev. Luke C. Walker.

Church of the Holy Comforter (97) and residence. Helper, Charley Councillor.

St. Albans Chapel (31) Samuel Medicine Bull, Catechist.

Chapel of the Messiah (56) Reuben Estes, Catechist.

Chapel of the Holy Faith (37) Samuel High Elk, Helper.

Chapel of the Holy Name (22) Thomas Bow. Helper.

Chapel of the Saviour (27) Samuel Jones, Helper.

St. Peter's Station (19) Joseph A. Thunder, Helper.

PINE RIDGE MISSION —Agency District—Rev. Neville Joyner.

Church of the Holy Cross (80) and residence, Catechist, George Fire Thunder.

Epiphany Station (49), Catechist, G. Fire Thunder.

Advent Station (26) Helper, Clarence Three Stars.

St. James Chapel (22) Helper, Henry Black Elk.

St. Peter's Chapel (36) and residence, Catechist, Thomas Tyon.

St. Julia's Chapel (57) and residence, Deacon, Rev. I. Tuttle.

St. Philip's Chapel (47) and residence, Catechist, John Bissonette.

St. Thomas Chapel (45) Helper, Jonas H. Rock.

Messiah Chapel (49) and residence, Catechist, Paul Hawk.

St. Mary's Chapel (43) Catechist, John Black Fox.

St. Mary's Grass Creek (45) Catechist Mark Spider.

St. Luke's Chapel (34) Helper, C. H. Wolf.

St. Paul's Chapel (40) and residence, Catechist, Jefferson King.

St. Matthew's Station (20) Helper, Eugene Hair Bird.

St. John's Station (15) Helper, Peter Stands.

St. Jude's (6) Helper, (6) Helper, Peter Stands.

Christ Station (11) Helper, T. H. Man.

Grace Chapel (43) Deacon, Rev. Joseph Marshall.

St. Mary's Sand Hills (25) Deacon, Rev. Joseph Marshall.

PINE RIDGE MISSION—Corn Creek District—Rev. Amos Ross.

Church of the Inestimable Gift (60) and residence, Rev. Amos Ross.

St. Barnabas Chapel (50) and residence, Helper, Charlie American Horse.

Mediator Chapel (20) and residence, Helper, Samuel B. Rope.

Gethsemane Chapel (17) and residence, Helper, Richard Lips.

Hope Station (8) Helper, Cuny White Deer.

Faith Station (6) Helper, Charlie American Horse.

Trinity Station (13) Helper, Edward Black Bear.

ROSEBUD MISSION—Rev. A. B. Clark.

The Church of Jesus (61) Catechist, Samuel Broken Rope.

Ephatha Chapel (32) Layreader, L. K. Travis. (St. Mary's School).

Trinity Chapel (34) and residence; Presbyter, Rev. Baptiste P. Lambert.

Holy Innocents Chapel (48) and residence. Sr. Catechist, Stephen Murray.

St. Peter's Chapel (35) and residence; Catechist, Samuel B. Rope.

St. Thomas's Chapel (40) and residence; Catechist, Edward Dark Face.

St. Paul's Chapel (27) Catechist, Hugh Charging Bear.

St. Barnabas Station (36) Helper, Joseph War Comet.

Mediator Chapel (42) and *St. Matthew's Station* and residence Deacon. Rev. Dallas P. Shaw.

Advent Chapel (41) and residence, Helper, Job Tokate.
Calvary Chapel (91) and *Cottonwood Station* and residence, Sr. Catechist, Lewis Darian.
St. James' Chapel (59) and residence; Catechist, John T. Henry.
St. Philip's Chapel (32) Helper, Clay Yellow Eagle.
Epiphany Chapel (33) and *St. Luke's Station* (17) Catechist. Thomas Owatanla.
St. John's Chapel (15) Catechist, James Clairmont.
St. George's Chapel (41) Helper. Lewis Greenwood.
St. Mark's Chapel (42) Catechist, James Otakte.
St. Andrew's Chapel (73) Helper, Oliver Eagle Feather.
All Saints Chapel (28) and residence; Deacon, Rev. Charles M. Jones
Ascension Chapel (25) Lay reader, John B. Clark.
Grace Station (6) Helper, Amos Moccasin.
SANTEE MISSION—Rev. William Holmes.
Church of our most Merciful Saviour Agency (153) and residence, Agency, Rev. William
    Holmes. Helper, William Abraham.
Chapel of our Blessed Redeemer (103) Deacon, Rev. William Saul.
Chapel of the Holy Faith (105) Catechist, George G. Lawrence. Catechist-at-large, John
    Kitto.
St. John's Ponca Agency, Chapel (38) and residence, Rev. William Holmes; Helper,
    Alfred Barker.
SISSETON MISSION—Rev. John Robinson; Rev. Victor Renville, Assistant.
St. Mary's Church (110) and residence, Thomas Cante, Catechist.
St. John Baptist Chapel (49) D. J. Robertson, Catechist.
St. James' Chapel (93) and residence, Richard Keble, Catechist.
St. Luke's Chapel (35) Moses Williams, Helper.
STANDING ROCK—Rev. P. J. Deloria.
St. Elizabeth's Church (184) Presbyter, Rev. P. J. Deloria. Deacon, Rev. Herbert Welch.
    Catechist, Josua Necklace.
Chapel of the Good Shepherd (56) Helper, Johnson Brown Eagle.
St. John the Baptist's Chapel (65) Sr. Catechist, Joseph White Plume.
St. Thomas' Chapel (41) Helper, William Walking Shield.
YANKTON MISSION—Rev. John Flockhart.
Church of the Holy Fellowship (228) and residence. Catechists, Robert Obashaw and
    Louis Claymore; Ministering Woman, Miss Mary G. Barney.
Chapel of the Holy Name (105) and residence. Deacon, Rev. Joseph Good Teacher.
Chapel of St. Philip (135) and residence, Catechist, John Rondell.
YANKTONNAIS MISSION—Rev. H. Burt.
Christ Church (35) and residence, Rev. H. Burt.
St. John Baptist Chapel (50). Ministering Woman, Miss J. B. Dixon.
All Saints Chapel (24) and residence. Deacon, Rev. David Tatiyopa.
St. Peter's Chapel (25) Helper, George Keble.
Ascension Chapel (23) Catechist, D. P. Fire Cloud.

EASTERN AND BLACK HILLS DEANERIES.
(Corrected to September 1st, 1910.)

Parishes.

Aberdeen, St. Mark's Church (182) and Rectory, Rev. J. W. Hyslop. Wardens; C. A.
    Lum, W. C. Lovejoy.
Deadwood, St. John's (60), Rev. Marshall Montgomery. Wardens, D. A. McPherson,
    W. E. Adams.

Huron, Grace Church (98), and Rectory, Rev. G. S. Keller. Wardens, J. W. Campbell. A. Lampe.

Lead City, Christ Church (105), and Rectory, Rev. Marshall F. Montgomery. Wardens, E. E. Fry, James Wilke, Sr.

Sioux Falls, Calvary Cathedral, (200), and Deanery, The Bishop. The Very Rev. George Biller, Jr., Dean. Wardens, Hon. John E. Carland, Dr. S. A. Brown.

Watertown, Trinity Church, (215), and Rectory, Rev. David Clark Beatty. Wardens, H. G. Walrath, George E. Cloyes.

Yankton, Christ Church, (168), Rev. B. S. McKenzie. Wardens, S. A. Boyles, J. W. Summers.

Organized Missions.

Arlington, (15), Rev. _____. Warden, A. J. Rohyl; Treas., Mrs. Allen Story; Clerk, Mrs. Adam Royhl.

Armour, St. Philip's (15), Rev. R. M. Hardman. Warden, Eli Thomas; Treas., William Moore; Clerk, R. E. Dana.

Belle Fourche, St. James Church, (45), Rev. A. W. Bell. Warden, D. J. Hull; Treas., W. B. Penfold; Clerk, R. E. Hall.

Brookings, St. Paul's (18), Rev. William Hall Williams. Warden, William Paul; Treas., Miss Alma Walter; Clerk, Mrs. W. H. Roddle.

Canton, Holy Innocents, (26), Rev. _____. Warden, O. S. Gifford; Treas., W. H. Miller; Clerk, Mrs. F. P. Smith.

Carter, All Saints, (5), Rev. W. B. Roberts. Warden, George W. Segrist; Treas., Ed Youngquist; Clerk, Ray Gould.

Chamberlain, Christ Church, (55), Rev. Elias Wilson. Warden, C. H. Miller; Treas. A. E. Cowie; Clerk, J. H. Bingham.

Dallas, Church of the Incarnation, (14), Rev. W. B. Roberts. Warden, Don H. Foster; Treas., Frank H. Jackson; Clerk, S. M. Winchell.

Dell Rapids, Church of the Living Water, (43), Rev. R. Doherty, D. D. Warden, _____; Treas., P. W. Dougherty; Clerk, Mrs. C. Keneflick.

De Smet, St. Stephen's (58), Rev. William Hall Williams. Warden, J. H. Carroll; Treasurer, W. H. Henney; Clerk, Donald A. Crawford.

East Sioux Falls, St. Peter's (11), Rev. G. Biller, Jr. Warden, John Stewart; Treas., Joseph Wright; Clerk, Frank Hoyt.

Elk Point, Church of the Saviour, (40), Rev. _____. Warden, W. J. Conway, M.D.; Treas., F. W. Ford; Clerk, N. J. Lund.

Fairfax, Trinity Mission, (9), Rev. W. B. Roberts. Warden, U. G. Stevenson; Treas., _____, Clerk, Z. K. Doane.

Flandreau, Church of The Redeemer, (124), Rev. R. Doherty, D. D. Warden, J. A. Smith; Treas., Mrs. Mina Tobin; Clerk, Henry A. Booth.

Fort Pierre, St. Peter's Church, (12), Rev. H. L. Russell. Warden, Dr. C. J. Lavery; Treas., Mrs. Anna McKillip: Clerk, E. A. Lorimer.

Gettysburg, Christ Church, (10), Rev. George McKay. Warden, Mrs. R. B. Fisk; Treas., F. M. Wright; Clerk, R. Jones.

Groton, Trinity Church. (20), Rev. _____. Warden, R. A. Mather; Treas., E. J. Mather; Clerk, W. J. Rawson.

Hot Springs, St. Luke's Church, (65), Rev. H. S. Paynter. Warden, F. G. Osmotherly; Treas., E. R. Juckett; Clerk, J. J. March.

Howard, Trinity Church, (61), Rev. _____. Warden, J. A. Holstrom; Treas., H. M. Hanson; Clerk, D. A. McCullough.

Hurley, Grace Church, (33), Rev. _____. Warden, Henry Anderson; Treas., Peter Allen; Clerk, Mrs. M. A. Robinson.

Kaspar, St. Stephen's (18), Rev. George McKay. Warden, S. L. Traverse; Treas., James Brown; Clerk, Joseph Wilding.

Lemmon, Trinity, (15), Rev. _____. Warden, L. T. Everett; Treas., F. E. de Malignon; Clerk, Dr. Horace Clark.

Madison, Grace Church, (86), Rev. _____. Warden, C. E. Preston; Treas., W. O. White; Clerk, Arthur Murray.

Milbank, Christ Church, (61), Rev. H. N. Tragitt. Warden, G. C. Middlebrook; Treas., P. C. Sanders; Clerk, J. W. Ross.

Mitchell, St. Mary's (52), Rev. F. B. Barnett. Warden, S. S. Bately; Treas., R. E. Cone; Clerk, J. D. Anderson.

Parker, Good Smaritan, (24), Rev. _____. Warden, F. C. Danforth; Treas., John Waterbury; Clerk, G. Trull.

Pierre, Trinity, (69), Rev. H. L. Russell. Warden, G. W. Lumley; Treas., C. H. Burke; Clerk, P. F. McClure.

Rapid City, Emmanuel Church, (66), Rev. _____. Warden, A. K. Thomas; Treas., I. M. Humphrey; Clerk, F. L. Ackerman.

Redfield, St. Georges, (50), Rev. George McKay. Warden, H. Packard; Treas., Dr. C. E. Stutenroth; Clerk, J. A. Sinclair.

Scotland, St. Andrew's, (16), Rev. R. M. Hardman. Warden, F. D. Wicks; Treas., H. A. Reeves; Clerk, _____.

Selby, Christ Church, (25), Rev. _____. Warden, _____, Treas., J. C. Pierce; Clerk, H. R. de Malignon.

Spearfish, Church of All Angels, (34), Rev. A. W. Bell. Warden, O. W. Hanson; Treas., Mrs. G. L. Smith; Clerk, A. L. Kenney.

Springfield, Ascension, (58), Rev. R. M. Hardman. Warden, C. M. Keeling; Treas., J. L. Turner; Clerk, H. M. Davison.

Sturgis, St. Thomas', (109), Rev. _____. Warden, Clarence M. Smith; Treas., E. Galvin; Clerk, Frank Sim Welch.

Vermillion, St. Paul's, (37), Rev. James Henderson. Warden, Alfred O. Hancock; Treas., Mrs. Arden Clark; Clerk, Will S. Hooper.

Webster, St. Mary's, (34), Rev. _____. Warden, W. H. Chard; Treas., _____, Clerk, S. Pearson.

Woonsocket, St. Luke's, (20), Rev. F. B. Barnett, Warden, Noah Keller; Treas., W. H. Allen; Clerk, J. L. Terry.

Unorganized Missions.

Blunt, (4), Rev. H. L. Russell.
Bristol, St. John's, (15), Rev. _____.
Buffalo Gap, (18), Rev. H. S. Paynter.
Colonn, (4), Rev. W. B. Roberts.
Hill City, (10), Rev. _____.
Morristown, (2), Rev. _____.
Mt. Vernon, Rev. E. Wilson.
Philip, (2), Rev. _____.
Pukwana, Rev. E. Wilson.
Sisseton, Gethsemane, (25), Rev. H. N. Tragitt.
Wall, Rev. _____.
Wilmot, (6), Rev. H. N. Tragitt.
Vale, (9), Rev. _____.

INSTITUTIONS.

Eastern Deanery.
All Saints School (for young ladies and children), Sioux Falls.
The Bishop, President.
Miss Helen S. Peabody, Principal.

Niobrara Deanery.
St. Mary's School (for girls), Rosebud Reserve.
The Bishop, President.
Mr. L. K. Travis, Principal.
Average Attendance, 70.
St. Elizabeth's School, (for boys and girls), Standing Rock Reserve
The Bishop, President.
J. L. Ricker, Principal.
Average Attendance, 55.8.

SUMMARY OF STATISTICS.
1909-1910.

	Indian Deanery	Other Deaneries	TOTAL
Clergy	22	21	43
Parishes and Missions	93	51	144
Baptisms—Infants	355	151	506
Baptisms—Adults	78	92	170
Baptisms—Total	433	250	683
Whole No. Baptized Persons	10848	4177	15025
Confirmations	264	326	580
Ordinations		2	2
Communicants	4652	2738	7390
Sunday School Scholars	1103	1768	2871
Contributions	$38,983.57	$39,576.85	$52,670.91

1935
LIST OF PARISHES AND MISSIONS

WHITE FIELD PARISHES
ABERDEEN—St. Mark
Rev. E. R. Todd. Wardens, A. F. Milligan, A. C. Fredrickson, Jr.; Clerk, Wilbur Kearns; Treasurer, A. C. Fredrickson; Vestry, Dr. A. E. Pittenger, E. C. Rhodes, C. H. Anderson, R. I. Hill, Wilbur Kearns, H. J. Jackson, N. L. Heinzen, Chris Cacavas and C. R. Morey.
DEADWOOD—St. John
Rev. A. E. Cash. Wardens, Clarence Snedeker, Harry Lathrop; Clerk, W. C. Pendered; Treasurer, G. P. Geistwhite; Vestry, E. V. Cooper, A. A. Coburn, Mrs. W. C. Elrod, Mrs. Francis Palmer, Mrs. Harold Bray.

HURON—Grace

Rev. John W. Smith. Wardens, Dr. H. D. Sewell, Mr. John B. Wheeler; Clerk, Mr. John Claymore; Treasurer, Mr. L. H. Cornell; Vestry, Frank Coffey, R. E. Cone, Frank Kent, Fred Lampe, Frank Meyers, Max Royhl, John P. Sauer.

LEAD—Christ

Rev. E. F. Siegfriedt. Wardens, E. R. Hall, E. J. Dingle; Clerk and Treasurer, John Adamson; Vestry, Fred Fielder, J. M. Bray, Richard Harris, John Gregory, Cecil Harris, Reginald S. Frazer and John Adamson.

MITCHELL—St. Mary's

Rev. J. Ethan Allen. Wardens, Robert Chatterly, C. R. Winter; Clerk, Sam F. Weller; Treasurer, Robert Chatterly; Vestry, Dr. G. G. Kimball, S. F. Seallin, W. E. Wendt, Mrs. William Rush, Arthur Sayer, S. F. Weller and Carl Rees.

PIERRE—Trinity

Rev. A. J. Haines. Wardens, B. W. Morse, W. C. Allan; Clerk, C. J. Loomer; Treasurer, W. C. Allan; Vestry, C. E. Robbins, E. W. Lower, K. R. Scurr, J. W. Raish, J. J. Murphy, G. J. Bensendorf, F. S. Williams and E. P. Theim.

RAPID CITY—Emmanuel

Rev. E. Jerome Pipes. Wardens, Dr. R. E. Jernstrom, Dr. M. C. Babington; Clerk, Dr. Chas. F. Bowles; Treasurer, C. J. Barker; Vestry, C. O. Knight, Walter Travis, Carl Quarnberg, Fred Parks, Ed. James, C. J. Laughlin and A. K. Thomas.

SIOUX FALLS—Calvary

Very Rev. E. B. Woodruff, D. D. Wardens, W. A. Beach, Dr. A. R. Pearce; Clerk, W. C. Leyse; Treasurer, C. D. Rowley; Vestry, 1936, Howard Shipley, Clarance Rowley, Dr. G. O. Goodman; 1937, Sioux K. Grigsby, Glenn Lockhart, C. W. Hermann; 1938, T. R. Johnson, Dr. P. R. Billingsley, George A. Carroll.

WATERTOWN—Trinity

Rev. Valentine Junker. Wardens, C. H. Lockhart, W. S. Peck; Clerk, W. F. Miller; Treasurer, H. D. Halibert; Vestry, J. L. Foster, Waldon Hancock, A. H. Hasche, Willard McIntosh, A. P. Munt, F. E. Paulis.

YANKTON—Christ

Rev. Wm. P. Reid. Wardens, E. J. Friedel, Dr. A. P. Larrabee; Clerk, Charles Smith; Treasurer, Del F. Manbeck; Vestry, Dr. Shelden Adams, Roy Milliken, Hugh Danforth, J. W. Summers and Ernest Ellerman.

MISSIONS

ARMOUR—St. Philip

Rev. Earl T. Kneebone. Warden, Dr. Harry Allen; Treasurer, Mrs. Matilda Dunbar; Clerk, Harold Bussell.

BELLE FOURCHE—St. Philip

Rev. A. E. Cash. Warden and Treasurer, W. B. Penfold; Clerk, Mrs. C. C. Bolles.

BONESTEEL—St. Andrew

Rev. Earl T. Kneebone. Warden, Al Balkkob; Treasurer, Mrs. Frank Burns; Clerk, Mrs. Wm. Hackett.

BRISTOL—St. John

Rev. Bruce W. Swain. Warden, Mrs. Dan Buckley; Clerk, Mrs. W. R. Stephenson; Treasurer, Mrs. Maude Anderson; Member, Mr. Everett Bennett.

BROOKINGS—St. Paul

Rev. Joseph S. Ewing. Warden, R. A. Mark; Clerk, Mrs. Frances Andren; Treasurer, J. G. Hutton; Committee, J. A. Bonell, Mrs. A. F. Grimm, Mrs. John Haney and Mrs. L. A. Arbogast.

BUFFALO GAP—Trinity

Rev. St. Clair Vannix. Warden, Mr. Guy Sewright; Clerk, Miss Verda Elton; Treasurer, E. D. Elton; Members, Mrs. P. B. Conger, Mrs. G. Griffis, Mrs. Guy Sewright and Mr. P. B. Conger.

CHAMBERLAIN—Christ

Rev. Robert Benedict. Warden and Treasurer, J. H. Drury; Clerk, Mrs. Arthur Burkholder; Other members, Mrs. J. H. Bingham, Mrs. George Pilger.

COLOME—St. Paul

Rev. A. C. Bussingham. Warden, Mrs. W. F. Edens; Clerk and Treasurer, Mr. Rex Bresley; other members, L. E. Bresley, Elizabeth B. Bradley.

CUSTER—Good Shepherd

Rev. St. Clair Vannix. Warden, Mr. Hobart Gates; Clerk, Mrs. Chas. Welty; Treasurer, Mrs. Tom Petty; Member, Mr. Chas. Welty.

DALLAS—Incarnation

Rev. A. C. Bussingham. Warden, H. R. Cassling; Clerk, H. P. Hetts; Treasurer, H. R. Cassling.

DELL RAPIDS—Living Waters

Warden, Wm. H. Beto; Clerk and Treasurer, Miss Alice A. Jones; other members, Fred Bowles, James Fairhurst, W. B. Milne and Mrs. Edna Krause.

DE SMET—St. Stephen

Rev. W. L. Johnson. Warden, Dr. P. L. Scoffield; Clerk and Treasurer, N. E. Tackaberry; other members, Wm. H. Haney and John Hasche.

DUPREE—St. Philip

John W. Clark. Wardens, Mose Denton, Oscar Hurst; Clerk, Douglas Brush; Treasurer, Mrs. Cornelia Menzel; Members, Mrs. Josie Pop, Mrs. Gertrude Rinehart.

FLANDREAU—Redeemer

Rev. Henry T. Praed. Warden, W. A. Simpson; Secretary and Treasurer, Mrs. Enos Albertson; Committee, Mrs. T. A. Spafford, Mrs. Hazal Babcock, Mrs. John Erickson.

FORT PIERRE—St. Peter

Rev. A. J. Haines. Wardens, Howard Henriksen and Guy L. Hart; Clerk, F. P. Carlisle; Treasurer, Howard Henriksen; Members, Mrs. C. C. Loupe, Mrs. C. Wagner and Mrs. G. S. Huston.

GARY—St. Barnabas

Rev. Valentine Junker. Warden, Anton Brevik; Clerk, Grant Stone; Treasurer, Arthur Bartells; Gilbert Brainard and Alfred Bresson.

GETTYSBURG—Christ

Captain W. B. Aukerman. Wardens, Kenneth Morgan, Albert Houck; Clerk, Albert Toomey; Treasurer, Joe Abourezk; Representatives of Guilds, Mrs. Whitlock and Miss Fern Cook.

GROTON—Trinity

Rev. E. R. Todd. Warden, R. A. Mather.

HENRY—St. Mark

Rev. W. L. Johnson. Warden, Dr. J. H. Lockwood; Clerk, D. B. Kelton; Treasurer, J. C. Aldous; other members, James A. Patterson, Guy M. Van Epps, G. S. Brando, S. D. Boyd, and H. H. Hilliard.

HOT SPRINGS—St. Luke

St. Clair Vannix. Warden, R. W. Southard; Clerk, Mrs. W. M. Knowlton; Treasurer, Mrs. Chas. Nicholls; Missionary Treasurer, Mrs. A. W. Fellows; Members, Mrs. F. W. Medbery, Mrs. C. T. C. Lollich, Mr. J. J. March and Dr. G. H. Spivey.

HOWARD—Trinity
  Rev. Henry T. Praed. Warden, E. M. Mumford; Treasurer, Mrs. A. Geer; Member, I. M. Mumford.
HURLEY—Grace
  Rev. D. G. L. Henning. Warden, Peter Allen; Treasurer, Mrs. B. F. Elliott.
LAKE ANDES—St. Peter
  Rev. Earl T. Kneebone. Warden, John Exon; Treasurer, Arlie Jenkins; Clerk, Val. Rheiner; Other Members, Judge James Exon, V. J. Pesicka, Earl Miller.
LEMMON—Trinity
  Rev. T. E. Hall. Warden, J. H. Pickering; Clerk, Mrs. A. E. Tubbs; Treasurer, Mrs. Coats; Member, Dr. H. P. Sinclair.
MADISON—Grace
  Rev. Henry T. Praed. Warden, O. W. Hanson; Clerk, J. E. Emberg; Treasurer, William Rae; Member, B. E. Ketcham.
MILBANK—Christ
  Rev. Bruce W. Swain. Warden, Dr. D. A. Gregory; Treasurer; G. C. Middlebrook; Clerk, A. A. Blomquist; Members, Thurm Portc:, Karl E. Bleser, Jos. S. Holden.
MILLBORO—Ascension
  Rev. A. C. Bussingham.
MOBRIDGE—St. James
  Rev. T. E. Hall. Wardens, W. Dunnicliff, Chas. E. Nath; Treasurer, H. A. Mosher; Committee, Dr. G. H. Twining, C. E. Tolkein, Paul Nylen, J. Keller, Fred Popple, J. E. Robertson and H. L. Steinstra.
NAPLES—All Saints'
  Rev. W. L. Johnson. Warden, Cameron Rider; Clerk, Mrs. T. O. Kenyon; Treasurer, Lester Scott; Other Member, Ben Kuester.
NEWELL—All Saints'
  Rev. E. Jerome Pipes. Warden, D. J. Hull; Treasurer, Mrs. Nellie Cheisman; Clerk, Mabel Kenaston.
PARKER—Good Samaritan
  Rev. D. G. L. Henning. Warden, Clarence Hetts; Treasurer and Clerk, Mrs. Nellie Bertelson.
PHILIP
  Rev. A. J. Haines. Warden, Dr. R. B. Driver.
REDFIELD—St. George
  Rev. H. C. Crellin. Warden, Dr. C. A. Stutenroth; Treasurer, Helene Engstrom; Clerk, Hanna Leighton; Members, Henry Schalkle, Paul Koschitzsky, F. A. Frederickson and Dr. W. S. Chapman.
ROSHOLT—St. Andrew
  Rev. Joseph DuBray. Warden, Wm. Weatherstone; Clerk, Elener R. Benson; Treasurer, Phyllis Weatherstone.
SCOTLAND—St. Andrew
  Rev. Wm. P. Reid. Warden, F. D. Wicks; Treasurer, Luther Breen; Clerk, Mrs. E. F. Ardery.
SIOUX FALLS—St. Peter
  Very Rev. E. B. Woodruff, D. D. Warden, George Haggar; Treasurer, Lillie E. Morris; Clerk, Oliver Marshall.
SISSETON—Gethsemane
  Rev. Joseph DuBray. Warden, Chris Olsen; Clerk and Treasurer, Al J. Adams; Members, Ben. Arnquist, Mary Wilcox, and Mrs. Kay Axness.

SPEARFISH—All Angels

Rev. A. E. Cash. Warden, Prof. F. C. Bennett; Clerk, L. C. Emerson; Treasurer, James M. Ramsey; Members, D. C. Booth and Mrs. H. G. Weare.

SPRINGFIELD—Ascension

Rev. Standish MacIntosh. Wardens, Dr. C. M. Keeling, Mr. H. M. Davison; Clerk, Mr. E. B. Dwight; Treasurer, Mrs. R. W. Kibble; Members, J. W. Turner, William Kirby and John R. Y. Kirk.

STURGIS—St. Thomas

Rev. A. E. Cash. Warden, Carl Lohman; Clerk, William Caton; Treasurer, Mrs. Jesse Harlow; Member, Mrs. J. A. Poznasky.

VERMILLION—St. Paul

Rev. D. G. L. Henning. Warden and Treasurer, Dr. W. H. Batson; Clerk, R. R. Reno; Committee, E. H. Shaw, Jr., J. E. Payne, T. C. Maude, B. B. Brackett, Earl Stevens, Joseph Garvis, Will Harrington, and Mrs. Lee Hester.

WEBSTER—St. Mary's

Rev. Bruce W. Swain. Wardens, Steve Pearson and Irving Woodworth; Clerk, Mrs. H. C. Peabody; Treasurer, Mrs. Chas. Bailly; Members, Chas. Bailly, A. C. Stockstead and Dr. P. D. Peabody.

WINNER—Trinity

Rev. Alfred C. Bussingham. Warden, W. H. Greives; Clerk, Fred Goode; Treasurer, L. D. Evans; Members, Windsor Doherty, H. B. Mosher, E. P. Fisher.

INDIAN FIELD

CHEYENNE RIVER MISSION

Rev. J. B. Clark, Superintending Presbyter, Mobridge, South Dakota; Rev. S. D. Frazier, Rev. Levi M. Rouillard, Assistant Priests.

St. John's Church, Rev. S. D. Frazier, Cheyenne Agency

Ascension Chapel, Norman Robertson, Catechist, Promise

Calvary Chapel, Rev. S. D. Frazier, Cheyenne Agency

Emmanuel, John Standing Cloud, Catechist, Timber Lake

St. Andrew's, Abel Thomas, Acting Helper, Cherry Creek

St. James', Mark Garter, Catechist, Lantry

St. Luke's Chapel, Rev. John Red Hawk, Dupree

St. Mark's Chapel, Paul Little Skunk, Helper, Eagle Butte

St. Mary's Chapel, Albert Yardley, Acting Helper, Promise

St. Paul's Chapel

St. Stephen's Chapel, Sidney Garfield, Helper, LaPlant

St. Thomas Chapel, Patrick Shields, Catechist, Eagle Butte

CROW CREEK MISSION

Rev. David W. Clark, Superintending Presbyter, Ft. Thompson.

All Saints' Chapel, Charles Long Fish, Helper, Ft. Thompson

Ascension Chapel, Joseph Dudley, Catechist, DeGrey

Christ Church, Melvin Lodge, Catechist, Ft. Thompson

St. John Baptist's, Rev. Paul Cekpa, Deacon, Pukwana

St. Peter's, Rev. Robert Benedict, Chamberlain

FLANDREAU MISSION

St. Mary's, Zenas Graham, Helper, Flandreau.

LOWER BRULE MISSION

Rev. D. W. Clark, Superintending Presbyter, Ft. Thompson.

Chapel of Messiah, Edward Pretty Head, Catechist, Iron Nation

Holy Comforter, Rev. Thomas Heminger, Lower Brule
Holy Name, Rev. Thomas Heminger, Lower Brule
St. Alban's, Rev. Thomas Heminger, Lower Brule
St. Michael's, Pierre Government Boarding School, Rev. David W. Clark, Ft. Thompson
PINE RIDGE AGENCY
Rev. Dr. Nevill Joyner, D. D., Superintending Presbyter, Pine Ridge Agency; Rev. F. M.
   Thorburn, Rev. Clayton High Wolf, Assistants.
Christ Church, Wilson Knee, Catechist, Bower
Holy Cross, Harry Little Soldier, Catechist, Pine Ridge Agency
Cleveland Memorial, Harry Little Soldier, Catechist, Pine Ridge Agency
Epiphany Station, Rev. Frank M. Thorburn, Pine Ridge Agency
King Memorial, Oliver Sun Bear, Catechist, Manderson
Messiah, William Center, Catechist, Wounded Knee
St. Alban's, Thomas Standing Elk, Catechist, Porcupine
St. James', Harry Little Soldier, Sr. Catechist, P. Ridge Agency
St. John's, Rev. Andrew White Face, Oglala
St. Jude's, Rev. Andrew White Face, Oglala
St. Julia's, Rev. Christian B. Whipple, Porcupine
St. Luke's, Rev. Christian B. Whipple, Deacon, Porcupine
St. Mark's, Rev. John Black Fox, Deacon, Rocky Ford
St. Matthew's, Joe Brave Heart, Catechist, Oglala
St. Paul's, Rev. Jefferson King, Deacon, Manderson
St. Peter's, Asa Ten Fingers, Catechist, Oglala
St. Philip's, Rev. Rob't White Plume, Deacon, Manderson
St. Thomas, Louis Shield, Catechist, Manderson
Stirk Station, Rev. Frank M. Thorburn, Pine Ridge Agency
Tuttle Station, Rev. Frank M. Thorburn, Pine Ridge Agency
St. George's Station, The Priest, Pine Ridge Agency, and Assistant Priest, Rev. Clayton
   High Wolf, Porcupine.
PINE RIDGE—Corn Creek Mission
Rev. Dallas Shaw, Superintending Presbyter, Allen, South Dakota.
All Saints', Rev. V. V. Deloria, Martin
Gethsemane, Rev. W. H. Zephier, Wanblee
Good Shepherd, Rev. V. V. Deloria, Martin
Grace Chapel, Rev. V. V. Deloria, Martin
Hope Station, Fred Standing Soldier, Helper, Kyle
Mediator, Daniel Red Eyes, Catechist, Kyle
S. Barnabas', Rev. H. Baker, Deacon, Kyle
S. Mary's, Sand Hills, Rev. V. V. Deloria, Martin
S. Philip's Station, Rev. W. H. Zephier, Kyle
Trinity, Edgar Yellow Bear, A-Helper, Allen
ROSEBUD MISSION
Rev. Paul H. Barbour, Superintending Presbyter, Mission.
Trinity Chapel, Mission, Bishop's Committee: Warden, Robt. Driving Hawk; Clerk,
   Lloyd Mengel; Member, John Mickel.
Church of Jesus, Rev. John DeCory, Mission
Advent, Solomon Slow Fly, Catechist, Mosher
All Saints', James Driving Hawk, Catechist, Herrick
Calvary, Rev. T. J. Rouillard, Okreek
Cedar Butte Station, Richard Standing Bear, A-Helper, Norris

Epiphany, Harrington Brings the Pipe, Catechist, Parmalee
Grace, Charles Charging Cloud, Helper, Rosebud
Holy Innocents', Rev. S. H. King, Silas Standing Bear, Helper, Parmalee
Holy Spirit, Ideal, James Winter Chaser, Helper, Ideal
Mediator, Dan Yellow Hair, Catechist, Wood
Our Saviour
St. Agnes'
St. Alban's
St. Andrew's, Charles Kills in Water, A-Helper, St. Francis
St. George's
St. James', James Kills Plenty, Catechist, White River
St. John's, Rev. Hugh Charging Bear, Deacon, Mission
St. Mark's, Chester Black Star, Helper, Parmalee
St. Paul's, Emmett Eagle Bear, A-Helper, Norris
St. Peter's, Amos Moccasin, Catechist, Parmalee
St. Philip's, Clay Yellow Eagle, Sr., Catechist, Westover
St. Thomas, Rev. Walter Williams, Deacon, Norris
S. Stephen's, Red Leaf, Samuel Bear, A-Helper, Norris

SANTEE MISSION

Rev. Walter V. Reed, Priest-in-Charge, P. O., Star Route, Niobrara, Nebraska.
Blessed Redeemer, Gabriel Rouillard, Helper, Niobrara, Nebr.
Holy Faith, Guy Lawrence, Helper, Bloomfield, Nebr.
Our Most Merciful Saviour, Harry Lockwood, A-Helper, Santee, Neb.

SISSETON MISSION

Rev. Joseph Dubray, Superintending Presbyter, P. O., Sisseton.
St. James Chapel, Quincy Plume, Catechist, Waubay, S. D., Clement White, Helper, Waubay, S. D.
St. John Baptist, Moses Williams, Catechist, Brown's Valley, Minn.
St. Luke's, Sam Robertson, A-Helper, Veblen, S. D.
St. Mary's, Rev. Henry H. Whipple, Peever, S. D.

STANDING ROCK MISSION

Rev. John B. Clark, Supterintending Presbyter, Mobridge.
St. Elizabeth's, Rev. John B. Clark, Mobridge, Rev. Sidney Bearsheart, Deacon, Wakpala
Good Shepherd, Joseph Packard, Catechist, Glencross
St. Paul's, Rev. C. C. Rouillard, Little Eagle, Paul Long Bull, Catechist, Little Eagle
St. John Baptist's, Rev. Harry Renville, Bullhead
St. Philip's and Holy Spirit, Johnson Brown Eagle, Catechist, Watauga
St. Thomas, John Little Bear, Helper, Kenel

YANKTON MISSION

Rev. I. M. S. MacIntosh, Priest-in-Charge, P. O., Greenwood.
Holy Fellowship, David Huapapi, A-Helper, Greenwood
Holy Name, George Selwyn, Helper, Dantee
St. Philip, Antoine Zephier, Helper, Lake Andes

INSTITUTIONS

ALL SAINTS SCHOOL

For girls, and young women. Situated at Sioux Falls. Curriculum includes grades and high school. President, the Bishop; Principal, Evangeline Lewis. The Executive Council is the legal trustee of the school.

HARE INDUSTRIAL SCHOOL

Vocational school for Indian high school boys. P. O., Mission, S. D. Principal, Mr. Lloyd Mengel.

ST. ELIZABETH'S SCHOOL

For Indian girls and young boys, P. O., Wakpala, S. D., Principal, Mrs. Mary G. MacKibbon.

ST. MARY'S SCHOOL

High School for Indian girls. Upper grades and high school. P. O., Springfield, S. D. Principal, Miss Grade Staple.

ASHLEY HOUSE

For training of Indian candidates for Orders. P. O., Mission, S. D. Warden, Rev. Paul H. Barbour.

CROW CREEK DORMITORY

For Indian girls. P. O., Ft. Thompson, S. D. Superintendent, Mrs. David W. Clark.

OTHER OFFICERS

Church Service League

President: Mrs. W. B. Roberts, 321 East 21st St., Sioux Falls.

Secretary-Treasurer: Mrs. J. H. Pirsch, Sioux Falls.

United Thank Offering: Treasurer, Mrs. R. W. Feyerharm, Yankton.

Bishop Biller Memorial Fund: Treasurer, Mrs. H. C. Sessions, 816 W. 8th Street, Sioux Falls.

Educational Secretary: Mrs. Standish MacIntosh, Greenwood.

Church Periodical Club: Under Educational Secretary.

Church League of the Isolated: Address Mrs. D. C. Vannix, McKennan Hospital, Sioux Falls.

Supply Secretary: Mrs. H. I. Fahnestock, 219 4th Ave. N. W., Watertown.

1945
LIST OF PARISHES AND MISSIONS

PARISHES

ABERDEEN—St. Mark's

Rev. Harry E. Nelson. Wardens, C. R. Morey, H. F. Wilson; Treasurer, A. C. Fredrickson; Vestry, C. Cacavas, W. R. Wells, W. T. Kearns, L. C. Lust, Allan Williamson, John Rawson, S. L. Mark, Ivan Huntsinger.

DEADWOOD—St. John's

Rev. L. R. S. Ferguson. Wardens, G. H. Hemminger, J. E. Chambers; Clerk, J. O. Horsfall; Treasurer, Oscar M. Blaisdell; Vestry, Lyle Elward, Stanley Nelson, Demarest Crary, William F. Greib, O. Kelley, Harold Norman, Ray H. Holst, Dr. J. J. Berry, Dr. T. H. Proctor.

HURON—Grace

Bishop. Wardens, Willis L. Walker, G. Edward Mackey; Clerk, Bert Reeve; Treasurer, Chester N. White; Vestry, R. M. Cowling, Karl Lampe, Walter Bonnemann, J. S. Foasberg, Charles W. Burnside, William M. Dunn, Charles H. Ward, Boyd M. Benson, Harry H. Graham, Carl J. Odegard.

LEAD—Christ

Rev. E. F. Siegfriedt, D. D. Wardens, F. C. Schadel, Madison Ballantyne; Clerk and Treasurer, John Adamson; Vestry, Clarance Cooper, A. E. Eklund, Elmer Nichols, Fred E. Bryan, Ben R. Stone, Jr., A. J. Nelson.

MITCHELL—St. Mary's
Rev. Walter Y. Whitehead. Wardens, Leo Stransky, A. F. Smith; Clerk, S. F. Scallin; Treasurer, Vera Jacoby; Vestry, Dr. E. W. Allen, Jack Bailey, W. R. Ronald, Charles Coury, C. F. Nelson, H. R. Lower, Mrs. A. F. Smith, A. N. Barnard, Mrs. J. Purcell.

PIERRE—Trinity
Rev. T. E. Hall, locum tenens. Wardens, E. B. Lee, Dr. Neil Plank; Clerk and Treasurer, F. M. Pinckney; Vestry, Dr. C. E. Robbins, Kenneth Scurr, George Hurst, Harper Hamilton, E. W. Stephens.

RAPID CITY—Emmanuel
Rev. E. Jerome Pipes. Wardens, Dr. R. E. Jernstrom, Dr. M. C. Babington; Clerk, J. A. Edstrom; Treasurer, F. W. Gormley; Vestry, Carl A. Quarnberg, Charles L. Bennett, George Thompson, Julius Sieler, Dr. J. P. Connolly, Fred Harter, Robert Swanson, L. Q. Ellis, Noel Klar.

SIOUX FALLS—Calvary Cathedral
Very Rev. Leland W. F. Stark. Wardens, Dr. R. G. Stevens, J. F. Dalton; Clerk, Tore Teigen; Treasurer, Ernest Raley; Vestry, F. A. Kreiser, E. C. Main, F. H. Weatherwax, K. J. Benz, T. R. Johnson, Raymond E. Dana, J. Nelson Shepherd.

WATERTOWN—Trinity
Rev. H. W. J. Urquhart. Wardens, A. P. Munt, J. O. Johnson; Clerk, Wilbur McBath; Treasurer, H. D. Hallberg; Vestry, Dale Freeburg, Reed Bard, Frank Morris, C. B. Chapin, Henry McClelland, Harvey Shaw.

YANKTON—Christ
Rev. H. N. Tragitt, Jr. Wardens, L. A. Boyles, E. J. Freidel; Clerk, J. W. Summers; Treasurer, Mrs. F. M. Otto; Vestry, W. F. Flint, G. H. Harvey, Dr. F. W. Haas, R. W. Feyerharm, M. P. Ohlman, H. A. Bussell, Rev. A. P. Larrabee.

MISSIONS

BELLE FOURCHE—St. James'
Rev. L. R. S. Ferguson. Senior Warden, Robert I. Howlett; Junior Warden and Clerk, Gale B. Wyman; Treasurer, George F. Johnson; Members, Ben Wood, Burton Penfold, Mrs. M. A. Gregg.

BONESTEEL—St. Andrews
Rev. Earl T. Kneebone. Warden and Treasurer, Al Blakkolb.

BRISTOL—St. John's
Rev. W. L. Johnson. Warden, Everett Bennett; Treasurer, Mrs. Maude Andersen.

BROOKINGS—St. Paul's
Rev. Wayne L. Johnson. Wardens, R. A. Mark, C. O. Gottschalk; Clerk, Mrs. John Haney; Treasurer, Mrs. Eric Green; Members, J. A. Bonell, Mrs. A. L. Moxon, A. D. Evenson.

BUFFALO GAP—Trinity
Rev. Philip W. Roberts. Warden, Eugene Griffis; Clerk, Mrs. W. Streeter; Treasurer, Pete Conger.

CHAMBERLAIN—Christ
Rev. Standish MacIntosh. Warden, J. H. Bingham; Clerk, Mrs. Robert Potter; Treasurer, J. H. Drury; Members, Mrs. Neil Fuller, Mrs. Adolph Gilbert.

DALLAS—Incarnation
Rev. Earl T. Kneebone. Warden and Treasurer, Robert Elliott.

DELL RAPIDS—Living Water
Rev. Elias Wilson, locum tenens. Warden, W. H. Beto; Clerk, Mrs. C. S. Reynolds; Treasurer, M. A. Haven; Members, Mrs. Edna Krause, Mrs. Walter Crisp, Jr., Mr. G. V. Reynolds, Mr. John Hoier.

DE SMET—St. Stephen's
   Bishop Coadjutor. Warden, P. L. Scofield; Clerk and Treasurer, N. E. Tackaberry;
   Members, L. A. Wakeman and Alfred Wyland.
DUPREE—St. Philip's
   Rev. S. D. Frazier. Wardens, Fred F. Nelson, Red Elm, and Frederick A. Menzel;
   Clerk, Lee M. Creamer; Treasurer, R. W. Douglass.
FLANDREAU—Redeemer
   Rev. Wayne L. Johnson. Warden, Stuart Ramsdell; Clerk, Mrs. W. Henry; Treasurer,
   A. J. Smith; Members, W. L. Ireland, Robert Dailey, Leslie Hawkins, Mrs. W. G.
   Cowles, Mrs. W. L. Rolfe.
FORT PIERRE—St. Peter's
   Rev. T. E. Hall, locum tenens. Wardens, Carl Wagner, Guy Hart; Clerk, Howard Hen-
   dricksen; Treasurer, Mrs. Elizabeth Huston.
GETTYSBURG—Christ
   Rev. S. D. Frazier. Wardens, Albert B. Tousley, Harry Brehl; Clerk, Albert Houck;
   Treasurer, John Hembd; Member, President of St. Margaret's Guild.
GROTON—Trinity
   Rev. Harry E. Nelson. Warden, R. A. Mather; Clerk, Emma Frommel; Treasurer, Mrs.
   M. J. Bingham.
HENRY—St. Mark's
   Rev. W. L. Johnson. Warden and Treasurer, Dr. James H. Lockwood; Clerk, J. C.
   Aldous; Member, S. D. Boyd.
HOT SPRINGS—St. Luke's
   Rev. Philip W. Roberts. Warden, S. O. Graham; Clerk, R. A. Peterson; Treasurer, R. W.
   Southard; Members, Mrs. E. A. L. Griffin, Miss Violet Chapman and D. G. Batchel-
   lor.
HOWARD—Trinity
   Rev. C. D. D. Doren. Wardens, Theodore Hanson, I. M. Mumford; Clerk and Treasurer,
   Sidney Davison; Members, Peter Olson, Robert Clark, Mrs. Chas. Hanson, President,
   Trinity Guild.
HURLEY—Grace
   Bishop Coadjutor. Warden and Treasurer, Mrs. Burton F. Elliott.
IGLOO
   Rev. P. W. Roberts
LAKE ANDES—St. Peter's
   Bishop Coadjutor. Warden, John J. Exon; Treasurer, Frank Svatos.
LEMMON—Trinity
   Rev. John B. Clark. Wardens, Dr. H. P. Sinclair, Mrs. Fred Voigt; Clerk, Mrs. Olive
   Ginther; Treasurer, Fred Voigt; Members, Miss Vida Thompson, Mrs. Effie Brooks.
MADISON—Grace
   Rev. C. D. D. Doren. Warden, John Emberg; Clerk and Treasurer, H. H. Green; Mem-
   bers, James Robson, Ed Reeve, Fred Fawkes.
MILBANK—Christ
   Rev. W. L. Johnson. Warden, George Middlebrook; Clerk and Treasurer, A. A. Blom-
   quist; Members, Joe Holden, Dr. D. A. Gregory.
MILLBORO—Ascension
   Rev. Earl T. Kneebone. Treasurer, Mrs. Fred Harvey.
MOBRIDGE—St. James'
   Rev. John B. Clark. Wardens, Charles K. Todd, Winston Hall; Clerk, Robert DeVinny;

Treasurer, Robert E. Stutenroth; Members, Jacob Keller, Frederick Popple, Raymond Miles, Chester Helmey.

NAPLES—All Saints'
Rev. W. L. Johnson. Warden, Raymond Rider; Treasurer, Lester Scott; Member, N. E. Harrison, Mrs. Margaret Kenyon.

NEWELL—All Saints'
Bishop Coadjutor, Treasurer, Mabel Kenaston.

PARKER—Good Samaritan
Bishop Coadjutor. Warden, Charles Dana; Clerk, Mrs. Hope Harris; Treasurer, J. C. Webster; Members, Rex Jones, A. M. Fisher.

PHILIP
Mrs. Harry L. Brown, Treasurer.

REDFIELD—St. George's
Rev. H. E. Nelson. Warden, Dr. C. E. Stutenroth; Clerk and Treasurer, H. J. Schalkle.

ROSHOLT—St. Andrew's
Rev. Vine V. Deloria. Warden, Ralph Weatherstone; Clerk, Elrod Robertson; Members, William Robertson, Spencer Weatherstone.

SCOTLAND—St. Andrews
Rev. H. N. Tragitt, Jr. Wardens, Hon. F. D. Wicks, Luther Breen; Clerk, E. F. Ardery; Treasurer, Donley Max; Members, George Yates, Wm. Erickson, Mrs. L. Breen.

SIOUX FALLS—St. Peter's
Very Rev. L. W. F. Stark. Warden, George Haggar; Clerk and Treasurer, Lillie E. Morris; Members, O. R. Marshall, Iva M. Bailey, Mrs. K. Haggar.

SISSETON—Gethsemane
Rev. Vine V. Deloria. Wardens, A. W. Powell, William J. Holland; Clerk, Dallas Butterbrodt; Treasurer, Charlotte Pearson; Members, Julian Pearson, Bert Wilcox, Ben Arnquist, T. N. Engdahl.

SPEARFISH—All Angels
Rev. E. F. Siegfriedt. Warden, Everett Ward; Clerk, F. L. Bennett; Treasurer, Rudolph Erickson; Members, Mrs. Charles Cooper, Mrs. Ernst Behrens, Emmanuel Russell, Martin Thompson.

SPRINGFIELD—Ascension
Bishop Coadjutor. Warden, John R. Kirk; Treasurer, Mrs. Vinta R. Kibble.

STURGIS—St. Thomas
Warden, Mr. Carl V. Lohmann; Clerk, Mrs. Lucille M. Poznasky; Treasurer, Mrs. Jessie Harlow.

VERMILLION—St. Paul's
Bishop Coadjutor. Warden and Treasurer, W. H. Batson; Clerk, E. H. Shaw; Members, C. S. Ball, A. M. Pardee, Morrison Barton, Harold Hinchcliff, Earl Stevens, E. T. Beadle, Mrs. C. S. Ball ex-Officio (President of St. Mary's Guild).

WAGNER
Rev. James Driving Hawk. Warden, Mr. Frank Rubertus; Clerk and Treasurer, Mrs. Frank Rubertus; Member, Mrs. Frank S. Strohbehn.

WEBSTER—St. Mary's
Rev. W. L. Johnson. Wardens, Dr. P. D. Peabody, Fenten Stewart; Clerk, C. J. Lee; Treasurer, Mrs. Charles Bailly; Members, Steve Pearson, Frank Gellerman, Mrs. F. W. Halbkat, Mrs. Frank Dickinson.

WINNER—Trinity
Rev. Earl T. Kneebone. Warden, W. H. Grieves; Clerk and Treasurer, John Lunn; Members, Ed King, E. P. Fisher, Dr. Janssen.

INDIAN FIELD

CHEYENNE RIVER MISSION

Rev. Stuart D. Frazier, Cheyenne Agency, Superintending Presbyter; Rev. Harry Renville, White Horse, Associate Priest.

St. John's, Rev. Stuart D. Frazier, Cheyenne Agency

Ascension, James Meeter, A-Helper, Moreau

Calvary, Rev. Stuart D. Frazier, Cheyenne Agency

Emmanuel, Rev. Harry Renville, White Horse

St. Andrew's, Felix Condon, A-Helper, Cherry Creek

St. James', Rev. S. D. Frazier

St. Luke's—Iron Lightening, William Red Bird, A-Helper

St. Luke's—Thunder Butte, Guy Bagola, A-Helper, Red Elm

St. Mary's, John DeWitt, Catechist, Promise

St. Paul's, Amos Eagle Boy, A-Helper, LaPlant

St. Stephen's, Rev. S. D. Frazier, Cheyenne Agency

St. Thomas', Felix Benoist, A-Helper, Eagle Butte

CROW CREEK MISSION

Rev. Standish MacIntosh, Fort Thompson, Superintending Presbyter.

All Saints', Charles Long Fish, Helper, Fort Thompson

Ascension, William Horn, A-Helper, Fort Thompson

Christ Church, Oscar Deloria, A-Helper, Fort Thompson

St. John Baptist, Hosea Ree, A-Helper, Fort Thompson

St. Peter, John Whippoorwill, A-Helper, Pukwana

FLANDREAU—St. Mary's

Warden, Ben Jones; Clerk, Mrs. Howard Robertson.

LOWER BRULE

Rev. Standish MacIntosh, Fort Thompson, Superintending Presbyter, Rev. T. J. Rouillard, Lower Brule.

Messiah Chapel, Jobe White, A-Helper, Kennebec

Holy Comforter, Reuben Estes, Sr-Catechist, Lower Brule

Holy Name, Rev. T. J. Rouillard, Lower Brule

St. Alban's, Rev. T. J. Rouillard, Lower Brule

PINE RIDGE MISSION

Rev. Frank M. Thorburn, Pine Ridge Agency, Superintending Presbyter; Revs. Harold S. Jones, Oglala; Stephen H. King, Wounded Knee, Associate Priests.

Holy Cross, Rev. Frank M. Thorburn, Pine Ridge Agency, Sister Annie A. Horner, Pine Ridge Agency

Advent, Harry Little Soldier, Sr-Catechist, Agency

Christ Church, Rev. Harold S. Jones, Oglala

Epiphany Station, Rev. Stephen H. King, Wounded Knee

Messiah, Rev. Stephen H. King, Wounded Knee

St. Alban's, Rev. C. B. Whipple, Porcupine, Thomas Standing Elk, Catechist, Porcupine

St. James', Rev. Harold S. Jones, Oglala, Harry Little Soldier, Sr-Catechist, Agency

St. John's, Rev. Harold S. Jones, Oglala

St. Jude's, Rev. Harold S. Jones, Oglala

St. Julia's, Rev. C. B. Whipple, Porcupine, James Locke

St. Luke's, Rev. C. B. Whipple, Porcupine

St. Mark's, Rev. John Black Fox, Deacon, Rocky Ford

St. Matthew's, James Roan Eagle, A-Helper, Agency

St. Paul's, Rev. Stephen King, Wounded Knee

St. Peter's, Rev. Harold S. Jones, Oglala

St. Philip's, Rev. Stephen S. King, Wounded Knee, Rev. Robert White Plume, Deacon, Manderson

St. Thomas', Rev. Stephen King, Wounded Knee, William Center, Catechist, Manderson

Tuttle Station, Rev. C. B. Whipple, Porcupine

St. George's Station, Rev. Frank M. Thorburn, Pine Ridge Agency

St. Mary's (King Memorial), Rev. Robert White Plume, Deacon, Manderson

PINE RIDGE

Corn Creek Mission—Rev. Dallas Shaw, Allen, Superintending Presbyter; Rev. Henry H. Whipple, Wanblee, Associate Priest.

Church of the Inestimable Gift, Rev. Dallas Shaw. Allen, Allen Last Horse, Sr-Catechist, Allen

St. Katharine's, Rev. Henry H. Whipple, Wanblee

Gethsemane, Rev. Henry H. Whipple, Wanblee

Good Shepherd, Rev. Henry H. Whipple, Wanblee

Grace, Rev. H. H. Whipple, Wanblee

Mediator, Edgar Brown Bear, Catechist, Kyle

St. Barnabas', Rev. Wallace Zephier, Deacon, Kyle

St. Mary's, Sand Hills, Rev. H. H. Whipple, Wanblee

St. Philip's Station, Rev. Henry Whipple, Wanblee

Trinity, Frank G. Elk

Hope St. Timothy, Rev. H. H. Whipple, Wanblee, George B. Rooks

ROSEBUD MISSION

Rev. Paul H. Barbour, D. D., Mission, Superintending Presbyter; Revs. C. C. Rouillard, Parmelee, and James Driving Hawk, Okreek, Associate Priests.

Trinity, Rev. Paul H. Barbour, Mission

Church of Jesus, Rev. Paul H. Barbour, Mission

Advent, Rev. James Driving Hawk, Okreek

All Saints', Dan Yellow Hair, Catechist, Herrick

Calvary, Rev. James Driving Hawk, Okreek, Everdell Wright, A-Helper, Okreek

Cottonwood Station, Rev. James Driving Hawk, Okreek

Epiphany, Walter Williams, Deacon, Rosebud

Grace, Rev. Walter Williams, Deacon, Rosebud

Holy Innocents, Rev. C. C. Rouillard, Parmelee, Sam Yellow Cloud, Catechist, Wood

Holy Spirit, Lloyd Winter Chaser, Catechist, Ideal

Mediator, Peter White Hawk

Our Saviour, Rev. James Driving Hawk, Okreek

St. Andrew, Mark Walking Eagle, Catechist, St. Francis

St. Agnes', Rev. P. H. Barbour, Mission

St. Alban's, Rev. Paul H. Barbour, D. D., Mission

St. George's, Rev. James Driving Hawk, Okreek

St. James', Charles J. Marshall, Catechist, White River

St. John's, James Yellow Cloud, Helper, Rosebud

St. Mark's, James Black Bull, Catechist, Parmelee

St. Paul's

St. Philip's, Clay Yellow Eagle, Sr-Catechist, Westover

St. Stephen's, Red Leaf, Samuel Bear, Catechist, Norris

St. Thomas', Rev. Hugh Charging Bear, Deacon, Norris

SANTEE MISSION

Rev. Andrew A. Weston, Star Route, Niobrara, Nebraska, Associate Priest.

Blessed Redeemer, Gabriel Rouillard, Catechist, Niobrara, Nebr.

Holy Faith, Guy Lawrence, Helper, Bloomfield, Nebr.

Our Most Merciful Saviour, Rev. A. A. Weston, Stephen Moose, Catechist, Santee

SISSETON

Rev. Vine V. Deloria, Sisseton, Superintending Presbyter; Rev. Paul Chekpa, Waubay, Associate Priest.

St. James', Rev. Paul Chekpa, Waubay

St. John Baptist, Moses Williams, Sr-Catechist, Browns Valley, Minn.

St. Luke's, Sam Robertson, Helper, Veblen

St. Mary's, Sam V. Renville, A-Helper, Peever

STANDING ROCK

Rev. John B. Clark, Mobridge, Superintending Presbyter; Rev. Levi M. Rouillard, Little Eagle, Associate Priest.

St. Elizabeth's, Rev. John B. Clark, Mobridge, Guy Lambert, Catechist, Wakpala, Isaac Hawk

Good Shepherd, Moses Mountain, Helper, Glencross

Holy Spirit, Rev. Levi M. Rouillard, McLaughlin

St. Paul's, Rev. Levi M. Rouillard, McLaughlin, Johnson Brown Eagle, Sr-Catechist, Little Eagle

St. John Baptist, John Standing Cloud, A-Helper, Bullhead

St. Philip's, Rev. Levi M. Rouillard, McLaughlin

St. Thomas', Truby Turning Heart, A-Helper, Kenel

YANKTON MISSION

Rev. James Driving Hawk, Greenwood.

Holy Fellowship, Rev. James Driving Hawk, Greenwood

Holy Name, James Mound, Catechist, Dante

St. Philip's, George Selwyn, Catechist, Lake Andes

St. Joseph's, Joseph Packard, Catechist, Marty

INSTITUTIONS

ALL SAINT'S SCHOOL

For girls and young women. Situated at Sioux Falls. Curriculum includes grades and high school. President, the Bishop; Principal, Edith P. Stickney, Ph.D.

SAINT ELIZABETH'S SCHOOL

For Indian girls and boys. P. O., Wakpala, S. D. Principal pro tem, Mrs. John R. Caton.

SAINT MARY'S SCHOOL

High School for Indian girls. P. O., Springfield, S. D. Principal, Miss G. Bernice Holland.

THE WOMAN'S AUXILIARY OF THE DISTRICT
Officers, 1945

President—Mrs. Charles I. Danforth, Yankton.

Secretary-Treasurer—Mrs. F. S. Strohbehn, Wagner.

U. T. O. Treasurer—Mrs. George G. Kimball, Mitchell.

Bishop Biller Treasurer—Mrs. Irving M. Mumford, Howard.

Church Periodical Club—Mrs. Frank Nemer, Winner.

Supply Secretary—Mrs. Harry W. Elliott, Rapid City.

Educational Secretary—Mrs. William H. Batson, Vermillion.

1960
LIST OF PARISHES AND MISSIONS

PARISHES

ST. MARKS—ABERDEEN

The Rev. George Gillespie. *Wardens:* Richard Hodgson, John Pagones; *Clerk:* John

Pagones; *Treasurer:* John Rawson; *Vestry:* William Emerson, Dr. Robert Murdy, Alan Hunter, John McDowell, Charles Todd, Dr. W. M. Reuett, Mrs. W. Kearns, Mrs. P. T. Spaulding, Howard Bastian.

ST. JAMES'—BELLE FOURCHE

The Rev. James W. Rice. *Wardens:* Gerry Breeding, Joseph Bonneman; *Clerk:* Mrs. Cyril Beeching: *Treasurer:* Richard Hall: *Vestry:* Dr. John H. Davis, James Lang, Doyle Ream.

ALL ANGELS'—SPEARFISH

The Rev. James W. Rice. *Wardens:* Donald E. Young, O. A. Kelley; *Clerk:* Wallace Velte; *Treasurer:* Rudolph Erickson: *Vestry:* Dr. Barnard S. Clark, Dr. Floyd Ward, Ernest Terrault.

ST. PAUL'S—BROOKINGS

The Rev. Frank M. Thorburn. *Wardens:* Alfred L. Musson, Donald Kratochvil; *Clerk:* David F. Pearson: *Treasurer:* Alfred G. Trump; *Vestry:* Miss Gertrude Young, Donald J. Biggar, William F. Railing.

ST. JOHN'S—DEADWOOD

The Rev. H. E. Nelson. *Wardens:* Lyle Elward, Rodger L. Thomas; *Clerk:* V. C. Edstrom; *Treasurer:* Rodger L. Thomas: *Vestry:* Leo Aldrich, V. C. Edstrom, Kenneth Ellis, Sam Morthland, A. F. Roberts, Larry Ryan, L. James Shedd, Robert C. Swanson, William Yeager.

GRACE CHURCH—HURON

The Rev. Donald J. West. *Wardens:* Willis Engel, A. M. Haskell, Jr.; *Clerk:* Gertrude Lampe; *Treasurer:* George Goodell; *Vestry:* R. C. Sandvig, R. H. Rowe, H. K. Wheeler, Ralph G. Roth, M. D. Morris, R. C. Deaton, Jr., B. M. Benson, M. H. Monheim, Miss Gertrude Lampe.

CHRIST CHURCH—LEAD

The Rev. Eric Wright. *Wardens:* John Bjorge, Don Williams; *Clerk:* Richard Furze; *Treasurer:* Merritt Olson; *Vestry:* E. R. McLaughlin, William Ausmann, Larry McKay, Ed Manseau, Fred Bryan, Glen Howe, A. Giachetto, William Taylor, H. Allen.

ST. MARY'S—MITCHELL

The Rev. Walter H. Jones. *Wardens:* Robert Rew. Burton Ayres; *Clerk:* Mrs. Myrna Stone; *Treasurer:* Mrs. Edith Wedehase; *Vestry:* Art Raymond, Wayne Clark, Don Leetch, William Belcher, Fred Shearer, George Janke, Darold Brooks, Iola Hathaway.

ST. JAMES'—MOBRIDGE

The Rev. George Pierce. *Wardens:* Winston Hall, Arthur Grothe; *Clerk:* William Kienast; *Treasurer:* Philip Hall; *Vestry:* E. J. Englerth, Ned E. Harris, Frances Grover, Amos White, A. G. Weishaar.

TRINITY CHURCH—PIERRE

The Rev. Walter Shroeder. *Wardens:* Buron Lindbloom, M.D., Clinton Gregory; *Clerk:*   ; *Treasurer:* L. A. Wheaton; *Vestry:* Ray Rummel, Walter Burke, The Hon. Charles Hanson, John Dobier, Jefferson Boyer.

EMMANUEL CHURCH—RAPID CITY

The Rev. E. Jerome Pipes. *Wardens:* John W. Vucurevich, Richard W. Klein; *Clerk:* R. E. Furois; *Treasurer:* F. W. Gormley; *Vestry:* John M. Costello, Don White, William Wilson, C. C. Reitz, Selmer Myron, Hoadley Dean, W. A. McCullen, Donald Shultz. Neil Simpson.

CALVARY CATHEDRAL—SIOUX FALLS

The Very Rev. Harry W. Henning, Jr., Dean; The Rev. Paul A. Clark, Canon. *Wardens:* Jean R. Kroeger, Cecil A. Schoeneman; *Clerk:* Harold D. Lindseth; *Treasurer:* Earle D. Johnson; *Vestry:* Kermit C. Andersen, John Foreman, Walter H. Naused, Thomas B. Shepard, Charles H. Stephenson, Sam Payne, Ray E. Dana, George Bottge, Arnold N. Petterson, R. Marshall Brandon, Ted F. Doolittle.

CHURCH OF THE GOOD SHEPHERD—SIOUX FALLS

The Rev. Michael Canfield; The Rt. Rev. W. Blair Roberts, Vicar Emeritus. *Wardens:* Marshall Stenson, Paul Batcheller; *Clerk:* Robert Berry; *Treasurer:* Mrs. K. E. Ball; *Vestry:* Ed Jacobson, Lowell Abrahamson, Dan McNitt, Walter Fischer, Robert Reynolds. Sullivan Barnes, C. A. Cummings, Robert Berry.

ST. THOMAS'—STURGIS

The Rev. James W. Munck. *Wardens:* Dr. R. M. Wood, LaVern Mitchell; *Clerk:* Mrs. Lillian Furze Carr; *Treasurer:* Stanley R. Pugh; *Vestry:* K. B. Nash, Fred Nelsen, John Varenhorst, Mrs. Isobel Grams, S. W. Martin.

TRINITY CHURCH—WATERTOWN

The Rev. E. L. Badenoch. *Wardens:* M. D. Stonebarger, Claude C. Paterson; *Clerk:* Wilbur McBath; *Treasurer:* Mrs. Margaret C. Reese; *Vestry:* Frank Bard, Dallas Butterbrodt, Walter Farl, Dale Freeburg, Wilbur McBath, A. F. Reese, Milton Rosen, Harlan Sampson, Donald Smith.

TRINITY CHURCH—WINNER

Wardens: Charles Hansen, Frank McCormick; *Clerk:* Richard Reyer; *Treasurer:* Mrs. Audrey Holm; *Vestry:* Ben Viedt, Jack Lapp, Paul Kositzky.

CHRIST CHURCH—YANKTON

The Rev. Alexander Wood. *Wardens:* Louis Boyles, Harold Modereger; *Clerk:* Mrs. Theodore M. Burleson; *Treasurer:* Hugh Danforth; *Vestry:* L. L. Larrabee, Tim Johnson, Dr. A. A. Fosterman, Emanuel Kozak, Mrs. Sidney W. Gurney.

MISSIONS

ST. ANDREW'S—BONESTEEL

The Rev. Daryl Stahl (d). *Wardens:* Paul Woerpel, Tony Kuleza; *Clerk:* Vernal Glynn; *Treasurer:* Vernal Glynn; *Bishop's Committee:* Neil Elston, Orville Hanson.

TRINITY CHURCH—BUFFALO GAP

The Rev. C. E. B. Harnsberger. *Warden:* Glen Smith; *Clerk:* Frances Thurston; *Treasurer:* Glen Smith; *Bishop's Committee:* Viola Bondurant, Glen Smith, Frances Thurston.

CHRIST CHURCH—CHAMBERLAIN

The Rev. James C. Wright; Captain Howard Galley, C. A. *Wardens:* Clifford A. Craft; *Clerk:* Art Remmele; *Treasurer:* Neil E. Fuller; *Bishop's Committee:* George Vranesh, Louis Knox, Donald Hamiel.

CARNATION—DALLAS

The Rev. Daryl Stahl (d). *Wardens:* George Grubbs, George Peabody; *Clerk:* Wayne Hotchkiss, *Treasurer:* Wayne Hotchkiss; *Bishop's Committee:* Dudley Herman, Charles Whitepipe, Sam La Fave, Holger Cassling, Web Lindsey.

CHURCH OF THE LIVING WATER—DELL RAPIDS

The Rev. Bruce W. Swain. *Wardens:* John Hoier, John Harlan; *Clerk:* Mrs. C. S. Reynolds; *Treasurer:* Mrs. B. J. Sweatt; *Bishop's Committee:* Mrs. B. J. Sweatt, Mrs. C. S. Reynolds, Dr. P. T. Anderson, Mrs. Edna Krause, Mrs. Walter Crisp, Mrs. Fred Voigt.

ST. STEPHEN'S—DESMET

The Rev. Bruce W. Swain. *Wardens:* A. J. Ryland, Merle Pratt; *Clerk:* Frank Rouser; *Treasurer:* P. L. Scofield; *Bishop's Committee:* Mrs. Lloyd Myers.

ST. PHILIP'S—DUPREE

The Rev. Anthony Morris. *Wardens:* Charles Hersey, Ralph Pesicka; *Clerk:* Mrs. Gene Burgee: *Treasurer:* Robert J. Burgee; *Bishop's Committee:* Darrel Sprague, Ruth Hersey, Lily Pesicka.

CHURCH OF THE REDEEMER—FLANDREAU

The Rev. Robert Wagner. *Wardens:* Robert Dailey, Sr.; Harold Schramm; *Clerk:* Mrs. Grace Fuller: *Treasurer:* Mrs. Roy McFarland; *Bishop's Committee:* Mrs. Grace Fuller, Mrs. Roy McFarland, Stuart Ramsdall, Raleigh Matson.

ST. PETER'S—FORT PIERRE

The Rev. Ronald Hennies. *Wardens:* Raymond Rheborg; *Clerk:* Mrs. Charles Carlisle; *Treasurer:* Lyle Henriksen; *Bishop's Committee:* Robert Schumaker, August Zieman, Meta Shifet, Inez Huckfeldt, Cynthia Fuller.

CHRIST CHURCH—GETTYSBURG

The Rev. Ronald V. Perrind. *Wardens:* Gordon Fawcett, Frederick Soule: *Clerk:* Dorothy Fawcett; *Treasurer:* Jane Hoover; *Bishop's Committee:* Louis A. Bartels, Orlow Eidam. Jack Hill.

ST. LUKE'S—HOT SPRINGS

The Rev. C. E. B. Harnsberger. *Wardens:* John Gray, Lawrence Kaudy; *Clerk:* Alfred Ward; *Treasurer:* Violet Chapman; *Bishop's Committee:* Ernest Reeves, Harry Whitehead, Dane Conger, Francis Reese, John Gray, Alfred Ward, Violet Chapman, James Kocer, Lionel McMillin, Charles Roe, Lawrence Kaudy, Kenneth Field.

TRINITY CHURCH—HOWARD

The Rev. Bruce W. Swain. *Wardens:* Eilers Grimme, E. M. Mumford, Jr.; *Clerk:* Sidney I. Davison: *Treasurer:* Dr. Dale J. Haugan; *Bishop's Committee:* S. I. Davison, Dr. D. J. Haugan, William Hepner, Robert Clark. Elmer Olson, I. M. Mumford, William Quinn, Mrs. Robert Clark.

ST. MARTIN'S—IGLOO

The Rev. C. E. B. Harnsberger. *Warden:* William Ottmann; *Clerk:* Sylvia Hoppes; *Treasurer:* Grant McCoy; *Bishop's Committee:* Vincent Goodman, Stanley Barnett, Grant McCoy, William Ottmann, Sylvia Hoppes, Fred Coates.

ST. PETER'S—LAKE ANDES

The Rev. Webster A. Two Hawk. *Wardens:* Albert Harvey, L. J. Hadd; *Clerk:* Dale Leonard; *Treasurer:* Mavis Clark; *Bishop's Committee:* Harry Parker, Thorald Brooks, Richard Dowell. Virginia LaBarge.

TRINITY CHURCH—LEMON

The Rev. William Fay; Captain Hubert J. Harris, C. A. Borad. *Wardens:* William Coats; *Clerk:* Mrs. Jean Borud; *Treasurer:* Ernest Borud; *Bishop's Committee:* Harold Gibbons, George Pixler, Carolyn Raney.

GRACE CHURCH—MADISON

The Rev. Bruce W. Swain. *Warden:* Merrill D. Hunter; *Treasurer:* Rex Page; *Bishop's Committee:* Homer Engelhorn, Forrest Cole, Mrs. Francis Sly, Mrs. D. W. Knappen, Mrs. Pat Baughman.

ST. KATHARINE'S—MARTIN

The Rev. Frederick C. H. Wald. *Wardens:* Harold Bates, Harold Kosmicke; *Clerk:* C. A. Houghlett; *Treasurer:* Warren Johnson; *Bishop's Committee:* James Ross, Myron Johnson, Richard Howe, Robert Pich, Mrs. Lucille Kosmicke, Mrs. Jennie Brown, Mrs. Alice Milliken, Mrs. Ione Olson, Mrs. Dorothy Ziegler.

CHRIST CHURCH—MILBANK

The Rev. Ralph R. Stewart. *Wardens:* Calvin D. Oamek, E. Norman Graves; *Clerk:* Mrs. Bette Vesecky; *Treasurer:* Clifford Dexter; *Bishop's Committee:* Dr. D. A. Gregory, Mrs. C. B. Lowe, Mrs. Hugo Magedanz.

TRINITY CHURCH—MISSION

The Rev. John B. Clark, locum tenens. *Wardens:* Richard Clausen, Robert Emery; *Clerk:* Philip Zoubek; *Treasurer:* Mrs. Hattie Marcus; *Bishop's Committee:* Willis Groves, John Artichoker, Glen Seadore, Fred Schmidt, Graydon Hallock, James Didier, Walter Wright.

GOOD SAMARITAN—PARKER

The Rev. Robert D. Crawford, D.D. *Warden:* Charles Dana; *Clerk:* Mrs. Juanita Jones; *Treasurer:* Mrs. Martha Overturf; *Bishop's Committee:* Rex Jones, Mrs. Juanita Jones, Mrs. Dorothy Garvey, Mrs. Martha Overturf.

ST. PHILIP'S—PHILIP

The Rev. Walter Schroeder. *Warden:* Howard Hopkins; *Clerk:* Mrs. Harry Brown; *Treasurer:* Mrs. Harry Brown.

ST. ANDREW'S—RAPID CITY

The Rev. Marvin A. Nordmeier. *Warden:* Clifford B. Henningsen; *Clerk:* Helen Derr; *Treasurer:* Norton E. Lawellin; *Bishop's Committee:* Mrs. Sally Paulson, Robert B. Frankenfeld, Mrs. Betty Coon, Dr. W. J. Martin, Herbert R. Martelon, Winfield. R. McCain, Delmar Aldrich.

ST. MATTHEW'S—RAPID CITY

The Rev. Edward O. Moore, Sister Daisy Kitchens, C.A. *Wardens:* Simon Iron Cloud, Emerson Packard; *Clerk:* Mrs. Lupe Romero; *Treasurer:* Raymond A. Fracek; *Bishop's Committee:* Benjamin Stead, Daniel D. Quilt, Nobel Moore, Mrs. Rudolph Wright, Mrs. Charles Tyburec, Rudolph Wright, Gilbert Wright, Nelson D. Jenesse, Jr., Hobart Little Cloud.

ST. GEORGE'S—REDFIELD

The Rev. Donald J. West; Captain E. Bruce Ackles, C. A. *Wardens:* Paul Kositzki, Floyd Morey; *Treasurer:* Omar Gavin; *Bishop's Committee:* Mrs. Jeanne Young, Mrs. Charlotte Hufteling, Floyd Morey, Omar Gavin.

ST. ANDREW'S—SCOTLAND

The Rev. Alexander Wood. *Warden:* Donley Max; *Treasurer:* Mrs. William S. Donley; *Bishop's Committee:* Mrs. Donley Max, Mrs. Mary Max.

ST. PETER'S—SIOUX FALLS

The Rev. Robert T. Wagner. *Wardens:* George Haggar, A. D. Kasch; *Clerk:* Sylvan Hauff; *Treasurer:* Arthur Lundgren; *Bishop's Committee:* Sylvan Hauff, Arthur Lundgren, Donald Haggar, Jim Gouge, M. Ray Sween.

GETHSEMANE CHURCH—SISSETON

The Rev. M. J. Dwyer. *Wardens:* C. E. Vanderlinden, William Holland; *Clerk:* Jack Adams; *Treasurer:* William Hooper; *Bishop's Committee:* Jack Adams, William Hooper, A. W. Powell, Julian Pearson, Herbert Axnes, Ruben LaBatte.

ASCENSION—SPRINGFIELD

Mr. Kenyon Cull, *Lay Vicar. Clerk:* Mrs. Vinta Kibble; *Treasurer:* Mrs. Vinta Kibble; *Bishop's Committee:* Kenyon Cull, Mrs. Vinta Kibble, Laurel Iverson, James Tucker, Irving Cressman.

ST. MARK'S—TIMBER LAKE

The Rev. George P. Pierce. *Warden:* Buck Simpson; *Clerk:* Mrs. J. P. Byington; *Treasurer:* F. L. McMacken; *Bishop's Committee:* James Byington, Glen French, Jack French, Sr.

ST. PAUL'S—VERMILLION

The Rev. Robert D. Crawford, D.D. *Warden:* J. K. Black; *Clerk:* James Jorgenson; *Treasurer:* William Barton; *Bishop's Commitee:* Dr. C. D. Cox, Robert Exon, Frederick Davis.

ST. MARY'S—WEBSTER

The Rev. Ralph R. Stewart. *Wardens:* Frank Gellerman, Roger Williams; *Clerk:* Mrs. C. J. Lee; *Treasurer:* William Evans; *Bishop's Committee:* J. H. Flagstad, Miss Pat Pearson, Mrs. F. W. Halbkat, Mrs. Donn Q. Thomas.

NIOBRARA DEANERY

Note: Italics Designate Lay Readers

CHEYENNE RIVER MISSION

The Rev. Andrew A. Weston, Eagle Butte; The Rev. Anthony Morris, Dupree; the Rev. William Fahsing, Eagle Butte.

St. John the Evangelist, Eagle Butte, The Rev. A. A. Weston; *Gus Kingman*

St. Andrew's, Cherry Creek, *Dan Afraid of Hawk*

St. James', Bear Creek, *Vern Howard*

St. Luke's, Iron Lightning, *Ed Clown*

St. Paul's, LaPlant, *Sam DeHorse*

St. Peter's, Thunder Butte, *James White Feather*

Ascension, Moreau, *Andrew LeBeau*

Emmanuel, White Horse, *Joseph Fiddler, Jr.*

St. Mary's, Promise, *Isaac Traversie*

St. Stephen's, Red Scaffold, *Mike Ward*

St. Thomas', On the Tree, The Rev. A. A. Weston

Calvary, Marksville, The Rev. William Fahsing

CHRIST CHURCH DAKOTA MISSION

The Rev. Alexander M. Wood, Yankton; *Steven Moose, James Hayes, Harley Zephier.*

CROW CREEK MISSION

The Rev. James C. Wright, Chamberlain; Capt. Howard Galley, C.A., Fort Thompson

Christ Church, Fort Thompson, *Stanley Jennesse*

Ascension, Harrold, *Capt. Howard Galley*

St. John the Baptist, Bedashosha Lake, *Capt. Howard Galley*

FLANDREAU MISSION

St. Mary's, The Rev. Frank M. Thorburn, Brookings

LOWER BRULE MISSION

The Rev. Ronald Hennies, Fort Pierre

Holy Comforter, Lower Brule, *Clyde G. Estes*

Holy Name, Fort George, The Rev. Ronald Hennies

Messiah, Iron Nation, *Jobe White*

St. Alban's, Fort Lookout, The Rev. Ronald Hennies

PIERRE MISSION

St. Michael's—The Rev. Ronald Hennies, Fort Pierre: Deaconess: D. J. King, Box 652, Pierre: *George Estes.*

PINE RIDGE MISSION

The Rev. Eric S. W. Cole, Pine Ridge; The Rev. Paul Chekpa, Pine Ridge: The Rev. Sidney U. Martin, Allen; The Rev. Stephen Moccasin, Wanblee; Miss Aline Cronshey, Pine Ridge.

Advent, Pine Ridge, *Leo American Horse*

Holy Cross, Pine Ridge, The Rev. E. S. W. Cole

Christ Church, Red Shirt Table, Rev. C. E. B. Harnsberger

Epiphany, Wolf Creek, The Rev. Paul Chekpa

Messiah, Wounded Knee, *Charles Moose*

St. Alban, Porcupine, *Dawson Little Soldier*

St. Andrew, Wakpamni Lake, *Dawson No Horse*

St. James', Oglala, The Rev. Paul Chekpa

St. John, Oglala, The Rev. Paul Chekpa

St. Jude, White River, The Rev. Paul Chekpa
St. Julia's, Porcupine, The Rev. E. S. W. Cole
St. Luke, Porcupine, *Garfield Wounded Head*
St. Mark, Rocky Ford, The Rev. E. S. W. Cole
St. Mary, Grass Creek, The Rev. E. S. W. Cole
St. Matthew, Slim Buttes, The Rev. Paul Chekpa
St. Peter, Oglala, *Basil Broken Nose*
St. Philip, Manderson, *William Eagle Bull*
St. Thomas', Manderson, *William Eagle Bull*
CORN CREEK DISTRICT OF THE PINE RIDGE MISSION
Gethsemane, Wanblee, *Fred Mesteth, Sr.*
Inestimable Gift, Allen, *Clarence Broken Rope*
Good Shepherd, Martin, *Stephen Marshall*
Mediator, Kyle, *Wilson W. Gay*
St. Barnabas, Kyle, *Amos Lone Hill*
St. Philip's, Hisle, *Stephen Marshall*
St. Timothy, Potato Creek, *George Rooks*
Trinity, Allen, *Morris No Horse*
Bad Wounds Station, Martin, *Stephen Marshall*
Kadoka Station, Kadoka, The Rev. Stephen Moccasin
ROSEBUD MISSION
The Rev. John B. Lurvey, Mission; The Rev. W. Harold Luxon, Rosebud; The Rev.
    William B. Locke, Mission.
Advent, Moṣher, The Rev. John B. Lurvey
Calvary, Okreek, The Rev. John B. Lurvey
Church of Jesus, Rosebud, The Rev. W. H. Luxon
Epiphany, He Dog Camp, The Rev. W. B. Locke
Grace, Soldier Creek, *James Provincial*
Holy Innocents, Parmalee, The Rev. W. H. Luxon
Mediator, Wood, The Rev. John B. Lurvey
St. Andrew, Spring Creek, *Charles Kills in Water*
St. Columba, Presho, The Rev. John B. Lurvey
St. James, Horse Creek, The Rev. John B. Lurvey
St. Mark, Lower Cutmeat, *James Black Bull*
St. Michael, Belvidere, The Rev. W. H. Luxon
St. Paul, Norris, The Rev. W. H. Luxon
St. Philip, Two Kettle, The Rev. John B. Lurvey
St. Stephen, Red Leaf, The Rev. W. H. Luxon
St. Thomas Norris, *Sam Bear*
All Saints, Ponca Creek, The Rev. Daryl Stahl, *Ed Godfrey*
Holy Spirit, Ideal, *Ed Eagle Star*
SANTEE MISSION NIOBRARA AND WINNEBAGO CITY MISSIONS
Rev. Donald Wilson, Santee, Nebraska
Our Most Merciful Saviour, Santee, The Rev. D. R. Wilson
Blessed Redeemer, Center, *George Selwyn*
Holy Faith, Lindy, *George Selwyn*
St. Paul's, Niobrara, *George Selwyn*
All Saints, Winnebago
SISSETON MISSION
The Rev. Martin J. Dwyer, Sisseton; Miss Eunice Olsen, Sisseton.

Gethsemane Evening Group, Sisseton, *Aaron Bernard*
St. James Enemy Swim, *Wilfred Rouillard*
St. Luke's, Veblen, The Rev. M. J. Dwyer
St. Mary's Old Agency, *Aaron Bernard*
St. John the Baptist, near Brown's Valley, Minnesota, *William Seaboy*
STANDING ROCK MISSION
The Rev. William M. Fay, Wakpala; Miss Alicia Thomas, McLaughlin.
Good Shepherd, Little Oak Creek, *Joseph Kills Crow*
Holy Spirit, Firesteel Creek, The Rev. William M. Fay
St. Elizabeth's, Wakpala, *Isaac Hawk*
St. John the Baptist, Bullhead, *Emmett Martin*
St. Paul, Little Eagle, *Vernon Ashley, Wilbur Bearsheart*
St. Philip, Watauga, The Rev. William M. Fay
St. Thomas, Kenel, *Abel White*
YANKTON MISSION
The Rev. Webster Two Hawk, Lake Andes.
Holy Fellowship, Greenwood, *Everade Jordan*
Holy Name, Dante, *William Black Lance*
St. Philip the Deacon, Lake Andes, *James E. Mound*
Wagner Station, Wagner, *Floyd Blankenfeld*

INSTITUTIONS

ALL SAINTS SCHOOL
An independent day school for boys and girls operated by All Saints School, Inc., Sioux
Falls. Nursery, Kindergarten, and grades 1-6. Accredited: Mrs. Mary L. Donaldson,
Acting Principal; Mr. Gilbert H. Paulton, President of the Board.
ST. MARY'S SCHOOL FOR INDIAN GIRLS, Springfield
5th grade through High School, Headmaster: Kenyon Cull, M.A.
BISHOP HARE SCHOOL
For Indian boys of grades 6-12, Mission, South Dakota. Principals: Mr. and Mrs. John
Artichoker; Chaplain: the Rev. John B. Clark.
ST. ELIZABETH'S SCHOOL
For Indian Boys and Girls, Wakapala, S. D. Directors, Mr. and Mrs. William McK.
Chapman; Chaplain: the Rev. William M. Fay.

THE EPISCOPAL MEN OF SOUTH DAKOTA

COMMITTEE OF FIVE:
Mr. Frank Coffey, 803 North Maple, Watertown; Mr. Redman Albaugh, Winner; Dr. Ben
Reifel, 1621 South Second, Aberdeen; Mr. Almer Steensland, Beresford; Mr. LaVern
Mitchell, Sturgis.

THE EPISCOPAL WOMEN OF SOUTH DAKOTA

President, Mrs. Marion Morris, 1107 Idaho Ave. SE, Huron
Secretary, Miss Goldie Wells, P.O. Box 433, Aberdeen
Treasurer, Miss Sibyl Pritchard, 403 N. Broadway, Watertown
First Vice President and Supply and Christian Social Relations Chairman, Mrs. Dudley
Herman, Gregory
Second Vice President and United Thank Offering Chairman, Mrs. Charles Bennett, 1424
W. Blvd., Rapid City
Altar Guild Director, Mrs. Ray Howard, 635 S. Dakota Ave., Sioux Falls

Church Periodical Club Director, Miss Gertrude Lampe, 1260 Dakota S., Huron
Chairman of Conference Center, Mrs. Robert Best, 2209 South Main, Sioux Falls
Girls' Friendly Society Director, Mrs. R. G. Albaugh, 542 Jefferson, Winner
Ecumenical Relations Chairman, Mrs. George Bruntlett, 903 Fulton, Rapid City
Christian Education Secretary and Yearbook, Mrs. C. F. Vagle, 1226 Ohio, SW, Huron
Personnel Director, Miss Helen Chaney, 10 Alert, Lead
Devotional Chairman, Mrs. Norman Gross, 410 Capital Street, Yankton

1970
LIST OF PARISHES AND MISSIONS

PARISHES

ST. MARK—ABERDEEN

The Rev. Robert W. Dunn. *Wardens:* Kenneth Anglin, Earl Sheldon; *Clerk:* Mrs. Harvey Hamman; *Treasurer:* Douglas D. Johnson; *Vestry:* Mrs. Ronald Angerhofer, Linda Dillavou, William Forschner, Harvey Hamman, David Lias, Gerald Lust, Emil May, William Norton, Alvin Zephier, Mrs. John Melin.

ST. JAMES—BELLE FOURCHE

The Rev. Thomas G. Russell. *Warden:* George Pridgeon; *Clerk:* Miss Marge McGregor; *Treasurer:* James S. Lang; *Vestry:* James Roberts, George Higashi, Michael Weaver.

ST. PAUL—BROOKINGS

The Rev. James W. Hauan. *Wardens:* Lee Jorgenson, F. Stan Kidwiler; *Clerk:* Mrs. Joseph Bonnemann; *Treasurer:* Alfred G. Trump; *Vestry:* Charles Cecil, Alfred L. Musson, Mrs. William Alexander.

ST. JOHN—DEADWOOD

The Rev. Milo D. Dailey. *Wardens:* Don Derosier, Ora J. Horsfall; *Clerk:* Lyle Elward; *Treasurer:* Robert C. Swanson; *Vestry:* Robert Dardis, Alvoro Ayres, Lyle Collins, Demarest H. Crary, A. F. Roberts, Dr. Peter Kryger, William Severns, Col. Melvin A. Hoherz, Donald G. Purchase.

GRACE—HURON

Wardens: Aldo Panerio, A. M. Haskell, Jr.; *Clerk:* Mrs. A. M. Fuller; *Treasurer:* Renford Rowe; *Vestry:* M. L. Gogolin, Nicholas J. Karras, Ronald Manolis, Kenneth Powell, Reed Sandvig, Mrs. Howard T. Shober, H. Kirke Wheeler, Willard Youtz.

CHRIST—LEAD

The Rev. Fenton H. Kovic. *Wardens:* Fred E. Bryan, A. E. Eklund; *Clerk:* Kenneth Lee; *Treasurer:* Mrs. Judy Urban; *Vestry:* Bill Ausmann, Melvin Mattson, Ed Rantapaa, Merritt Olson, Robert Magers, Mrs. Donald Mueller.

ST. MARY—MITCHELL

The Rev. Dennis A. Tippett. *Wardens:* Fred Shearer, George Karedis; *Clerk:* Betty Milliken; *Treasurer:* Richard Opp; *Vestry:* Norman Bouton, Maxine Leetch, Leo Stedman, Howard Petersen, Jerry Wegman, Kay Meyers.

ST. JAMES—MOBRIDGE

The Rev. James P. Barton. *Wardens:* Elmer Newcomb, William Hauff; *Clerk:* Mrs. Bernice Broe; *Treasurer:* Mrs. Corrine Morris; *Vestry:* Winston Hall, Natalie Guerrant, Larry Bearsheart, Albert Simpson, Mrs. Ann Higham, Mrs. Dorothy Condon, Mrs. Dorothy Horn, Charles Hare.

TRINITY—PIERRE

The Rev. Robert T. Hodgen. *Wardens:* Michael H. Shaw, Dr. B. O. Lindbloom; *Clerk:* Mrs. Dale Wagner; *Treasurer:* James E. Terwilliger; *Vestry:* Cecil W. Moore, Richard Duncan, Donald Haggar, Forrest Koos, Lyle Martin, John Dobier, Lois Manning, James Hopkins, Neele Kruse, Gene A. Sougstad.

EMMANUEL—RAPID CITY

The Rev. Hanford L. King, Jr., Ph.D., Rector. The Rev. Hewes W. Phillips, Assistant. *Wardens:* Lloyd Pugh, Lt. Col. A. H. Haberkorn; *Clerk:* Miss Mary Keller; *Treasurer:* Mrs. L. William Melvin; *Vestry:* James W. Ayres, Fred Gellerman, Kirk Goodwin, Dr. Ralph Huntsinger, George Kroetch, Mrs. M. P. Merryman, Wallace Milne, Col. Hudson Stuart, Dr. F. R. Williams.

ST. ANDREW—RAPID CITY

The Rev. Charles G. du Bois. *Wardens:* Gerald J. Paulson, Herbert Martelon; *Clerk:* Mrs. R. B. Frankenfeld; *Treasurer:* Mrs. C. M. Lockwood; *Vestry:* The Hon. Thomas Parker, Mrs. Duane Corning, Albert Wright, Mrs. James A. Cline, Delmar Aldrich, Robert Frankenfeld, Robert N. Coon, Mrs. Selmer Myron, R. T. Pitsor.

CALVARY CATHEDRAL—SIOUX FALLS

The Very Rev. Paul J. Davis, Dean. The Rev. Edwin K. Sisk, Canon-Pastor. *Wardens:* Robert W. Best, Harry J. Carleton, Jr.; *Clerk:* Mrs. Richard Wamsley; *Treasurer:* Earle D. Johnson; *Vestry:* Mrs. H. A. Bradfelt, Irwin Nolt, Donald Reaves, Harley Roddel, John P. Foster, Mrs. Robert Haggar, Thomas Sheeley, Dr. Loyd Wagner, Marvin Keller, William Robbins, Roger Van Twisk.

CHURCH OF THE GOOD SHEPHERD—SIOUX FALLS

The Rev. Robert D. Wright. *Wardens:* Don Healy, William Lenker; *Clerk:* Esther E. Sutcliffe; *Treasurer:* George Peterson; *Vestry:* Dr. Malcolm Jameson, Roger Schmidt, Leon Organ, Harold Huber, Gene Haggar, Dr. R. J. Briggs, Mrs. Inez Olson, Merle Bach.

CHURCH OF ALL ANGELS—SPEARFISH

The Rev. Andrew Jensen. *Wardens:* William Skillern, Maurice Clarkson; *Clerk:* Mrs. A. E. Mead; *Treasurer:* Mrs. Mary Ann Brandeberry; *Vestry:* Mrs. Bernard S. Clark, Mrs. Floyd Ward, John Ward, Mrs. Robert W. Brown, Ernest J. Tetrault, Mrs. Fred Gerber, H. A. Sullivan.

ST. THOMAS—STURGIS

The Rev. Eric Wright. *Wardens:* John Morgan, Harold Kelley; *Clerk:* Nora Hussey; *Treasurer:* Morgan Elton; *Vestry:* Dr. R. H. Riedesel, Al Elliott, Herman Walker, W. D. Hogue, William Kampa, LaVern Mitchell, Mrs. Harriet Kelley, George L. Parsons, Dr. W. Trumpe, Lee Wright.

TRINITY—WATERTOWN

Wardens: Leslie Rose, Lewis Feuerstein; *Clerk:* Miss Etta Marie Lamb; *Treasurer:* Miss Sibyl Pritchard; *Vestry:* John Davies, Martin Cormier, Harold Gray, Dr. Thomas Reul, Mrs. R. K. Newcomb, Jerry Eggen, Paul Below, Russell Lehman.

TRINITY—WINNER

The Rev. Richard H. McGinnis. *Wardens:* Leon Miller, C. G. Wilson; *Clerk:* Mrs. Ethel Sals; *Treasurer:* Mrs. Esther Enders; *Vestry:* Walt Pharris, Fred Harvey, William Day, Dennis Pospisil, Cham Wilson, Donald Mason, Dr. Wayne Jackson.

CHRIST CHURCH—YANKTON

The Rev. James W. Munck. *Wardens:* Elza L. Anderson, James Branaugh,; *Clerk:* Mrs. Robert Shoemaker; *Treasurer:* Mr. E. J. Freidel; *Vestry:* Mrs. Charles Danforth, William Harris, Charles Rees, Dr. R. A. Beilby, Dennis Hayward.

MISSIONS

ST. ANDREW—BONESTEEL

The Rev. Dwain A. Jenista. *Bishop's Committee:* Paul Woerpel, Pearl Mulford, Miss Gladys Sutton, Ronald Gustafson, Ralph Marts, Billie H. Sutton, Mrs. Eva Marts, Mrs. Ida Woerpel.

CHRIST—CHAMBERLAIN

The Rev. John K. Vallensis. *Bishop's Committee:* Ray Steckelberg, Mrs. Ruth Potter, E. J. Buckingham, George Gilbert, Mrs. Helen Knox, Mrs. Norman Fuegen.

CHURCH OF THE LIVING WATER—DELL RAPIDS

The Rev. Frank M. Thorburn (Ret.). *Bishop's Committee:* Dr. P. T. Anderson, Mrs. Walter Crisp, Mrs. Fred Voigt.

ST. STEPHEN—DE SMET

The Rev. Leonard J. Adams. *Bishop's Committee:* Merle Pratt, Mrs. P. Scofield, Edward Gummer, Lloyd Meyers, Alfred Ryland, Willis Engel.

CHURCH OF ST. MARY AND OUR BLESSED REDEEMER—FLANDREAU

The Rev. Frank M. Thorburn (Ret.). *Bishop's Committee:* Vance Sneve, Kingsmill Jones, Mrs. Ramona Zephier, Mrs. Bernice Jones, Mrs. Bonnie MacFarland, Howard Robertson, Emmett Jones, Mrs. Vera Weston.

ST. PETER—FORT PIERRE

The Rev. John B. Lurvey. *Bishop's Committee:* Charles Carlisle, Cynthia Fuller, Louis Hackett, Martin Schutteree. Mrs. Robert Schumacher, Mrs. Ramon Roubideaux.

CHRIST—GETTYSBURG

The Rev. James P. Barton. *Bishop's Committee:* Eldon Smith, Gordon Fawcett, Mrs. Dorothy Fawcett, Mrs. Dora Voorhes, Orlow K. Eidam, Jack Hall.

INCARNATION—GREGORY

The Rev. Dwain A. Jenista. *Bishop's Committee:* William Wernke, Charles W. Fillmore, George Grubbs, Dudley R. Herman, Stephen J. Boxa, Jerry McCance, Charles R. Johnson.

ST. LUKE—HOT SPRINGS

Bishop's Committee: Laurence Kaudy, Harry Whitehead, Mrs. Ella Mae Reese, John Gray, Joe Kern, Mrs. Carl Ottmann, Mrs. R. W. Southard, Mrs. Steve Hoy, Dan V. Goodman, Sr., Wallace A. Murray, Mrs. G. R. Brown, William M. Arnold, Mrs. Edith Brendmoen.

TRINITY—HOWARD

The Rev. Leonard J. Adams. *Bishop's Committee:* Robert Clark, Eilers Grimme, Mrs. Eilers Grimme, Donald Raabe, J. Baumbach, Sid Davison, Mrs. W. Hepner.

ST. PETER—LAKE ANDES

The Rev. Edward G. Vock. *Bishop's Committee:* Ralph Town, Albert Harvey, Mrs. Virginia LaBarge, R. Pesicka, Mrs. R. Dowell, Dale Leonard, Gregory Leonard, Leo Soulek, Wayne Hotchkiss.

GRACE—MADISON

The Rev. Leonard J. Adams. *Bishop's Committee:* Mrs. L. G. Boyd, Homer Engelhorn, Charles Skinner, Merrill Hunter, Rex Page, Mrs. Gloria Burke.

ST. KATHARINE—MARTIN

The Rev. Gordon R. Plowe. *Bishop's Committee:* Richard Howe, Clyde Rayhill, Doris Hicks, Marvin Howe, Darlene Pich, Harold Bates, Cleon Boomer, Mrs. Marvin Harris, Mrs. Grace Hays, Linn McCoy, Mrs. Vern Olson, Charles Sasse.

CHRIST—MILBANK

The Rev. Henry J. Cluver. *Bishop's Committee:* William E. Hooper, James Adler, Francis Comstock. Clifford Dexter, Dr. D. A. Gregory, C. Bryan Lowe, Arthur Magedanz, Ray Nelson, Thomas H. Tippett.

TRINITY—MISSION

The Rev. Noah Brokenleg. *Bishop's Committee:* John Artichoker, Glen Tucker, Mrs. Frances Halligan, Mrs. Elda Abourezk, Mrs. Carlene Tucker, Hubert Dillon, Pat LeBeau, Mrs. Paula Coleman, Bernard Halligan, Walter Wright, Mrs. Hattie Marcus, Willis Groves.

ST. MATTHEW—RAPID CITY

The Rev. Donald S. Walch. *Bishop's Committee:* Gilbert Wright, Sheridan Quilt, Anne Armstrong, Lloyd Crisman, Gus Kingman, Dan Quilt, Joe Dudley, Matthew Yellow Eagle, Marlene Packard.

ST. GEORGE—REDFIELD

The Rev. Robert W. Dunn. *Bishop's Committee:* Omar Gavin, Floyd Morey, Galen Gillette, Mrs. Charlotte Hufteling, Jerald Gavin.

ST. ANDREW—SCOTLAND

The Rev. James W. Munck. *Bishop's Committee:* Donley Max. Mrs. Donley Max, Mrs. J. S. Donley, E. F. Ardery.

CHURCH OF THE HOLY APOSTLES—SIOUX FALLS

Bishop's Committee: A. D. Kasch, Claude Hinman, Miss Madeline Haggar, James Heinzman, James Gouge, Gordon Anderson, Mrs. Forrest Rode.

GETHSEMANE CHURCH—SISSETON

The Rev. J. Dean Maurer. *Bishop's Committee:* George Johnston, Edwin Robertson, Mrs. Dorothea Axness, Mrs. Ruth Vanderlinden, Jack Adams, Herbert Axness, Neil Harcum, William Holland, Julian Pearson, C. E. Vanderlinden, Albert Pfeifle, Jr.

ASCENSION—SPRINGFIELD

Mr. Kenyon Cull, Lay Vicar. *Bishop's Committee:* Kenyon Cull, Laurel Iverson.

ST. MARK—TIMBER LAKE

Bishop's Committee: James Byington, Mrs. James Byington, Francis L. McMacken.

ST. PAUL—VERMILLION

The Rev. Vine V. Deloria, (locum tenens). *Bishop's Committee:* Dr. Wellborn R. Hudson III, Thomas E. Poe, Jr., Dr. Josephine Moore, Leonard Cook, Mrs. Elizabeth Kerns.

ST. MARY—WEBSTER

The Rev. Henry J. Cluver. *Bishop's Committee:* Rodney A. Upton, Cornelius Wells, Mrs. C. J. Lee, W. F. Evans, Don Q. Thomas, J. H. Flagstad.

NIOBRARA DEANERY

Note: Italics Designate Lay Readers

CHEYENNE RIVER MISSION

The Rev. Andrew A. Weston, Eagle Butte; Capt. William Black Lance, C.A., Dupree
St. John the Evangelist, Eagle Butte, *Guy Bagola*
Ascension, Moreau, *Andrew LeBeau*
Calvary, Marksville, *Andrew LeBeau*
Emmanuel, White Horse, *Joseph Fiddler*
St. Andrew, Cherry Creek, *Captain William Black Lance*
St. James, Bear Creek, *Raymond Clown*
St. Luke, Iron Lighning, *Captain William Black Lance*
St. Mary, Promise, *Isaac Traversie*
St. Paul, LaPlant, The Rev. Andrew A. Weston
St. Peter, Thunder Butte, *Captain William Black Lance*
St. Philip, Dupree, *Captain William Black Lance*
St. Stephen, Red Scaffold, *Mark Ward*
St. Thomas, On the Tree, *Timothy Red Dog*
Isabel Station, *Norman Blue Coat*

CROW CREEK MISSION

Ft. Thompson, The Rev. John K. Vallensis, Chamberlain.
Christ Church, Fort Thompson, *Everett Jones*

St. John, Pukwana, *Everett Jones*
St. Peter, Shelby, *Everett Hopkins*
St. Columba, Presho, The Rev. John K. Vallensis

LOWER BRULE MISSION
Lower Brule, The Rev. John B. Lurvey, Fort Pierre.
Holy Comforter, Lower Brule, *John Estes*
Holy Name, Fort George, The Rev. John B. Lurvey
Messiah, Iron Nation, *Nathan Middletent*
St. Alban, Fort Hale, The Rev. John B. Lurvey
Cedar Creek Station, The Rev. John B. Lurvey

PIERRE MISSION
Pierre. The Rev. John B. Lurvey, Fort Pierre; Warden : David Marks; Treasurer: Mrs. George Van Wald; Clerk: Mrs. Barbara LeBeau.
St. Michael, Pierre, The Rev. John B. Lurvey

PINE RIDGE MISSION
The Rev. William M. Fay, Superintending Presbyter, Pine Ridge; the Rev. Wilbur A. Bearsheart, Porcupine; the Rev. Ronald A. Campbell, Pine Ridge; the Rev. Charles G. Morgan (d), Wanblee; Sister Margaret Hawk, C. A., Pine Ridge; Captain Gilford Noisy Hawk, C. A. Manderson.
Holy Cross, Pine Ridge, The Rev. William M. Fay, *Harley Zephier*
Advent, Pine Ridge, *Leo American Horse*
Christ Church, Red Shirt Table, *The Rev. Ronald A. Campbell*
Epiphany, Wolf Creek, The Rev. William M. Fay
Messiah, Wounded Knee, *Charles Moose*
St. Alban, Porcupine, *Dawson Little Soldier*
St. Andrew, Wakpamni Lake, *Vincent Two Lance*
St. James, Oglala, *William Eagle Bull*
St. John, Oglala, *William Eagle Bull*
St. Jude, White River, The Rev. Ronald A. Campbell
St. Julia, Porcupine, The Rev. Wilbur A. Bearsheart
St. Luke, Porcupine, *Dawson Little Soldier*
St. Mark, Rockyford, The Rev. Wilbur A. Bearsheart
St. Mary, Grass Creek, The Rev. Wilbur A. Bearsheart
St. Matthew, Slim Buttes, The Rev. William M. Fay
St. Peter, Oglala, *Tex Broken Nose*
St. Philip, Manderson, *Capt. Gilford Noisy Hawk, C.A.*
St. Thomas, Manderson, *Capt. Gilford Noisy Hawk, C.A.*
Batesland Station, *Vincent Two Lance*

CORN CREEK DISTRICT OF THE PINE RIDGE MISSION
Gethsemane, Wanblee, The Rev. Charles G. Morgan (d), *Milton Milk*
Good Shephard, Martin, The Rev. Gordon R. Plowe, *Amos Ghost Bear*
Inestimable Gift, Allen, *Ellsworth Brown*
Mediator, Kyle, *Wilson Gay*
St. Barnabas, Kyle, The Rev. Charles G. Morgan (d)
St. Philip, Hisle, *Oliver Bad Wound*
St. Mary, Kadoka, The Rev. Charles G. Morgan (d)
St. Timothy, Potato Creek, *Orville Reddest*
Trinity, Allen, *Daniel Makes Good*
Bad Wounds Station, Martin, *Oliver Bad Wounds*

ROSEBUD MISSION
The Rev. Frederick E. Jessett, Rosebud; The Rev. C.E.B. Harnsberger, White River: the Rev. Noah Brokenleg, Mission.
Advent, Mosher, The Rev. Noah Brokenleg
Calvary, Okreek, The Rev. Noah Brokenleg, *Norman Knox, Everdell Wright*
Church of Jesus, Rosebud, The Rev. Frederick E. Jessett, *Theodore Lunderman*
Epiphany, Parmelee, The Rev. C.E.B. Harnsberger, *Leo Running Horse*
Grace, Mission, The Rev. Frederick E. Jessett, *James Provincial*
Grass Mountain Community, The Rev. Frederick E. Jessett
Holy Innocents, Parmelee, The Rev. C.E.B. Harnsberger, *James Black Bull, Sr.*
Mediator, Wood, The Rev. Noah Brokenleg
St. Andrew, St. Francis, The Rev. Frederick E. Jessett, *Charles Kills in Water*
St. Mark, Parmelee, The Rev. C.E.B. Harnsberger
St. Paul, Norris, The Rev. C.E.B. Harnsberger, *Joseph Kills Crow*
St. Philip and St. James, The Rev. C.E.B. Harnsberger, *Joseph Marshall*
St. Stephen, Norris, The Rev. C.E.B. Harnsberger, *Sam Bear*
St. Thomas, Norris, The Rev. C.E.B. Harnsberger, *Sam Bear*
All Saints, Herrick, The Rev. Dwain A. Jenista, *Ed Godfrey, Sr.*
Holy Spirit, Ideal, The Rev. Richard H. McGinnis, *Lloyd Winter Chaser*
SANTEE MISSION
The Rev. Sidney U. Martin, Niobrara, Nebraska.
Our Most Mercyful Saviour, Santee, *C. Theodore Robertson*
Blessed Redeemer, Howe Creek, *Benjamin Kitto*
Holy Faith, Lindy, The Rev. Sidney U. Martin
St. Paul, Niobrara, *Albert Thomas*
SISSETON MISSION
The Rev. J. Dean Mauer, Sisseton; the Rev. George L. Selwyn, Waubay.
St. James, Enemy Swim Lake, Waubay, The Rev. George L. Selwyn
St. John, Brown's Valley, *Moses Quinn*
St. Luke, Veblen, The Rev. J. Dean Maurer
St. Mary, Old Agency, Peever, The Rev. George L. Selwyn, *Winfield Kampeska*
STANDING ROCK MISSION
The Rev. Clyde G. Estes, McLaughlin.
Good Shepherd, Little Oak Creek, *Henry Red Legs*
St. Elizabeth, Wakpala, *James Mound*
St. John the Baptist, Bullhead, *Ambrose Running Hawk*
St. Paul, Little Eagle, *Victor and Levi Brown Eagle*
St. Peter, McLaughlin, *William Archambault*
St. Thomas, Kenel, The Rev. Clyde G. Estes
St. Philip, Watauga, The Rev. Clyde G. Estes
YANKTON MISSION
The Rev. Edward G. Vock, Pickstown; the Rev. William F. Fahsing, Wagner.
Holy Fellowship, Greenwood, The Rev. William F. Fahsing, *Everard Jordan*
Holy Name, Dante, *Sampson Ree*
St. Philip the Deacon, Lake Andes, The Rev. Edward G. Vock

CHURCH ARMY PERSONNEL
Captain William Black Lance, Dupree
Captain Gilford Noisy Hawk, Manderson
Sister Margaret Hawk, Pine Ridge
Captain Fred M. Nussbaum, Mission

Martin Kelsey Brokenleg
David Lloyd Seger
Francis Charles Apple

POSTULANTS

Capt. William Black Lance, C. A.
Morris Bull Bear
Everett Jones
Fred Mesteth, Jr.
Marion D. Morris
Lyle Noisyhawk

INSTITUTIONS

ALL SAINTS SCHOOL

A school for boys and girls operated by All Saints School, Inc., Sioux Falls. Nursery, kindergarten and grades 1-6. Mrs. Robert Manthe, Headmistress.

ST. MARY'S SCHOOL FOR INDIAN GIRLS, Springfield

5th grade through high school, Mr. Kenyon Cull, M.A., Headmaster.

BISHOP HARE MISSION HOME

For Indian boys of grades 7-12, Mission, South Dakota. Captain Fred M. Nussbaum, C.A., Director.

ST. ELIZABETH'S MISSION

Wakpala, South Dakota. Mr. Joseph Skye, Director. A training center 1970-71—The Rev. David R. Cochran.

THE EPISCOPAL CHURCHWOMEN OF SOUTH DAKOTA

President: Mrs. Norman C. Gross, 410 Capitol, Yankton, SD 57078
Vice-Pres: Mrs. Stan Beecher, 1521 S. Van Eps, Sioux Falls, SD 57105
Secretary: Mrs. Robert Jones, Box 99, Yankton, SD 57078
Treasurer: Mrs. Robert Streedbeck, 601 S. Sneve Ave., Sioux Falls, SD 57103
United Thank Offering: Mrs. Aldo Panerio, 776 Wisconsin SW, Huron, SD 57350
Church Periodical Club: Mrs. Frank Stickney, Box 37, Elk Point, SD 57025
Christian Social Relations: Mrs. Bernard Halligan, Mission, SD 57555
Christian Education: Mrs. William Fay, Pine Ridge, SD 57770
Supply & M.R.I: Mrs. R. E. Furois, 4038 West Main St., Rapid City, SD 57701
Ecumenical Relations: Mrs. Bessie Hildebrand, 1116 N. Burr, Mitchell, SD 57301
Devotions: Mrs. Lois Howe, Martin, SD 57551
Conference Center: Mrs. Robert Best, 127 S. Duluth, Sioux Falls, SD 57102
Christian Ministries: Sister Margaret Hawk, Pine Ridge, SD 57770
Altar Guild: To be appointed by Bishop Jones

1975

LIST OF PARISHES AND MISSIONS

PARISHES

ST. MARK—ABERDEEN

The Rev. Robert W. Dunn. *Senior Warden:* Mr. Elmer Newcomb; *Junior Warden:* Mr. John Zemina; *Treasurer:* Mr. Douglas D. Johnson; *Clerk:* Mrs. Richard L. Lawton; *Vestry:* Mrs. Kenneth Anglin, Mrs. William Lamont, Mr. James D. Powell, Mrs. Thomas Berbos, Mr. Neil Dewhirst, Mrs. Douglas Johnson, Mr. Clark Newman, Mr. Jerry Richards, Mr. Robert Salmi, Mr. Joseph Skye, Mrs. Edward White.

ST. JAMES—BELLE FOURCHE

The Rev. Winston F. Jensen. *Senior Warden:* Dr. E. C. Smart; *Junior Warden:* Mr. Mike Weaver; *Treasurer:* Mr. James Lang; *Clerk:* Mrs. James Roberts; *Vestry:* Ms. Janet Rix, Mrs. Joan Mead, Mr. Claire Smith, Mr. James Roberts, Mrs. Nadine Wood, Mr. George Higashi, Mr. George Pridgeon, Mr. Gene Hovland, Mr. Mike Reade, Mr. Amos Davis.

ST. PAUL—BROOKINGS

The Rev. James W. Hauan. *Senior Warden:* Mr. Joseph J. Bonnemann; *Junior Warden:* Mr. Frederick Bunce; *Treasurer:* Mrs. Jean Lacher and Mrs. Kay Clever; *Clerk:* Mrs. Winnie Baker; *Vestry:* Mrs. Eva Gilkerson, Mr. David Pearson, Mrs. Elizabeth Williams, Mr. James McLellan.

ST. JOHN—DEADWOOD

The Rev. Ronald G. Hennies, *Lead Senior Warden:* Mr. Larry Ryan; *Junior Warden:* Mr. James Shedd; *Treasurer:* Mr. R. C. Swanson; *Clerk:* Mr. Lyle Elward; *Vestry:* Mr. Malcolm H. Allen, Mr. Jene Melton, Mr. Wayne H. Kincaid, Mr. Kenneth Ellis, Col. Melvin Hoherz, Mr. J. Ora Horsfall, Mr. Lloyd West, Mr. Gary Darland, Mrs. Myrtle Auer, Mrs. Dorothy J. Hoherz, Mrs. Yvonne Derosier.

GRACE—HURON

Senior Warden: Mr. Clarke H. Christiansen; *Junior Warden:* Mr. Ronald J. Wheeler; *Treasurer:* Mr. Frederick E. Olmsted; *Clerk:* Mrs. Tessie Coffey; *Vestry:* Mr. Gene Bigelow, Mr. James Kopka, Mr. Gary Enright, Mr. Aldo Panerio, Mr. Elmer Drapeau, Mr. Dennis Dunlay, Mrs. Maxie Smith.

CHRIST—LEAD

The Rev. Ronald G. Hennies. *Senior Warden:* Mr. Homer Arbogast; *Junior Warden:* Mr. Ted Pascoe; *Treasurer:* Mrs. Dorothy Henderson; *Clerk:* Mr. Robert Magers; *Vestry:* Mr. A. E. (Bill) Eklund, Mrs. Florence Adamson, Mr. John Bjorge, Mr. Dan Regan, Mr. Tom Regan.

ST. MARY—MITCHELL

The Rev. Gordon R. Plowe. *Senior Warden:* Mr. Jerry Wegman; *Junior Warden:* Mr. Leo Stedman; *Treasurer:* Mrs. Kay Meyers; *Clerk:* Mrs. Betty Milliken; *Vestry:* Mr. Cortland Kelly, Mr. Toy Coury, Mr. Richard Goudy, Mr. Darald Brooks, Mr. Andrew Radford, Mr. William Timmins, Mrs. Myrna Stone.

ST. JAMES—MOBRIDGE

The Rev. James P. Barton. *Senior Warden:* Mr. Winston Hall; *Junior Warden:* Mr. Charles Hare; *Treasurer:* Mrs. Billie Lewellen; *Clerk:* Mrs. Dorothy Horn; *Vestry:* Mr. Robert Stutenroth, Mr. Arthur Grothe, Mr. Richard Adams, Mrs. Natalie Guerrant.

TRINITY—PIERRE

The Rev. Robert T. Hodgen. *Senior Warden:* Mr. Laurel Iverson; *Junior Warden:* Mrs. Mary K. Burke; *Treasurer:* Mr. James S. Hopkins; *Clerk:* Mrs. Gladys Gifford; *Vestry:* Mr. John A. Dobier, Mrs. Anne Gentle, Mrs. Muriel Jarman, Mrs. Phyllis Lindbloom, Mrs. Aileen Sougstad, Mr. Robert H. Travis, Mrs. Carol Valentine, Mr. C. Wayne Ward, Dr. Robert Westaby, Mr. Arthur Wilner.

EMMANUEL—RAPID CITY

The Rev. Hewes W. Phillips, Rector. The Rev. Paul A. Clark, Assistant. *Senior Warden:* Mr. Phil McCauley; *Junior Warden:* Mr. Don Dickinson; *Treasurer:* Mr. Joe Mustard; *Clerk:* Mrs. Kay Gay; *Vestry:* Mrs. Carole Hillard, Mr. Ken Kirkeby, Mr. Bill Cromett, Mr. David Sieler, Mr. Tom Vucurevich, Mr. Wallace McCullen, Dr. Streeter Shining, Mr. Rosco Brooks.

ST. ANDREW—RAPID CITY

The Rev. Charles G. du Bois. *Senior Warden:* Capt. Robert Neben; *Junior Warden:* Mr. Doyle Ream; *Treasurer:* Mr. Herbert R. Martelon; *Clerk:* Mrs. Lorraine Quarnberg; *Vestry:* Mr. Ralph Byrkit, Capt. Fred Williams, Lt. Michael Mazzaro, Mr. Peter

Geyerman, Ms. Kathryn Humphrey, Mr. L. Michael McKay, Mrs. Mary Martin, Mr. Ben Yetter.

CALVARY CATHEDRAL—SIOUX FALLS

The Very Rev. Paul J. Davis, Dean. The Rev. Canon Edwin K. Sisk, Pastor. The Rev. Marion D. Morris, Assistant. *Senior Warden:* Mr. Ray Slechta; *Junior Warden:* Mr. Ray Loftesness; *Treasurer:* Mr. Larry Cornell; *Clerk:* Mrs. Donald Malcomb; *Vestry:* Mr. Jim Fravel, Mrs. Fran Van Twisk, Dr. Harold Wheeler, Mrs. Ginger Ziegler, Mr. Bill Winn, Lt. Col. Donald Bowman, Mr. Brian Stuart, Mr. Nels Turnquist, Mr. Donald Davis, Mrs. Gen Schoenenberger, Mr. William H. Shannon.

CHURCH OF THE GOOD SHEPHERD—SIOUX FALLS

The Rev. Robert D. Wright. *Senior Warden:* Dr. Barry Pitt-Hart; *Junior Warden:* Mr. Dale Lewis; *Treasurer:* Mr. Marshall Stenson; *Clerk:* Mr. Gary Conradi; *Vestry:* Mrs. Lenore Walter, Mr. Gerald Kisecker, Mr. Ed Poole, Dr. B. J. Williams, Mr. Mead Bailey, Mrs. Sue Sailer, Mr. Deane Grav, Mr. Robert Schmidt.

CHURCH OF ALL ANGELS—SPEARFISH

The Rev. Milo D. Dailey. *Senior Warden:* Mr. Bill Lynn; *Junior Warden:* Dr. Bernard Clark; *Treasurer:* Mrs. Mary Ann Brandeberry; *Clerk:* Mrs. Darlene Young; *Vestry:* Mrs. Gless Clarkson, Mrs. Bee Brown, Mr. Richard Hicks, Mr. Robert Pesicka, Mr. Donald Wince, Mr. Robert Dardis, Dr. Thomas Mead, Mr. Donald Young, Mr. Alan Hardin.

ST. THOMAS—STURGIS

The Rev. Clayton T. Holland. *Senior Warden:* Mr. John Shepard; *Junior Warden:* Mr. Duayne Rhoden; *Treasurer:* Mr. Morgan Elton; *Clerk:* Mrs. Lillian Carr; *Vestry:* Mr. William Brown, Mr. Larry Burtzlaff, Mr. Harvey Hamman, Mr. Erwin Hartmann, Mr. W. D. Hogue, Mr. John Hughes, Mr. LaVern Mitchell, Mr. William Moore, Mr. Wilfred Stieg, Dr. Charles Townsend. Mr. Robert L. Wang, Mr. Duane Erickson.

TRINITY—WATERTOWN

The Rev. Field H. Hobbs. *Senior Warden:* Mr. Dallas Butterbrodt; *Junior Warden:* Mr. Paul Below; *Treasurer:* Mr. Jerry D. Eggen; *Clerk:* Mrs. Dorothy Thomas; *Vestry:* Mr. Alex Johnson, Mr. Donald Smith, Mrs. Margery Tauber, Mr. Russell Lehman, Mr. David Marquardt, Mrs. Barbara Miller, Mrs. Shirley Clark, Mrs. Dee Feuerstein, Mr. Ray Thomas.

TRINITY—WINNER

The Rev. Richard H. McGinnis. *Senior Warden:* Mr. Robert Maule; *Junior Warden:* Mr. Dennis Pospisil; *Treasurer:* Mrs. A. L. Jorgenson and Miss Winona Viedt; *Clerk:* Mrs. L. E. Nicholson; *Vestry:* Mr. Leon Miller, Mr. Charles Hansen, Mr. Don Mason, Mr. Dick Janak, Mr. Jack Lapp, Mr. Walt Pharris.

CHRIST—YANKTON

The Rev. James W. Munck. *Senior Warden:* Mr. E. W. Boyles; *Junior Warden:* Mr. H. J. Modereger; *Treasurer:* Mr. E. J. Freidel; *Clerk:* Mrs. George Greenlee; *Vestry:* Mr. J. L. Gray, Sr., Mr. Lesel Reuwsaat, Mr. Charles Magedanz, Mrs. F. F. Otto, Mrs. James Cope, Mr. Robert Kennedy.

AIDED PARISHES

ST. LUKE—HOT SPRINGS

The Rev. C. E. B. Harnsberger. *Bishop's Committee:* Mr. Marshall Truax, Mr. Rodney Millar, Mr. Joe Kern, Mrs. Marcia Wolfe, Mrs. Marjorie Brown, Mr. Laurence Kaudy, Mr. John Gray, Dr. Richard King, Mrs. Anita Gallentine.

ST. KATHARINE—MARTIN

The Rev. Philip A. Nevels. *Senior Warden:* Mr. Harold Kosmicke; *Junior Warden:* Mr. Charles Sasse; *Treasurer:* Mr. Marvin Howe; *Clerk:* Mr. Joy C. Fairhead; *Vestry:* Mr.

Louis Livermont, Mrs. Emil Stanec, Mr. Linn McCoy, Mr. Jack Trumble, Mr. Jim Bradford, Mr. Clyde Rayhill, Mr. Bob Rayhill, Mrs. Neil Hicks, Mrs. Linn McCoy.

ST. PAUL—VERMILLION

The Rev. Ronald A. Campbell. *Senior Warden:* Mr. Dell Colwell; *Junior Warden:* Mr. Creighton Robertson; *Treasurer:* Mrs. Virginia Carmack; *Clerk:* Dr. Josephine Moore; *Vestry:* Mrs. Veronica Barstow, Mrs. Maxine Johnson, Mr. John McLain, Mr. Dave Colwell, Mr. James Taylor, Mrs. Diane Solger.

ORGANIZED MISSIONS

ST. ANDREW—BONESTEEL

The Rev. Kenneth C. Fieber. *Gregory Bishop's Committee:* Mr. Sam LaFave, Mr. Darwin Leslie, Mr. Ronald J. Gustafson, Mrs. Anita Leslie, Mr. Floyd Nelson, Mrs. Orese Speidel.

CHRIST—CHAMBERLAIN

The Rev. John W. Barkley. *Bishop's Committee:* Mr. Ray Steckelberg, Mr. Walter Labidee, Mrs. Sondra Zingler, Mr. Don Hamiel, Mr. Joe Drury, Mr. Art Remmele.

CHURCH OF THE LIVING WATERS—DELL RAPIDS

The Rev. Thomas Ŵ. Campbell. *Madison Bishop's Committee:* Mrs. Fred Voigt

ST. STEPHEN—DE SMET

The Rev. Thomas W. Campbell. *Madison Bishop's Committee:* Mr. A. J. Ryland, Mr. Merle E. Pratt, Mr. Edward Gummer.

ST. MARY & OUR BLESSED REDEEMER, FLANDREAU

The Rev. Thomas W. Campbell. *Madison Bishop's Committee:* Mr. Philip Dudley, Mr. Vance Sneve, Mrs. Virginia Sneve, Mrs. Josephine Monteau, Mr. Howard Robertson.

ST. PETERR—FORT PIERRE

Bishop's Committee: Mrs. Lola Ricketts, Mrs. Cynthia Fuller, Mrs. Flora Ziemann, Mrs. Edna Dirksen, Mr. Martin Schutterlee, Mr. Charles Carlyle, Ms. Bozanna Hart.

CHRIST—GETTYSBURG

The Rev. James P. Barton. *Mobridge Bishop's Committee:* Mr. Orlow Eidam, Mr. Abner Johnson, Mrs. Sybil Houck, Mrs. Dorothy Paulson, Mr. Frederick Soule.

CHURCH OF THE INCARNATION—GREGORY

The Rev. Kenneth C. Fieber. *Bishop's Committee:* Mr. Larry Schweigert, Mr. William Sherman, Mrs. Bernita Schweigert, Miss Kari Wernke, Mr. William Wernke, Mr. George Peabody.

TRINITY—HOWARD

The Rev. Thomas W. Campbell. *Madison Bishop's Committee:* Mr. Robert Clark, Mr. Eilers Grimme, Mr. S. I. Davison, Mrs. Tillie Kitchen.

ST. PETER—LAKE ANDES

The Rev. James D. Marrs, Sr. *Bishop's Committee:* Mr. Albert Harvey, Mr. Leo Soulek, Mr. L. J. Hadd, Mrs. Virginia LaBarge, Mr. James Templeton. Mr. William Grajkowske.

TRINITY—LEMMON

The Rev. Harold S. Gibbons. *Bishop's Committee:* Mr. Lyman Patee, Mr. William E. Coats, Mrs. Eleanor F. Coats, Mr. George Pixler.

GRACE—MADISON

The Rev. Thomas W. Campbell. *Bishop's Committee:* Mr. Merrill Hunter, Mr. Rex Page, Mrs. L. G. Boyd, Mrs. Gloria Burke, Mr. Eric Johnson.

CHRIST—MILBANK

The Rev. Henry J. Cluver, Ret'd, *Webster. Bishop's Committee:* Mr. William E. Hooper, Mr. Clifford Dexter, Mr. C. B. Lowe, Mr. Francis Comstock, Mr. Ray O. Nelson, Mr. Arthur Magedanz, Mr. James Adler, Mr. Thomas H. Tippett.

ST. MATTHEW—RAPID CITY

The Rev. LaVerne LaPointe. *Bishop's Committee:* Mr. Gus Kingman, Mr. William Wilcox, Mrs. JoAnn Trask, Mrs. Marie Rogers, Miss Caroline Packard, Mrs. Laura Wilcox, Mrs. Mary Wright, Mr. Gregg Trask.

ST. ANDREW—SCOTLAND

The Rev. James W. Munck, *Yankton. Bishop's Committee:* Mr. Donley Max, Mr. Leonard Layne, Jr., Mrs. Donley Max, Mr. E. F. Ardery.

CHURCH OF THE HOLY APOSTLES—SIOUX FALLS

The Rev. William J. B. Giovetti. *Bishop's Committee:* Mr. Darwin Marshall, Mr. James Heinzman, Miss Madeline Haggar, Mrs. Ernest Veigh, Mrs. Phyllis Beecher, Mr. Warren Shoberg, Mrs. C. R. Streedbeck, Mrs. Kenneth Salisbury.

GETHSEMANE—SISSETON

The Rev. Richard S. Miller. *Bishop's Committee:* Mr. Jack Adams, Mr. Andrew Miller, Mrs. Martha Pfeifle, Mrs. Charlotte Pearson, Mr. George Johnston, Mr. Tom Renville, Mr. Al Pfeifle, Sr., Mr. Ed Robertson, Mr. William Holland, Mr. Neil Harcum.

ASCENSION—SPRINGFIELD

Bishop's Committee: Mr. Kenyon Cull, Mrs. Linda Morrison, Mrs. Vera Tucker.

ST. MARY—WEBSTER

The Rev. Henry J. Cluver, Ret'd. *Bishop's Committee:* Mr. Cornelius Wells, Dr. Cyril Grace, Mr. Donn Q. Thomas, Mrs. C. J. Lee, Mrs. Kay Knott, Mr. S. Robert Pearson, Mr. Monte Rougemont, Dr. Joseph Lovering, Mr. F. W. Stewart, Mr. Roger Williams.

NIOBRARA DEANERY

Note: Italics Designate Lay Readers

CHEYENNE RIVER MISSION

The Rev. Andrew A. Weston, Eagle Butte; The Rev. John B. Lurvey, Eagle Butte; The Rev. Dr. John P. Edwards (d), Eagle Butte;

St. John the Evangelist Butte, *Joseph Fiddler, Homer LeBeau*

Ascension, Moreau, *Andrew LeBeau*

Calvary, Marksville

Emmanuel, White Horse

St. Andrew, Cherry Creek, *Levi Runs After*

St. James, Bear Creek, *Joseph Kills Crow*

St. Luke, Iron Lightning

St. Mary, Promise, *James White Feather*

St. Paul, LaPlant

St. Peter, Thunder Butte, *Raymond Clown, Earl Red Bird*

St. Philip, Dupree, *Guy Bagola*

St. Stephen, Red Scaffold, *Gilbert Little Thunder*

St. Thomas, On the Tree, *Cecil Curley*

Isabel Station, *Norman Blue Coat*

CROW CREEK MISSION

The Rev. Clyde G. Estes, Fort Thompson;

Christ, Fort Thompson, *Arline Voice*

St. John, Pukwanna, The Rev. John W. Barkley

St. Peter, Shelby

LOWER BRULE MISSION

The Rev. Clyde G. Estes, Fort Thompson;

Holy Comforter, Lower Brule, *John Estes, Sr., Mark Estes, Harlan Rus*

Holy Name, Fort George
Messiah, Iron Nation
St. Alban, Fort Hale, The Rev. John W. Barkley
Cedar Creek Station
ALL SAINTS, HERRICK
    The Rev. Kenneth C. Fieber, Gregory; *Edward Godfrey, Sr.*
HOLY SPIRIT, IDEAL
    The Rev. Richard H. McGinnis, Winner; *George Medicine Eagle, Clarence Stands, Ed
    Eagle Star*
ST. MICHAEL, PIERRE
    The Ven. Vine V. Deloria, Ret'd
PINE RIDGE MISSION
    The Rev. George P. Pierce, Superintending Presbyter, Pine Ridge; Sister Margaret
    Hawk. C.A., Pine Ridge; The Rev. Vincent Two Lance (d), Pine Ridge; The Rev.
    Francis C. Apple, Porcupine; Captain Gilford Noisy Hawk, C.A., Manderson; The
    Rev. Lyle M. Noisy Hawk, Wanblee; the Rev. Daniel Makes Good (d), Allen;
    Holy Cross, Pine Ridge, *Alvin Zephier, Robert Mesteth, Benjamin Tyon, Irv Stabnow*
    Advent, Pine Ridge, *Leo American Horse, Denver American Horse*
    Christ, Red Shirt Table, *Robert Two Bulls, Roger Campbell, James Two Bulls, Alex
        Wright, Todd Fast Bull*
    Epiphany, Wolf Creek, *Mel Lone Hill*
    Messiah, Wounded Knee, *Warfield Moose, Charles Moose*
    St. Alban, Porcupine, *Dawson Little Soldier*
    St. Andrew, Wakpamni Lake, *Dawson No Horse, Dennis Yellow Thunder*
    St. James, Oglala, *Leo American Horse*
    St. John, Oglala
    St. Jude, Little White River, *Robert Two Bulls*
    St. Julia, Porcupine, *Garfield Wounded Head, Fred Mesteth, Francis Apple, Jr., Cheryl
        Wounded Head*
    St. Luke, Porcupine, *Dawson Little Soldier, Guy L. Byrd, John High Hawk, Pedro Quick
        Bear*
    St. Mark, Rockyford, *Alvin Twiss*
    St. Mary, Grass Creek
    St. Matthew, Slim Buttes, *Wilbert Yellow Horse*
    St. Michael, Batesland, *Peter Red Owl, Sandra Two Lance, Peter Plenty Wound, Wilson
        Two Lance*
    St. Peter, Oglala, *Tex Broken Nose, Stephen White Magpie*
    St. Philip, Manderson
    St. Thomas, Manderson, *Dawson Protector, Rachel Eagle Bull*
CORN CREEK DISTRICT OF THE PINE RIDGE MISSION
Mission Churches:
    Gethsemane, Wanblee, *Isaac White Bull*
    Inestimable Gift, Allen, *Chris Conquering Bear, Arlene Garnette, Rosalyn Marshall*
    Mediator, Kyle, *Willard Kill-In-Water, Wilson Gay, Daniel Lone Hill*
    St. Barnabas, Kyle, *Luke Broken Rope, Delano Featherman, Royal Bull Bear, Ray War
        Bonnette*
    St. Timothy, Potato Creek, *Orville Reddest*
    Trinity, Allen
Stations:
    Good Shepherd, Martin, *Jasper Milk*

St. Mary, Kadoka, *Leland Bear Heels*
St. Phillip, Hisle, *Oliver Bad Wound*
Bad Wound Station, Martin, *Oliver Bad Wound*

ROSEBUD MISSION

The Rev. Noah Brokenleg, Rosebud; The Rev. Edward G. Vock, Mission; The Rev.
   Francis C. Cutt (d), White River;

Organized Churches:
Church of Jesus, Rosebud, *A. Leslie Brokenleg*
Trinity, Mission, *Derril H. Wright*

Mission Churches:
Calvary, Okreek, *Theodore Lunderman, Norman Knox*
Epiphany, Parmelee, *Leo Running Horse*
Grace, Soldier Creek, *James Provancial, Sr.*
Holy Innocents, Parmelee, *James Black Bull, Sr., Kenneth Austin*
Mediator, Wood
Mni Wiconi, Grass Mountain, *Vine Good Shield*
St. Andrew, St. Francis, *Charles Kills in Water*
St. Mark, Parmelee, *James Black Bull, Sr., Keith Matzke*
St. Paul, Norris
Ss. Philip & James, White River, *William Black Lance*
St. Stephen, Norris, *Sam Bear*
St. Thomas, Norris, *Sam Bear*

Stations:
Advent, Mosher
St. Michael, Belvidere

SANTEE MISSION

The Rev. Ronald A. Campbell, Vermillion;
Our Most Merciful Saviour, Santee, *Albert Thomas, Guy Lawrence*
Blessed Redeemer, Howe Creek
Holy Faith, Lindy
St. Paul, Niobrara

SISSETON MISSION

The Rev. Richard S. Miller, Sisseton;
St. James, Enemy Swim Lake, Waubay, *Ishmael Shepherd, Aaron Bernard, John Two
   Stars, Philip Dorsch, Vernon Cloud, James Strutz*
St. John, Brown's Valley, *Moses Quinn, Aaron Bernard, John Two Stars*
St. Luke, Veblen, *James D. Crawford, Narcisse Necklace, John Two Stars*
St. Mary, Old Agency, Peever, *Vernon Cloud, Philip Dorsch, Aaron Bernard, John Two
   Stars, Harold Frank, Ken Seaboy*

STANDING ROCK MISSION

The Rev. Lester I. Kills Crow, Wakpala: The Rev. Sidney U. Martin, Ret'd Mobridge;
Good Shepherd, Little Oak Creek, *Henry Red Legs*
St. Elizabeth, Wakpala, *Wilbur Three Legs, John Four Bears*
St. John the Baptist, Bullhead, *Ambrose Running Hawk*
St. Paul, Little Eagle, *Levi Brown Eagle*
St. Peter, McLaughlin, *William Archambault*
St. Thomas, Kenel

YANKTON MISSION

The Rev. James D. Marrs, Sr., Pickstown;
Holy Fellowship, Greenwood

Holy Name, Dante, *Samson Ree*
St. Philip the Deacon, Lake Andes, *William O'Connor*

CHURCH ARMY PERSONNEL

Captain Gilford Noisy Hawk, Manderson
Sister Margaret Hawk, Pine Ridge

RURAL DEANS

BLACK HILLS, The Rev. Winston F. Jensen
CENTRAL, The Rev. Clyde G. Estes
EASTERN, The Rev. Ronald A. Campbell
NIOBRARA, The Rev. Noah Brokenleg
NORTHERN, The Rev. Field H. Hobbs
NORTHWEST, The Rev. John B. Lurvey
PINE RIDGE, The Rev. F. Charles Apple
ROSEBUD, The Rev. Kenneth C. Fieber

INSTITUTIONS

ALL SAINTS SCHOOL
   A School for boys and girls operated by All Saints School, Inc., Sioux Falls. Nursery, kindergarten, and grades 1-6. The Rev. F. Douglas Henderson, Headmaster.
ST. MARY'S SCHOOL FOR INDIAN GIRLS
   5th grade through high school, Springfield, S. D., Mr. Kenyon Cull, M.A., Headmaster
BISHOP HARE MISSION HOME
   For Indian boys of grades 7-12, Mission, S. D. The Rev. David G. DeVore, Director.

SOUTH DAKOTA EPISCOPAL CHURCH WOMEN
BOARD — 1975

President: Mrs. R. E. Furois (Betty), 4038 West Main St., Rapid City, S. Dak. 57701
Vice-President: Mrs. William Harris (Inez), 904 Pearl St., Yankton, S. Dak. 57078
Secretary: Mrs. Ronald Gustafson (Louise), R.R. 1, Box 26, Butte, Nebr. 68722
Treasurer: Mrs. A. E. Eklund (Esther), 413 Spark St., Lead, S. Dak. 57754
Church Periodical Club: Mrs. Laurel Iverson (Irene), 513 N. Van Buren, Pierre, S. Dak. 57501
United Thank Offering: Mrs. James Hauan (Alice), 519-8th Ave., Brookings, S. Dak. 57006
Christian Ministries: Sister Margaret Hawk, C.A., P.O. Box 319, Pine Ridge, S. Dak. 5770
Ecumenical Relations: Mrs. Gertrud Bonnemann, 734 Montana Ave., S.W., Huron, S. Dak. 57350
M.R.I. and Christian Social Relations: Mrs. Ray Loftesness (Mary), 1817 S. Sherman, Sioux Falls, S. Dak. 57105
Christian Education: Mrs. Phyllis J. Beecher, 1512 S. Van Eps, Sioux Falls, S. Dak. 57105
Devotions: Mrs. Richard L. Lawton (Cora Jane), 1410 S. 1st St., Aberdeen, S. Dak. 57401
Diocesan Altar Guild: Mrs. Marion Morris (Hazel), 633 S. Main Ave., Apt. 12, Sioux Falls, S. Dak. 57104
Conference Center: Mrs. Robert Best (Betty), 127 S. Duluth, Sioux Falls, S. D. 57104

.∧.∧∧∧.

Historical Sketch of the White Field

(as compiled in 1898)

I.

Memoranda, quite imperfect, of:

a. First services, when and by whom held.

b. Date of organization.

c. Date of building first church.

THE EASTERN DEANERY.

YANKTON:

a. In 1860, by Bishop Talbot, of Indiana, and the Reverend M. Hoyt. Dr. Hoyt came to Yankton to reside in 1862. b. 1862. Probably the first ecclesiastical organization in the Territory. c. 1866. This building was probably the first house of worship erected in the Territory.

SIOUX FALLS:

a. Probably as early as 1863, by Bishop Clarkson. Reverend W. H. H. Ross had charge in 1871, probably the first pastor; Reverend J. M. McBride from 1882 to 1884. b. 1871. c. 1872. Calvary Cathedral erected in 1888.

SPRINGFIELD:

a. Probably in 1863, by Dr. Hoyt. b.

ELK POINT:

a. About 1863, by Dr. Hoyt; Reverend W. W. Fowler in 1876; Reverend Joshua V. Himes, 1881 to July 27, 1895 b.   c. Not ascertained. The first building having been destroyed by fire, a beautiful church was erected in 1895, as a Memorial of the daughter of a devout churchwoman, who defrayed the expense of building, furniture and organ.

PARKER:

a. About 1863, by Dr. Hoyt. b.   c. About 1885.

HURLEY:

a. 1863, by Dr. Hoyt. b. about 1864. c. quite early; probably in 1865. A parsonage in 1885.

SCOTLAND:

a. 1863 or 1864, by Dr. Hoyt. Reverend John Morris had charge in 1883. Dr. Hoyt removed to Scotland in 1886, and died there, Jan. 2, 1888. b.   c. 1887.

VERMILLION:

a. In 1866, by Dr. Hoyt. Reverend W. W. Fowler from 1876 to 1879. Reverend Joshua V. Himes from 1879 to 1889. b.

CANTON:
a. In 1871, by Reverend W. W. Fowler. Reverend J. M. McBride in 1881, and Reverend W. J. Wicks from 1884 to 1887. b.   c. In 1883.

HURON:
In 1875 probably by Dr. Hoyt. Dr. Hoyt had charge from 1881 to 1884. b. Probably 1875. c. Church begun in 1887; finished in 18____.

DELL RAPIDS:
a. In 1879, by Bishop Clarkson. b.   c. In 1895.

MITCHELL:
a. In 1880, by Reverend John Morris. Reverend David A. Sanford was the first settled pastor, 1882 to 1883; he was succeeded by Reverend C. C. Harris in 1884. b. In 1881. c. In 1881.

GROTON:
a. Probably in 1882, by Reverend D. A. Sanford, who was in charge in 1883. b.

MILBANK:
a. Probably 1883, by Reverend R. E. Metcalf. b.

ABERDEEN:
a.   b. Probably by Dr. Hoyt, who was the first pastor. Reverend D. A. Sanford was in charge in 1883.

PIERRE:
a. Probably in 1883, by Reverend Henry T. Bray. Reverend J. M. McBride took charge in 1884. b.   c. 1885.

ALEXANDRIA:
a. In 1884, by Reverend C. C. Harris. b.   c. In 1886.

CHAMBERLAIN:
a. Not certainly known when and by whom the first services were held, but Reverend C. C. Harris held services in 1884. b. 1890. c. 1893.

PLANKINTON:
a. 1884, by Reverend C. C. Harris. b. 1890. c. No church edifice.

MADISON:
a. Probably 1884, by Reverend John Morris. b. In 1884. c. Not known. A beautiful stone church was erected in 1895.

HOWARD:
a. Probably 1864, by Reverend John Morris. b. In 1884. c. In _____. It was burnt down in 1897 and a new one was erected in 1898.

CARTHAGE:
a. As early as 1884, by Reverend John Morris. b.   c.

BROOKINGS:
a. In 1884, by Reverend John Morris. b.

WOONSOCKET:
a. In 1885, by Reverend John Morris. b. 1887. c. In 1888 and parsonage same year.

FLANDREAU, (THE REDEEMER):
a. In 1887, charge of Reverend F. Gardner and Reverend J. H. Molineaux. b.   c. In 1895.

WEBSTER:
a. 1887, by Reverend E. Ashley. b.   c.

GETTYSBURG:
a. In 1888, by Reverend J. M. McBride. b. 1888. c.

ST. LAWRENCE:
a. As early as 1888, by Mr. B. T. Ives, Lay Reader. b.

PARKSTON:
  a. 1890, by Reverend R. M. Doherty; by Reverend J. H. Babcock from December 1890 to December 1892. b.

WAUBAY:
  a. 1895, by Reverend T. H. J. Walton. b.   c.

THE BLACK HILLS DEANERY.

DEADWOOD:
  a. By Rev'd. E. Ashley, 1877, July, 1878 to May, 1879, Reverend E. K. Lessell, Bishop Hare's first visitation to the Black Hills, was in November, 1879. Reverend George C. Pennell came in 1879; died there May, 1882. b.

LEAD CITY:
  a. Probably in 1879, by Bishop Hare. Reverend R. M. Doherty in 1886-7. b. About 1885. c. About 1888. A large and handsome church was nearly finished in 1898.

RAPID CITY:
  a. In 1884, (probably), by Mr. G. G. Ware, Lay Reader. b. In 1885. c. In 1890.

STURGIS:
  a. 1887, by Bishop Hare. Reverend F. North Tummon, present pastor, came in 1893. b. 1893. c. 1893.

SPEARFISH:
  a. In 1887, by Bishop Hare. b.   c.

HOT SPRINGS:
  a. Probably in 1891, by Reverend G. G. Ware. b. In 1891. c.

II.
SUMMARY OF STATISTICS OF THE WHITE FIELD

THE EASTERN DEANERY

	1860 1870	1877	1883	1898
Souls	200 ?	?	1500	3000
Communicants	50 ?	200 ?	600	1300
Clergy	4	6	10	13
Parishes and Missions	6	10	30	33

THE BLACK HILLS DEANERY.

	1878	1898
Souls		1400
Communicants		500
Clergy	1	4
Parishes and Missions		10

TOTALS IN THE WHITE FIELD.

	1898
Souls	4400
Communicants	1800
Clergy	17
Parishes and Missions	43

The Population of the Territory of Dakota in 1877 was about 50,000; that of the State of State of South Dakota in 1898 is about 400,000. (John H. Babcock)

ʌʌʌʌ
.ʌ.ʌ.ʌ.ʌ.

Annual Convocations of the Missionary District of South Dakota

1. 1884, Sioux Falls
2. 1885, Sioux Falls
   1886, Unknown
3. 1887, Sioux Falls
4. 1888, Sioux Falls
5. 1889, Sioux Falls
6. 1890, Mitchell
7. 1891, Sioux Falls
8. 1892, Aberdeen
9. 1893, Yankton
10. 1894, Huron
11. 1895, Sioux Falls
12. 1896, Madison
13. 1897, Sioux Falls
14. 1898, Aberdeen
15. 1899, Yankton
16. 1900, Aberdeen
17. 1901, Sioux Falls
18. 1902, Howard and Madison
19. 1903, Sioux Falls
20. 1904, Sioux Falls
21. 1905, Sioux Falls
22. 1906, Sioux Falls
23. 1907, Yankton
24. 1908, Sioux Falls
25. 1909, Sioux Falls
26. 1910, Mitchell
27. 1911, Huron
28. 1912, Sioux Falls
29. 1913, Mitchell
30. 1914, Lead
31. 1915, Watertown
32. 1916, Sioux Falls
33. 1917, Aberdeen
34. 1918, Sioux Falls
35. 1919, Huron
36. 1920, Watertown
37. 1921, Lead and Deadwood
38. 1922, Mitchell
39. 1923, Yankton
40. 1924, Aberdeen
41. 1925, Pierre
42. 1926, Huron
43. 1927, Rapid City
44. 1928, Sioux Falls
45. 1929, Sioux Falls
46. 1930, Watertown
47. 1931, Aberdeen
48. 1932, Deadwood and Lead
49. 1933, Mitchell
50. 1934, Pierre
51. 1935, Yankton
52. 1936, Rapid City
53. 1937, Huron
54. 1938, Watertown
55. 1939, Mitchell
56. 1940, Aberdeen
57. 1941, Sioux Falls
58. 1942, Huron
59. 1943, Pierre
60. 1944, Yankton
61. 1945, Mitchell
62. 1946, Sioux Falls
63. 1947, Aberdeen
64. 1948, Lead
65. 1949, Huron
66. 1950, Mitchell
67. 1951, Yankton

68. 1952, Deadwood
69. 1953, Watertown
70. 1954, Rapid City
71. 1955, Aberdeen
72. 1956, Brookings
73. 1957, Rapid City
74. 1958, Sioux Falls
75. 1959, Lead and Deadwood
76. 1960, Mitchell
77. 1961, Yankton
78. 1962, Rapid City
79. 1963, Aberdeen
80. 1964, Sioux Falls
81. 1965, Lead and Deadwood
82. 1966, Brookings
83. 1967, Martin
84. 1968, Huron
    1968, Special Convocation,
        Sioux Falls
85. 1969, Belle Fourche
    1970, Special Convocation,
        Pierre
86. 1970, Sioux Falls.

.\.\.\.\.\

Annual Conventions of the Diocese of South Dakota

87. 1971, Primary Convention,
    Pierre
88. 1972, Second Convention,
    Sioux Falls
89. 1973, Third Convention,
    Springfield
90. 1974, Fourth Convention,
    Mitchell
91. 1975, Fifth Convention,
    Rapid City
92. 1976, Sixth Convention,
    Watertown

/\.\/\.\/\.\

Niobrara Deanery Convocations

1. 1870, Santee Agency, Nebraska
2. 1871, Santee Agency, Nebraska
3. 1872, Santee Agency, Nebraska
4. 1873, Santee Agency, Nebraska
5. 1874, Yankton Agency, D.T.
6. 1875, Yankton Agency, D.T.
   1876, No Convocation
7. 1877, Yankton Agency, D.T.
8. 1878, Yankton Agency, D.T.
9. 1879, Yankton Agency, D.T.
10. 1880, Rosebud Agency, D.T.
11. 1881, Yankton Agency, D.T.
12. 1882, Yankton Agency, D.T.
13. 1883, Lower Brule Agency, D.T.
14. 1884, Yankton Agency, D.T.
15. 1885, Crow Creek Agency, D.T.
16. 1886, Yankton Agency, D.T.
17. 1887, Ft. Bennett, Cheyenne River Reserve, D.T.
18. 1888, Pine Ridge Agency, D.T.
19. 1889, Crow Creek Agency, D.T.
20. 1890, St. Elizabeth's Church, Standing Rock Reserve
21. 1891, Near St. Mary's School, Rosebud Reserve
22. 1892, Cheyenne Agency
23. 1893, Santee Agency, Nebraska
24. 1894, Pine Ridge Agency
25. 1895, Lower Brule Agency
26. 1896, St. Elizabeth's Church, Standing Rock Reserve
27. 1897, Near St. Mary's School, Rosebud Reserve
28. 1898, Sisseton Agency
29. 1899, Yankton Agency
30. 1900, Ascension Chapel, Cheyenne River Reserve
    1901, No Convocation
31. 1902, Black Pipe Creek, Rosebud Reserve
32. 1903, St. John the Baptist Chapel, Crow Creek Reserve
33. 1904, Bear Creek, Cheyenne River Reserve
34. 1905, St. Philip's Chapel, White Swan, Yankton Reserve
35. 1906, Santee Agency, Nebraska
36. 1907, Trinity Chapel, Rosebud Reserve
37. 1908, St. Mary's Chapel, Pine Ridge Reserve
38. 1909, Messiah Chapel, Lower Brule
39. 1910, Yankton Agency
40. 1911, St. Elizabeth's Church, Standing Rock Reservation
41. 1912, Christ Church, Ft. Thompson
42. 1913, St. Mary's Church, Sisseton Agency
43. 1914, Emmanuel Church, White Horse
44. 1915, Trinity Chapel, Rosebud
45. 1916, Holy Comforter, Lower Brule
46. 1917, Inestimable Gift Church, Allen
47. 1918, Holy Fellowship Church, Greenwood
48. 1919, St. Elizabeth's Church, Wakpala
49. 1920, Our Most Merciful Saviour Church, Santee, Nebraska
50. 1921, Calvary Church, Okreek
51. 1922, St. James Church, Waubay

52. 1923, Emmanuel Church, White Horse
53. 1924, Holy Cross Church, Pine Ridge
54. 1925, Holy Fellowship Church,
    Greenwood
55. 1926, Christ Church, Fort Thompson
56. 1927, Holy Cross Church, Pine Ridge
    Agency
57. 1928, Good Shepherd Church,
    Glencross
58. 1929, Trinity Church, Mission
59. 1930, Holy Comforter Church, Lower
    Brule
60. 1931, St. Mary's Church, Sisseton
61. 1932, Ascension Church, Promise
62. 1933, Inestimable Gift Church, Allen
63. 1934, Holy Fellowship Church,
    Greenwood
64. 1935, St. Elizabeth's Church, Wakpala
65. 1936, Holy Innocent's, Parmelee
66. 1937, Our Most Merciful Saviour,
    Santee, Nebraska
67. 1938, Holy Cross, Pine Ridge Agency
68. 1939, St. John's Chapel, Pukwana, Crow
    Creek
69. 1940, St. John Baptist Chapel, Sisseton
    Reservation
70. 1941, Emmanuel Church, Cheyenne
71. 1942, Inestimable Gift Church, Corn
    Creek
72. 1943, St. James Church, Rosebud
73. 1944, Holy Fellowship Church,
    Greenwood
    1945, Reservation Meetings
74. 1946, Good Shepherd Chapel, Standing
    Rock Reservation
75. 1947, Messiah Chapel, Pine Ridge
    Reservation
76. 1948, Holy Comforter, Lower Brule
77. 1949, Holy Innocent's, Parmelee
78. 1950, St. Barnabas', Kyle
79. 1951, St. Elizabeth's School, Wakpala
80. 1952, Our Most Merciful Saviour,
    Santee, Nebraska

81. 1953, Christ Church, Fort Thompson
82. 1954, St. Peter's, Pine Ridge
83. 1955, St. John's, Cheyenne Agency
84. 1956, Calvary Church, Rosebud
85. 1957, St. Mary's, Sisseton
86. 1958, Holy Comforter, Lower Brule
87. 1959, St. Paul's, Little Eagle, Standing
    Rock Mission
88. 1960, Church of the Holy Fellowship,
    Greenwood, Yankton Mission
89. 1961, Messiah, Wounded Knee, Pine
    Ridge Mission
90. 1962, St. John the Baptist, Browns
    Valley, Sisseton Mission
91. 1963, St. Mary's, Promise, Cheyenne
    River Mission
92. 1964, St. Peters, Crow Creek
93. 1965, Holy Innocents, Parmelee,
    Rosebud Mission
94. 1966, Our Most Merciful Saviour,
    Santee Mission, Nebraska
95. 1967, Inestimable Gift, Corn Creek
    District of the Pine Ridge
    Mission, Allen
96. 1968, St. James, Waubay, Sisseton
    Mission
97. 1969, Holy Comforter, Lower Brule —
    L.B. Mission
98. 1970, Holy Cross, Pine Ridge, Pine
    Ridge Mission
99. 1971, Holy Innocents, Parmelee,
    Rosebud Mission
100. 1972, St. Thomas on the Tree, Cheyenne
    River Mission
101. 1973, St. John The Baptist, Sisseton
    Mission
102. 1974, St. Elizabeth's, Standing Rock
    Mission
103. 1975, Mediator, Kyle, Corn Creek,
    District of the Pine Ridge Mission
104. 1976, Our Most Merciful Saviour,
    Santee, Nebraska

Bibliography

Addison, James Thayer, *The Episcopal Church in the United States, 1789–1931,* Charles Scribner's Sons, New York, 1951.

Ashley, Rev. Edward, letter to Bishop Hare, March 28, 1884, South Dakota Protestant Episcopal Church Diocesan Archives, Sioux Falls, South Dakota, (hereinafter referred to as Diocesan Archives).

Ashley, Rev. Edward, papers, Diocesan Archives, Sioux Falls.

Barbour, Rev. Paul H., letter to author, February 24, 1975, "Bishop Hare School for Dakota Boys, Mission, South Dakota," School Circular, no date.

Board of Missions Reports, (pamphlet), Bible House, New York, 1873.

The Bugle, Centennial Edition, St. Mary's Episcopal School, Springfield, South Dakota, June, 1973.

Burleson, the Rt. Rev. Hugh L., *The Conquest of the Continent,* Domestic and Foreign Missionary Society, New York, 1911.

Burleson, Rt. Rev. Hugh L., papers, Diocesan Archives, "Chronology of Indian Missions, *Seventh Annual Report of the Niobrara League,* American Church Press, New York, 1878-79.

"Chronology of the Episcopal Church's Indian Mission Work in South Dakota, 1860–1878," Diocesan Archives.

The Church News, Missionary District of South Dakota, Diocesan Archives Collection, Vols: 1886–1895.

"The Church and the Indians," *Indian Pamphlets,* no publisher, 1876.

Cook, Rev. Joseph, *Diary,* May 1875–1902, Diocesan Archives.

Deloria, Ella, *Speaking of Indians,* Friendship Press, New York 1944, Deloria File, Diocesan Archives.

Deloria, the Rev. Vine V., letter to author, September 23, 1975.

Furois, Betty, "History of South Dakota Episcopal Church Women," unpublished, compiled for the 1976 Church History project.

First Annual Report of the Indian Commission, pamphlet, Bible House, New York, 1872.

The First 100 Years of the Grand Lodge A. F. & A. M. of South Dakota, Centennial Committee, 1974.

Gesner, the Rt. Rev. Conrad H., unpublished autobiographic sketch to author, April 1, 1975.

Girton, Polly, *Protestant Episcopal Indian Missions of Dakota Territory,* unpublished Master's Thesis, University of South Dakota, 1960.

218

Handbook of the Church's Mission to the Indians in Memory of William Hobart Hare, An Apostle to the Indians, Church Missions, Hartford, Connecticut, 1914.

Hare, Rt. Rev. William Hobart, papers, Diocesan Archives.

Hare, Rt. Rev. William Hobart, papers, Houghton Library, Harvard University, call number 58-11.

Hare, Rt. Rev. William Hobart, *Annual Reports of the Missionary Bishop of Niobrara,* Bible House, New York, 1873-1893.

Heard, Issac, V. D., *History of the Sioux Wars and Massacres of 1862 and 1863,* Harper and Brothers, New York, 1863.

"Historic St. John's Episcopal Church, Deadwood, South Dakota, 1876-1976," unpublished parish history.

"History of Christ Church, Gettysburg, South Dakota," unpublished parish history.

"History of Christ Church, Yankton, South Dakota," unpublished parish history.

Hinman, the Rev. S. D., *Diary and Journal,* 1869, Diocesan Archives.

"Hope School, Springfield South Dakota," School Circular, 1885.

Howe, M. A. DeWolf, *Life and Labors of Bishop Hare,* Sturgis & Walton, New York, 1911.

Hyde, George E., *A Sioux Chronicle,* University of Oklahoma Press, Norman, Oklahoma, 1956.

Indian Tribes and Missions, Church Missions Publishing Company, Hartford, 1926.

Investing in Life, pamphlet, Missionary District of South Dakota, no date.

Jennewein, J. Leonard, Boorman, Jane, *Dakota Panorama,* Dakota Territory Centennial Commission, 3rd Printing, Brevet Press, Sioux Falls, 1973.

Journals, 1873-1975, bound pamphlets of the journals of annual convocations and miscellaneous reports of the Missionary District (Diocese) of South Dakota.

Joyner, Neville, *The Oglala Sioux Indians of Pine Ridge,* pamphlet, published by author, no date.

Kingsbury, George W., *History of Dakota Territory,* Vols, I & II, S. J. Clarke Publishing Company, Chicago, 1915.

Klock, Irma H., "Christ Church Episcopal, Lead," unpublished parish history, 1975.

Macgregor, Gordon, *Warriors Without Weapons,* University of Chicago Press, Chicago, 1946.

Marrs, James David, Sr., *Grant's "Quaker" Policy and the Bishop of Niobrara,* unpublished Master's Thesis, Department of History, University of South Dakota, 1970.

Meyer, Roy, *History of the Santee Sioux,* University of Oklahoma Press, Norman, 1967.

The Mobridge Tribune, Mobridge, South Dakota, Vol. LI, No. 39, May 8, 1958.

The Minnesota Missionary, Diocese of Minnesota, Vol. LXVIII, No. 2, February, 1945.

A Month Among the Indian Missions, pamphlet, American Church Press Company, New York, 1872, (no page numbers).

"100 Years on the Rosebud," unpublished manuscript file, Rosebud Diocesan Archives.

Parker, Donald D., *Early Churches and Towns in South Dakota,* History Department, South Dakota State College, Brookings, South Dakota, 1957.

Parker, Donald D., *Founding the Church in South Dakota,* History Department, South Dakota State College, Brookings, South Dakota, 1962.

Powell, Shirley J., *History of St. Mary's School,* unpublished Master's Thesis, University of South Dakota, Vermillion, South Dakota, 1954.

Riggs, Stephen, *Mary and I: Forty Years Among the Sioux,* Blakely, Brown and Marsh, Chicago, 1880.

Robinson, Doane, *A History of the Dakota or Sioux Indians,* South Dakota Department of History, Ross & Haines reprint, Minneapolis, 1967.

Roberts, the Rt. Rev. W. Blair, papers, Diocesan Archives.

"St. Mary's Episcopal School for Indian Girls," School Circular, no date.

"St. Paul's Episcopal Church History, Vermillion, South Dakota," parish history, no date.

"Seventy-fifth Anniversary, St. Mary's Church, Mitchell, 1875–1950," unpublished parish history.

Smith, George Martin, *South Dakota,* Vol. III, S. J. Clark Publishing Company, Chicago, 1915.

South Dakota Annual Reports and Miscellaneous, 1894–1901, Missionary District of South Dakota.

The South Dakota Churchman, Protestant Episcopal Missionary District of South Dakota, 1913–January, 1976.

South Dakota Historical Collections, Pierre, South Dakota, Vols. X, XXII, XXVII, XXVIII.

South Dakota Historical Review, pamphlet, South Dakota Historical Society, Pierre, S. Dak., Vol. II, No. 4, July, 1937.

Spirit of Missions, Missionary Magazine, New York, Vols. 1862–1897.

A Study of the Missionary District of South Dakota, Home Department of the National Council of the Protestant Episcopal Church, 1955–1958, Vols. I, II, III, IV, mimeographed.

Swift Bird, The Indians Bishop, Church Missions Publishing Co., Hartford, 1926.

Talbot, Rt. Rev. Ethelbert, *My People of the Plains,* Harper and Brothers, New York, 1906.

Tibbles, Thomas H., *The Ponca Chiefs,* University of Nebraska Press, Lincoln, 1972.

Thorburn, Rev. Frank, "Peyote Cult, Yuwipi, Back-sliders," unpublished paper for the S. Dak. Episcopal Church History Project, February, 1975.

"Trinity Church, Pierre, South Dakota," unpublished parish history, 1975.

Welsh, Herbert, *Four Weeks Among the Sioux Tribes of Dakota and Nebraska,* pamphlet, Horace F. McCann, Philadelphia, 1882.

Welsh, William, *Our Mission to the Poncas,* pamphlet, no publisher, no date.

Welsh, William, *Semi-Official Report,* pamphlet, letter to Hon. J. D. Cox, no publisher, 1870.

Welsh, William, *Sioux and Ponca Reports to the Missionary Organizations of the Protestant Episcopal Church,* pamphlet, M'Calla and Stavely Printers, Philadelphia, 1870.

Whipple, Rt. Rev. Henry Benjamin, *Lights and Shadows of a Long Episcopate,* Macmillan Company, New York, 1899.

Wilkins, Robert P. and Wynona H., *God Giveth the Increase,* North Dakota Institute for Regional Studies, Fargo, 1959.

Young, Gertrude S., "Correspondence of a Niobrara Archdeacon," *Historical Magazine of the Protestant Episcopal Church,* Vol. XXXII, No. 1, March, 1963.

Young, Gertrude S., *William Joshua Cleveland,* pamphlet, South Dakota State College, Brookings, no date.

Index